Heather
Lodinsky

The
BLOCK
COLLECTION

150 Inspiring Stash-Busting
Shapes to Knit and Crochet

Search Press

First published in 2011 as
150 Blocks to Knit & Crochet by
Search Press Ltd
Wellwood
North Farm Road
Tunbridge Wells
Kent TN2 3DR
United Kingdom

This edition published in 2021

ISBN: 978-1-78221-987-3
ebook ISBN: 978-1-78126-982-4

QUAR.KCBL

Conceived, edited and designed by
Quarto Publishing, an imprint of
The Quarto Group
The Old Brewery
6 Blundell Street
London N7 9BH
www.QuartoKnows.com

Project Editor: Victoria Lyle
Art Editor: Emma Clayton
Designer: Julie Francis
Copyeditor and Pattern Checker: Luise Roberts
Illustrator: Coral Mula
Photographer: Phil Wilkins
Proofreader: Liz Jones
Indexer: Helen Snaith
Art Director: Caroline Guest
Creative Director: Moira Clinch
Publisher: Samantha Warrington

Printed in China

FOREWORD

Both knit and crochet items are great 'take-along' projects when they are worked in smaller parts. This book is full of fun and interesting shapes that can be worked together into larger pieces, or left to 'shine' on their own.

I have been a knitter for more years than I have crocheted, but I have always thought the most gorgeous sweaters, blankets and other projects included both knit and crochet elements. Needless to say, I have become an avid crocheter as well! A book of blocks just wouldn't be complete without both knitted and crocheted shapes.

This book is a valuable reference for knitters, crocheters and all who would like to learn new techniques. As a knitting and crochet teacher, I have chosen blocks from beginner to advanced, with a variety made either in the round, side-to-side, from the inside or outside, and top to bottom. There is something here for everyone!

Heather Lodinsky

Heather Lodinsky

ABOUT THIS BOOK

DIRECTORY (pages 6–15)

Flip through this colourful visual selector, choose your design, and then turn to the relevant page of instructions to create your chosen block. The Directory is organized by shape and each shape is colour themed; you can use these or your own choice of colours.

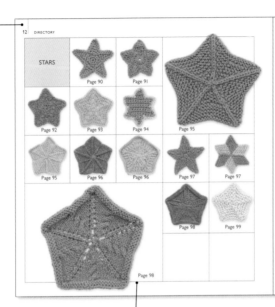
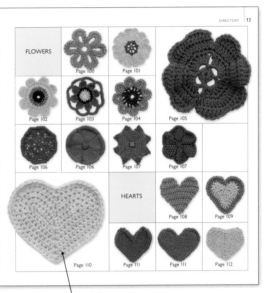

Each block is labelled with a number that corresponds to the relevant instructions in the Technical Instructions chapter, and a page number.

Each block is shown.

UNDERSTANDING THE SYMBOLS

Each pattern is accompanied by one or more symbols indicating how each pattern is worked, and a symbol indicating whether the pattern is knit or crochet and its degree of difficulty.

Worked in rows

 This symbol shows that the block has been worked backwards and forwards in rows.

Worked in rounds

 This symbol is used for blocks worked in the round from the centre outwards.

 This symbol is used for blocks worked in the round from the outside to the centre.

You will find some blocks, for example number 30 (page 40), are accompanied by both symbols as they have part of the pattern worked in rows and part in rounds.

Knit/Crochet, level of difficulty

 Crochet, beginner block

 Crochet, some experience required

 Crochet, challenging

 Knit, beginner block

Knit, some experience required

Knit, challenging

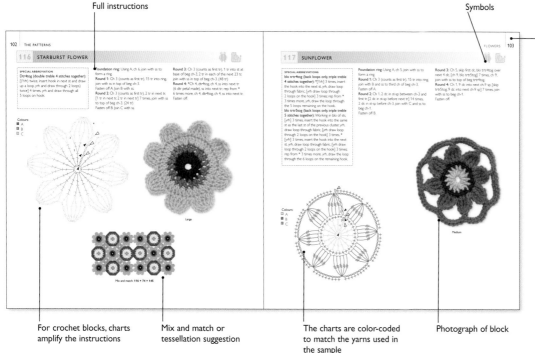

Full instructions

Symbols

116 STARBURST FLOWER

117 SUNFLOWER

For crochet blocks, charts amplify the instructions

Mix and match or tessellation suggestion

The charts are color-coded to match the yarns used in the sample

Photograph of block

THE PATTERNS
(pages 18–125)

Here you'll find instructions on how to create the blocks featured in the Directory. Organized by shape, this chapter contains full instructions, a photograph and helpful symbols to aid you in the creation of your chosen design. Mix and match or tessellation suggestions are occasionally given.

THE PROJECTS
(pages 128–131)

The Projects section includes plans for making two afghans, a bag, a scarf and a cushion using a selection of blocks from the book. Each design is accompanied by details of the finished item, the type of yarn and colours used, as well as the names and reference numbers of the component blocks.

TECHNIQUES
(pages 132–139)

This section explains how to fit the different shaped blocks together, as well as how to use and adapt connectors for your particular project. Details of blocking and joining blocks are demonstrated and tips on choosing and calculating yarn are also included.

READING PATTERNS AND CHARTS
(pages 140–141)

This section includes a list of the abbreviations and chart symbols used as well as a diagram showing how to read a crochet chart.

SIZE

- All the blocks in this book have been made using worsted weight yarn on 4.5 mm (size 7) knitting needles or a J-10 crochet hook. They fall into four size categories:
  1. **Small:** 9–12cm (3½–4¾in)
  2. **Medium:** 12–15cm (4¾–6in)
  3. **Large:** 15–18cm (6–7in)
  4. **Extra large:** 18–21cm (7–8¼in)
- The size of your blocks will depend on the yarn you use and the tension at which you knit. See Yarn Choices (page 137) and Tension (page 138) for further details.
- Depending on their shape, it may be possible to mix and match same-size blocks together. See Fitting blocks together (pages 132–133) for further details.

CONTENTS

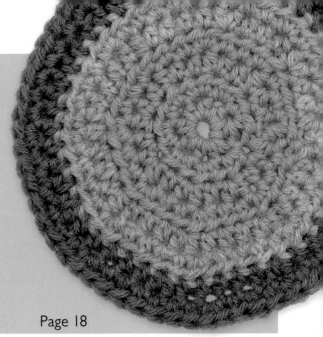

Page 18

CIRCLES

Page 19

Page 20

Page 21

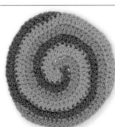

Page 22

Page 25

Page 23

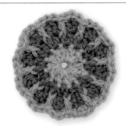

Page 23

Page 24

Page 26

Page 26

Page 27

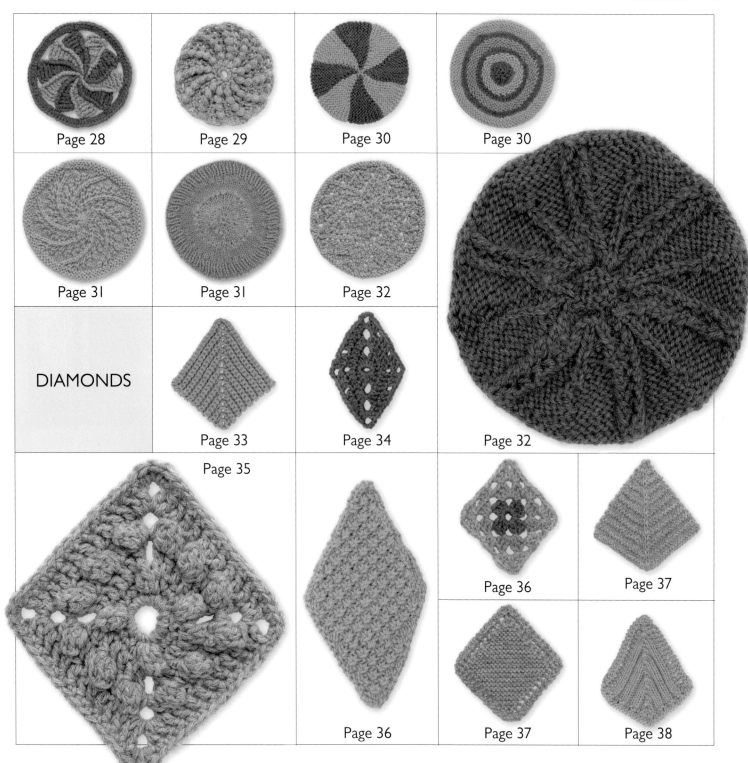

Page 28

Page 29

Page 30

Page 30

Page 31

Page 31

Page 32

DIAMONDS

Page 33

Page 34

Page 32

Page 35

Page 36

Page 36

Page 37

Page 37

Page 38

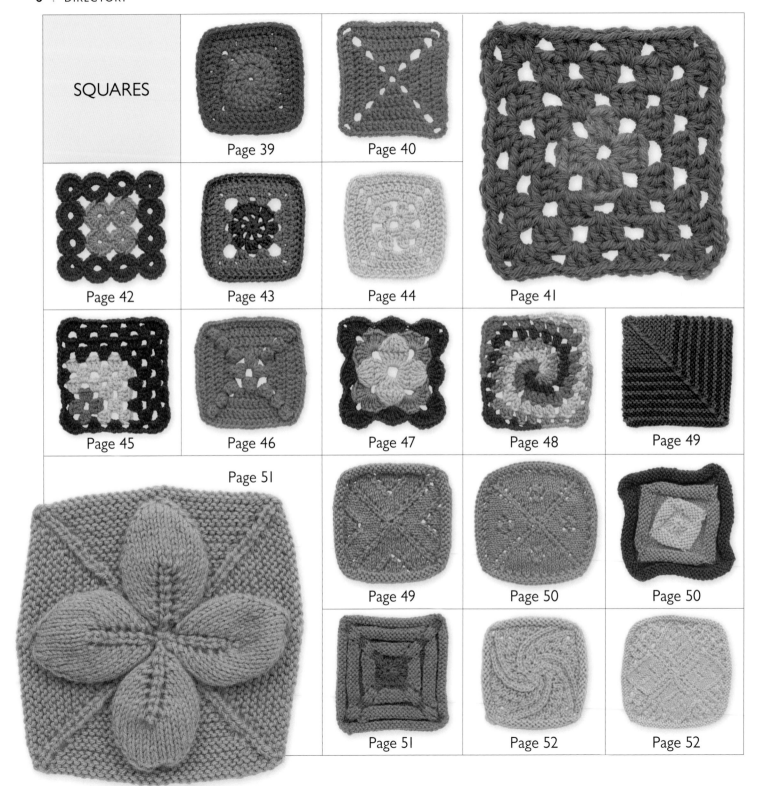

SQUARES

Page 39

Page 40

Page 41

Page 42

Page 43

Page 44

Page 45

Page 46

Page 47

Page 48

Page 49

Page 51

Page 49

Page 50

Page 50

Page 51

Page 52

Page 52

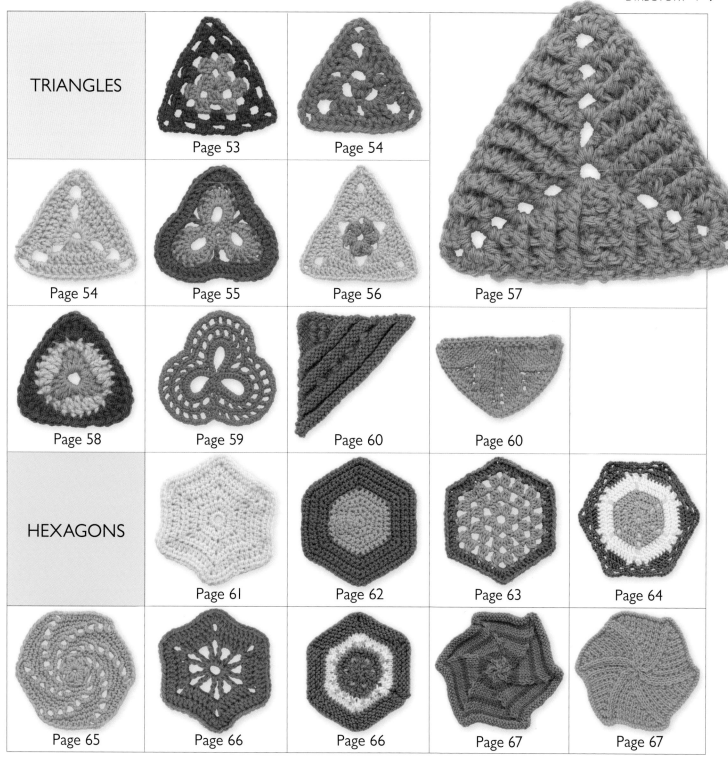

TRIANGLES

Page 53

Page 54

Page 54

Page 55

Page 56

Page 57

Page 58

Page 59

Page 60

Page 60

HEXAGONS

Page 61

Page 62

Page 63

Page 64

Page 65

Page 66

Page 66

Page 67

Page 67

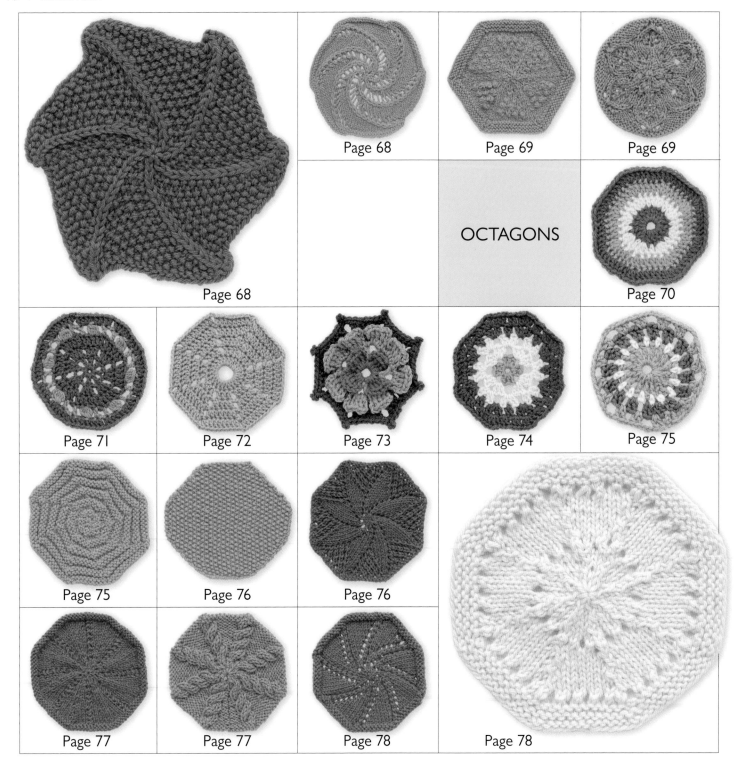

Page 68

Page 68

Page 69

Page 69

OCTAGONS

Page 70

Page 71

Page 72

Page 73

Page 74

Page 75

Page 75

Page 76

Page 76

Page 77

Page 77

Page 78

Page 78

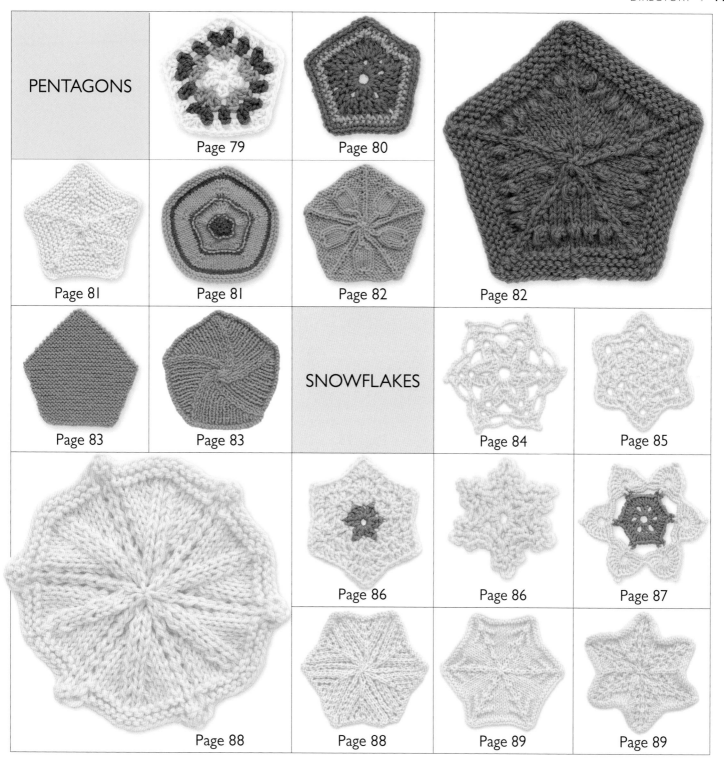

PENTAGONS

Page 79

Page 80

Page 81

Page 81

Page 82

Page 82

Page 83

Page 83

SNOWFLAKES

Page 84

Page 85

Page 88

Page 86

Page 86

Page 87

Page 88

Page 89

Page 89

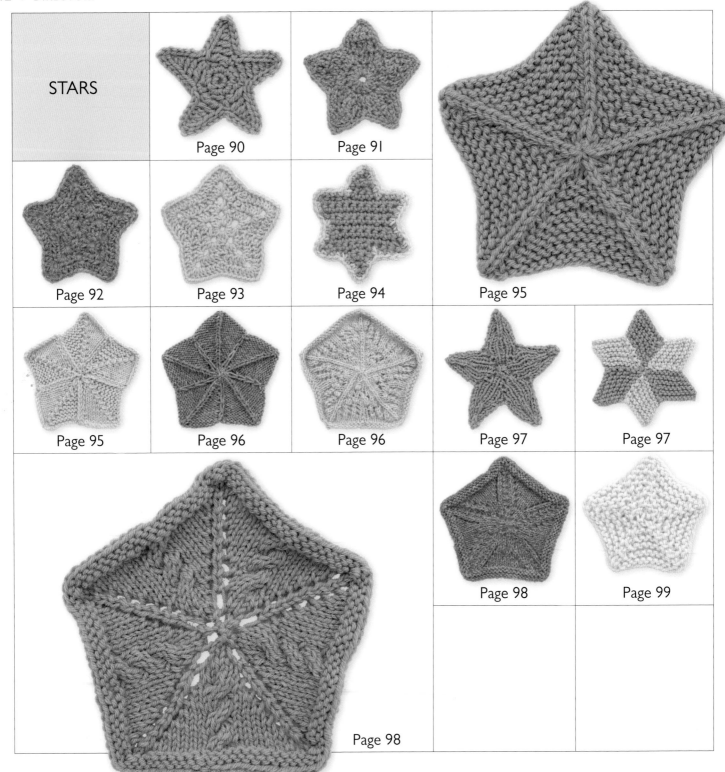

STARS

Page 90

Page 91

Page 92

Page 93

Page 94

Page 95

Page 95

Page 96

Page 96

Page 97

Page 97

Page 98

Page 98

Page 99

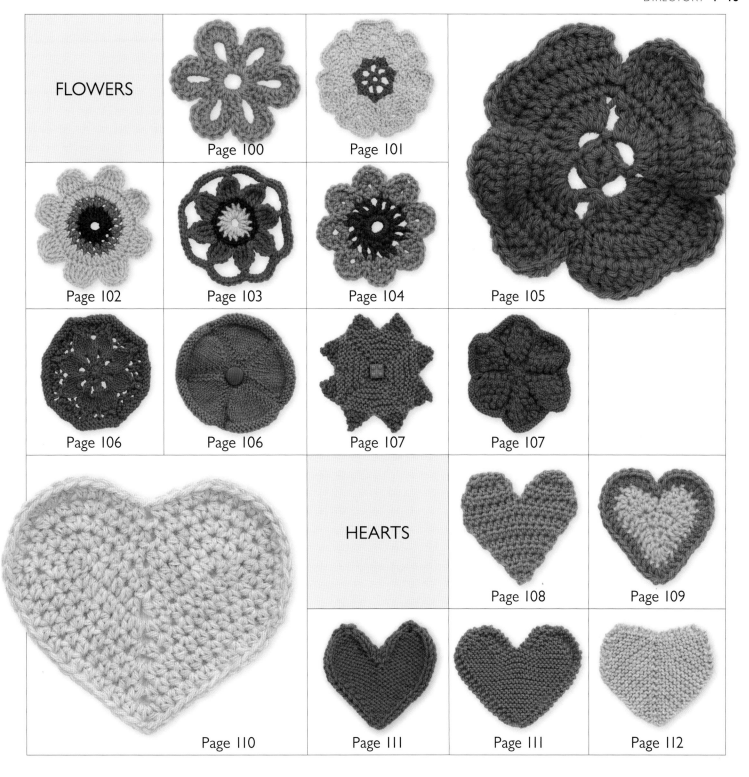

FLOWERS

Page 100

Page 101

Page 102

Page 103

Page 104

Page 105

Page 106

Page 106

Page 107

Page 107

HEARTS

Page 108

Page 109

Page 110

Page 111

Page 111

Page 112

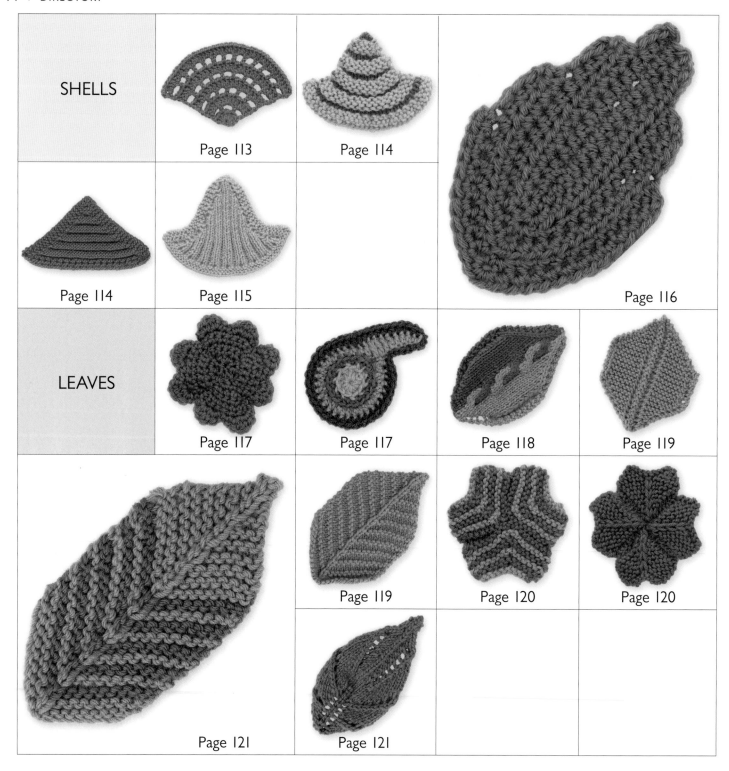

SHELLS

Page 113

Page 114

Page 114

Page 115

Page 116

LEAVES

Page 117

Page 117

Page 118

Page 119

Page 119

Page 120

Page 120

Page 121

Page 121

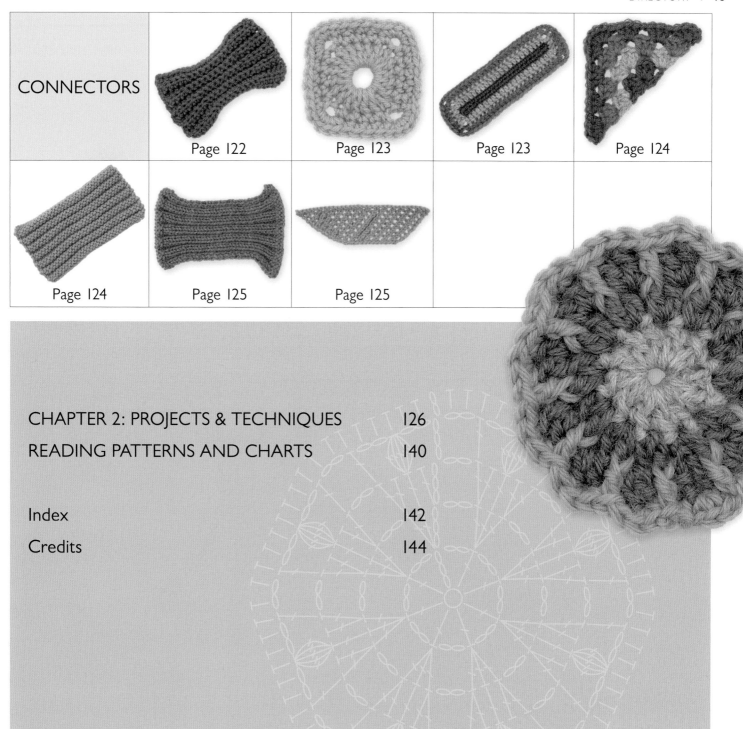

| CONNECTORS | Page 122 | Page 123 | Page 123 | Page 124 |
| Page 124 | Page 125 | Page 125 | | |

CHAPTER ONE

THE PATTERNS

Organized by shape, this chapter contains full instructions for all the blocks, a photograph of each and helpful symbols to aid you in the creation of your chosen design.

1 TRI-COLOUR BULLSEYE

Foundation ring: Using A, ch 4, join with ss to form a ring.

Round 1: Ch 2, 8 htr in ring, join with ss in beg ch-2, turn. (8 sts)

Round 2: Ch 2, 2 htr in each htr; join with ss in beg ch-2, turn. (16 htr)

Round 3: Ch 2, [1 htr in next htr, 2 htr in next htr] 8 times, join with ss in beg ch-2, turn. (24 htr)

Round 4: Ch 2, [1 htr in each of the next 2 htr, 2 htr in next htr] 8 times, join with ss in beg ch-2, turn. (32 htr)
Fasten off A. Join B.

Round 5: Ch 2, [1 htr in each of the next 3 htr, 2 htr in next htr] 8 times, join with ss in beg ch-2, turn. (40 htr)

Round 6: Ch 2, [1 htr in each of the next 4 htr, 2 htr in next htr] 8 times, join with ss in beg ch-2, turn. (48 htr)
Fasten off B. Change to C.

Round 7: Ch 2, 1 htr in each of the next 3 htr; 2 htr in next htr, [1 htr in each of the next 5 htr; 2 htr in next htr] 7 times, 1 htr in each of the next 2 htr; join with ss in beg ch-2, turn. (56 htr)

Round 8: Ch 2, 1 htr in each of the next 4 htr, 2 htr in next htr, [1 htr in each of the next 6 htr; 2 htr in next htr] 7 times, 1 htr in each of the last 2 htr; join with ss in beg ch-2, turn. (64 htr)
Fasten off.

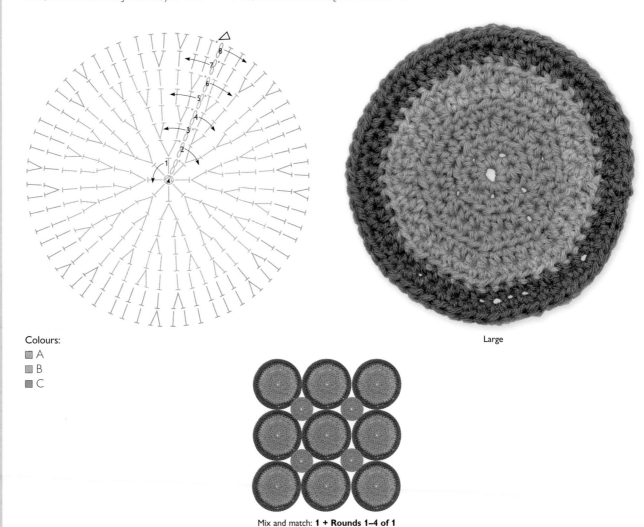

Colours:
- A
- B
- C

Large

Mix and match: **1 + Rounds 1–4 of 1**

Symbols and abbreviations
Turn to pages 140–141 for a full explanation of the symbols and abbreviations used.

2 PICOT SPIRAL

NOTE
Place marker to indicate beginning of round.
Move marker up as each round is completed.

Foundation ring: Ch 4, join with ss to form a ring.
Round 1: Ch 1, 9 dc in ring, do not join.
Round 2: [2 htr in next dc] 9 times. (18 htr)
Round 3: [2 tr in next htr, ch 1, skip next htr] 9 times. (18 tr and 9 ch-1 sp)
Round 4: [2 tr in next tr, 1 tr in next tr, ch 1, skip ch-1 sp] 9 times.
Round 5: [2 tr in next tr, 1 tr in each of next 2 tr, ch 1, skip ch-1 sp] 9 times.
Round 6: [2 tr in next tr, 1 tr in each of next 3 tr, ch 1, skip ch-1 sp] 9 times.
Round 7: [2 htr in next tr, 1 htr in next 4 tr, ch 1, skip next ch-1 sp] 9 times.
Round 8: 1 dc in next htr, ss in each htr and ch1 sp to the end of round.
Fasten off.

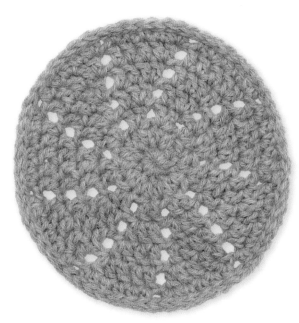

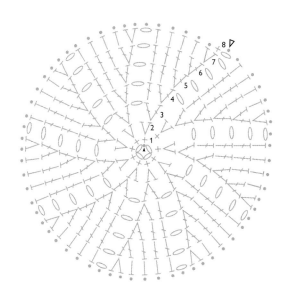

Colour:
A ▢

Large

Mix and match: **2 + Rounds 1–2 of 24**

3 TRI-COLOUR GRANNY

SPECIAL ABBREVIATION

puff st: [Yrh, insert hook into foundation ring, draw up loop] twice, yrh, draw loop through all 5 loops on hook.

Foundation ring: Using A, ch 4, join with ss to form ring.

Round 1: Ch 3, 1 htr into ring (counts as first puff st), ch 1, [puff st into ring, ch 1] 7 times, join with ss to top of first puff st.

Round 2: Ss to next ch sp, ch 3, 1 tr into ch sp at base of ch-3, ch 2 [2tr, into next ch-1 sp, ch 2] 7 times, join with ss to top of beg ch-3.

Round 3: Ss to next ch sp, ch 3, [1 tr, ch 1, 2 tr] into ch sp at base of ch-3, ch 1, *[2 tr, ch 1] twice into next ch-2 sp; rep from * 6 times more, join with ss to top of beg ch-3.

Fasten off A. Join B with ss into next ch-1 sp.

Round 4: Ch 3, 2 tr into ch sp at base of ch-3, ch 1, [3 tr into next ch-1 sp, ch 1] 15 times, join with ss to top of beg ch-3.

Fasten off B. Join C with ss into next ch-1 sp.

Round 5: Ch 3, 3 tr into ch sp at base of ch-3, ch 1 [4 tr into next ch-1 sp, ch 1] 15 times, join with ss to top of beg ch-3.

Round 6: Ch 1 (counts as first dc), 1 dc in each tr and each ch sp to end of round, join with a ss to top of beg ch-1.

Fasten off.

Colours:
■ A
■ B
■ C

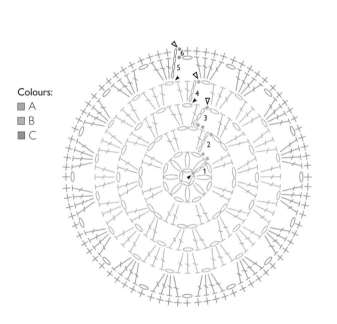

Large

4 WATER WHEEL

Foundation ring: Ch 4, join with ss to form a ring.

Round 1: Ch 3 (counts as first tr), 1 tr into ring, [ch 2, 2 tr into ring] 5 times, ch 2, join with ss to top of beg ch-3.

Round 2: Ch 3 (counts as first tr), 2 tr into base of ch-3, 1 tr into next tr; *ch 3, skip ch-2, 3 tr into next tr, 1 tr into next tr; rep from * 4 times more, ch 3, skip ch-2, join with ss to top of beg ch-3. (6 rep of 4 tr and ch 3)

Round 3: Ch 3 (counts as first tr), 2 tr into base of ch-3, 1 tr into next tr; tr2tog over next 2 tr; *ch 4, skip ch-3, 3 tr into next tr, 1 tr into next tr; tr2tog over next 2 tr; rep from * 4 times more, ch 4, skip ch-3, join with ss to top of beg ch-3.

Round 4: Ch 3 (counts as first tr), 2 tr into base of ch-3, 1 tr into each of next 2 tr, tr2tog over next 2 tr, *ch 5, skip ch-4, 3 tr into next tr, 1 tr into each of next 2 tr, tr2tog over next 2 tr;

rep from * 4 times more, ch 5, skip ch-4, join with ss to top of beg ch-3.

Round 5: Ch 1 (counts as first dc), 1 dc in each tr and ch to the end of the round, join with ss to beg ch-1.

Fasten off.

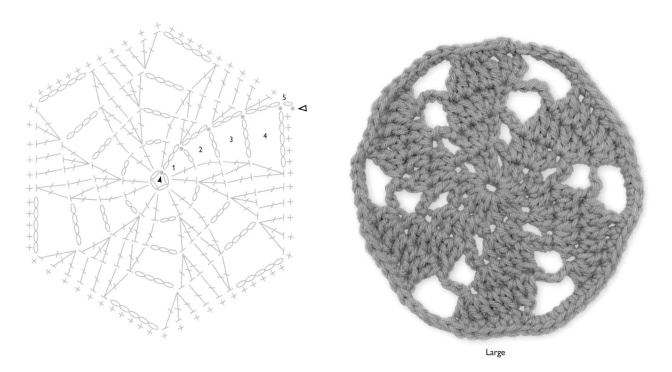

Colour:
A ▢

Large

Same-block tessellation: **4**

5 COLOUR SWIRL BLOCK

NOTE
Place working loops not in use onto a split-ring marker or safety pin.

Foundation chain: Using A, ch 2.
Round 1: Insert hook into second ch from hook [1 dc, 1 htr; 2 tr], remove hook from loop A, join B with dc in same ch, [1 htr; 2 tr] in same ch, remove hook from loop B, join C with dc in same ch, [1 htr; 2 tr] in same ch, remove hook from loop C, gently tighten chain into which sts have been worked. (4 sts each of A, B and C)

Round 2: Using A, *2 tr in next 4 sts, remove hook from loop A; rep from * with colours B and C. (8 sts each with A, B and C)
Round 3: Using A, *[2 tr in next st, tr in next st] 4 times, remove hook from loop A; rep from * with colours B and C. (12 sts each with A, B and C)
Round 4: Using A, *[2 tr in next st, 1 tr in next 2 sts] 4 times, remove hook from loop A; rep from * with colours B and C. (16 sts each with A, B and C)
Round 5: Using A, *[2 tr in next st, 1 tr in next 3 sts] 4 times, remove hook from loop A; rep from * with colours B and C. (20 sts each with A, B and C)

Round 6: Using A, *[2 tr in next st, 1 tr in next 4 sts] 4 times, remove hook from loop A; rep from * with colours B and C. (24 sts each with A, B and C)
Round 7: Using A, *[2 tr in next st, 1 tr in next 5 sts] 4 times remove hook from loop A; rep from * with colours B and C. (28 sts each with A, B and C)
Round 8: Using A, *1 htr in next st, 1 dc in next st, ss in next st, fasten off remove hook from loop A; rep from * with colours B and C.
Fasten off.

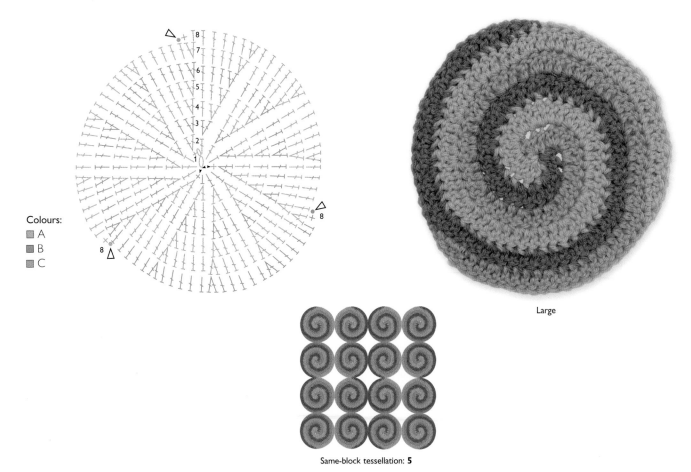

Colours:
■ A
■ B
■ C

Large

Same-block tessellation: 5

6 GEOMETRIC WHEEL

Foundation ring: Ch 10, join with ss to form a ring.

Round 1: Ch 3 (counts as first tr), work 29 tr into ring, join with ss to top of beg ch-3. (30 tr)

Round 2: Ch 6 (counts as first tr and ch 3), skip next 2 tr, [1 tr into next tr, ch 3, skip next 2 tr] 9 times, join with ss to third ch of beg ch-6.

Round 3: Ch 3 (counts as first tr), 2 tr into the base of ch-3, ch 3,

[3 tr into next tr, ch 3] 9 times, join with ss to top of beg ch-3.

Round 4: Ch 3 (counts as first tr), 1 tr into each of next 2 tr, ch 4, [1 tr into each of next 3 tr, ch 4] 9 times, join with ss to top of ch-3.

Round 5: Ch 2, (counts as first htr), 1 htr in each tr and ch to the end of round, join with ss to beg ch-2.

Fasten off.

Colour:
■ A

Large

7 TRI-COLOUR MEDALLION

SPECIAL ABBREVIATION

FPtr (Front Post treble crochet): Yrh, insert hook from front to back to front around post of indicated stitch; yrh and draw up loop, [yrh and draw up through 2 loops on hook] twice.

Foundation ring: Using A, ch 4, join with ss to form a ring.

Round 1 (RS): Ch 3 (counts as first tr), 11 tr into ring, join with ss in top of beg ch-3. (12 tr) Fasten off A. Join B with ss in any tr.

Round 2: Ch 3 (counts as first tr), 1 tr into base of ch-3, 2 tr in each st to end of round, join with ss in top of beg ch-3. (24 sts)

Round 3: Ch 3 (counts as first tr), 1 tr into base of ch-3, ch 1, skip next st, *2 tr in next st, ch 1, skip

next st; rep from * 10 times more, join with ss in top of beg ch-3. (12 ch-1 sp and 24 tr) Fasten off B. Join C.

Round 4: Ch 2, 2 dc in next tr, working in front of next ch-1 sp FPtr around skipped st in 2 rounds below, *1 dc in next tr, 2 dc in next tr, working in front of next ch-1 sp FPtr around skipped st in 2 rounds below; rep from * 10 times more, join with ss in beg ch-2. Fasten off.

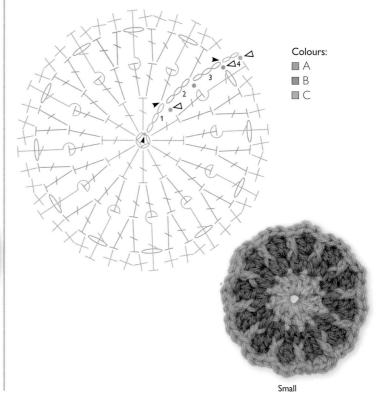

Colours:
■ A
■ B
■ C

Small

8 POPCORN CIRCLE

SPECIAL ABBREVIATIONS

beg popcorn: Ch 3, 4 tr into base of ch-4, drop loop from hook, insert hook from front to back in first tr of the popcorn catch working loop, yrh, draw through loop and st.

popcorn: 5 tr in next st, drop loop from hook, insert hook from front to back in first tr of the popcorn catch working loop, yrh, draw through loop and st.

Round 1: Using A, ch 4 (counts as ch 1 and first tr), 15 tr into fourth ch from hook, join with ss in top of beg ch-3. (16 tr)

Round 2: Beg popcorn, 2 tr in next tr; [popcorn in next tr, 2 tr in next] 7 times, join with ss in top of beg popcorn. (8 popcorns)

Round 3: Ch 3 (counts as first tr), tr into top of popcorn at base of ch-3, 1 tr in next tr, [2 tr in next st or popcorn, tr in next st or popcorn] 11 times, join with ss in top of beg ch-3. (36 tr) Fasten off A. Join B.

Round 4: Ch 3 (counts as first tr), 1 tr into base of ch-3, popcorn in next tr; [2 tr in next tr, popcorn in next tr] 17 times, join with ss in top of beg ch-3 to join. (18 popcorns)

Round 5: Ch 1 (counts as first dc), 1 dc in each st or popcorn to the end of round, join with ss in beg ch-1.
Fasten off.

Colours:
■ A
■ B

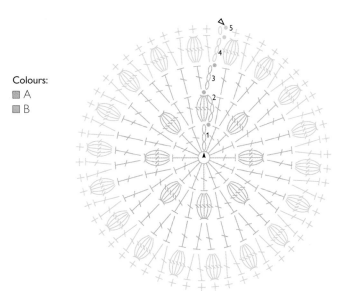

Medium

9 POST STITCH SPOKE WHEEL

SPECIAL ABBREVIATION

FPtr (Front Post treble crochet): Yrh, insert hook from front to back to front around post of indicated stitch, yrh, draw up loop, [yrh and draw up through 2 loops on hook] twice.

Foundation ring: Ch 4, join with ss to form a ring.
Round 1 (RS): Ch 3 (counts as first tr), 11 tr in ring, join with ss in top of beginning ch-3. (12tr)
Round 2: Ch 3 (counts as first tr), FPtr around beg ch-3 Round 1, [1 tr in next tr, FPtr around tr at the base of last tr worked] 11 times, join with ss in top of beg ch-3. (24 sts)
Round 3: Ch 3 (counts as first tr), 1 tr in next st, FPtr around FPtr at the base of last tr worked, [1 tr in next 2 sts, FPtr around FPtr at the base of last tr worked] 11 times, join with ss in top of beg ch-3. (36 sts)
Round 4: Ch 3 (counts as first tr), 1 tr in next 2 sts, FPtr around FPtr at the base of last tr worked, [1 tr in next 3 sts, FPtr around FPtr at the base of last tr worked] 11 times, join with ss in top of beg ch-3. (48 sts)
Round 5: Ch 3 (counts as first tr), 1 tr in next 3 sts, FPtr around FPtr at the base of last tr worked, [1 tr in next 4 sts, FPtr around FPtr at the base of last tr worked] 11 times, join with ss in top of beg ch-3. (60 sts)
Round 6: Ch 3 (counts as first tr), 1 tr in next 4 sts, FPtr around FPtr at the base of last tr worked, [1 tr in next 5 sts, FPtr around FPtr at the base of last tr worked] 11 times, join with ss in top of beg ch-3. (72 sts)
Round 7: Ch 2 (counts as first htr), 1 blo htr in st to end of round, join with ss in top of beg ch-2. Fasten off.

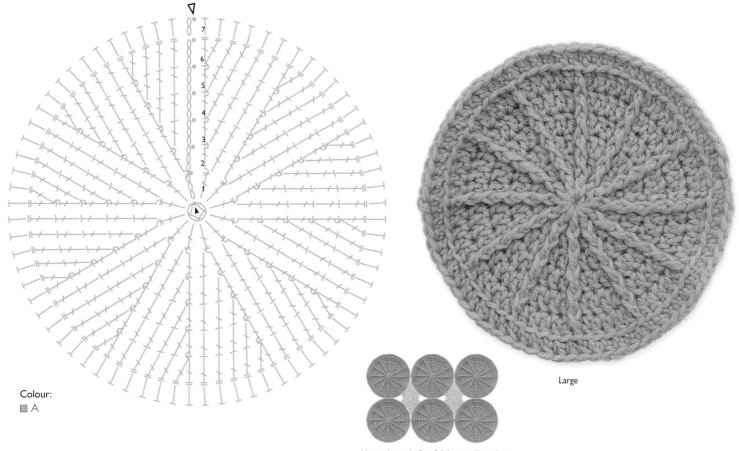

Colour:
■ A

Large

Mix and match: **9 + 94 (extending the chains on the last round to fit the shape)**

10 FLOWER MEDALLION

Foundation ring: Using A, ch 6, join with ss to form ring.
Round 1: Ch 4 (counts as first dtr), 2 dtr into ring, [ch 1, 3 dtr into ring] 5 times, ch 1, join with ss to top of ch-4.
Fasten off. Join B, turn.
Round 2: Ss into first ch-1 sp, ch 7, [1 dc into next ch-1 sp, ch 6] 5 times, join with ss to beg ch-1. Do not turn.
Round 3: Ss to first ch-6 sp [1 htr; 2 tr, 3 dtr, 2 tr, 1 htr] into each ch-6 sp around, join with ss to first htr. (6 petals)
Fasten off. Turn, join C to first htr of a petal.
Round 4: Ch 4 (counts as first dtr), * 1 tr into each of next 2 tr, 1 htr into each of next 3 dtr, 1 tr in each of next 2 tr, 1 dtr into each of next 2 htr; rep from * 5 times more, skip last dtr of last rep, join with ss to top of ch-4.
Fasten off.

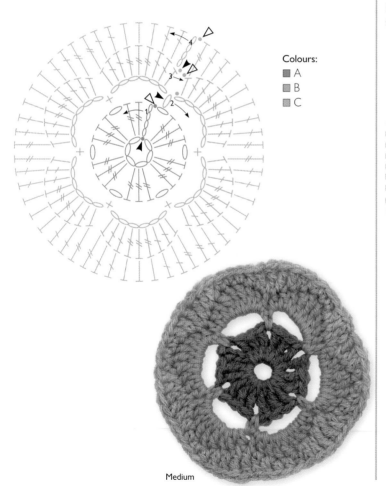

Colours:
■ A
■ B
■ C

Medium

11 BOBBLE BORDER WHEEL

SPECIAL ABBREVIATION
MB (Make Bobble): Work 5 tr into next st until 1 loop of each remains on hook, yrh and draw through all 6 loops on hook.

Foundation ring: Ch 4, join with ss to form a ring.
Round 1: Ch 5 (counts as first tr and ch 2), [1 tr into ring, ch 2] 7 times, join with ss to the third ch of beg ch-5.
Round 2: Ch 3 (counts as first tr), 2 tr into base of ch-3, ch 2, [3 tr into next tr, ch 2] 7 times, join with ss to top of beg ch-3.
Round 3: Ch 3, 1 tr into base of ch-3, 1 tr into next tr, 2 tr into next tr; ch 2 [2 tr into next tr, 1 tr into next tr, 2 tr into next tr; ch 2] 7 times, join with ss to top of beg ch-3.
Round 4: Ch 5 (counts as first tr and ch 2), skip next tr, MB into next tr, ch 2, skip 1 tr, 1 tr into next tr, ch 2, [1 tr into next tr, ch 2, skip 1 tr, MB into next tr, ch 2, skip 1 tr, 1 tr into next tr, ch 2] 7 times, join with ss to top of beg ch-5.
Round 5: Ch 2 (counts as first htr), 1 htr in each stitch and ch to end of round, join with ss to top of beg ch-2. Fasten off.

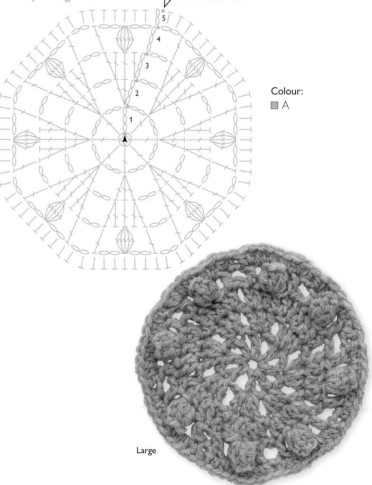

Colour:
■ A

Large

12 SPOKE WHEEL

Foundation ring: Using A, ch 4, join with ss to form ring.

Round 1: Ch 3 (counts as first tr), 9 tr into ring, join with ss in top of beg ch -3. (10 tr) Fasten off A. Join B.

Round 2: Ch 4 (counts as first tr and ch 1), [1 tr in next tr, ch 1] 9 times, join with ss in third ch of beg ch-4.

Round 3: Ch 3, 1 tr into base of ch-3, ch 2, [2 tr in next tr, ch 2] 9 times, join with ss in top of beg ch-3.
Fasten off B. Join C.

Round 4: Ch 3, 1 tr into base of ch-3, 1 tr in next tr, ch 2, [2 tr in next tr, 1 tr in next tr, ch 2] 9 times join with ss in top of beg ch-3.
Fasten off C. Join A.

Round 5: Ch 3, 1 tr into base of ch-3, 1 tr in next tr, 2 tr in next tr, ch 2, [2 tr in next tr, 1 tr in next tr, 2 tr in next tr, ch 2] 9 times, join with ss in top of beg ch-3.

Round 6: Ch 3 (counts as first tr), 1 tr into base of ch-3, 1 tr in next 3 tr, 2 tr next tr, ch 2, [2 tr in next tr, 1 tr in each of next 3 sts, 2 tr in next tr, ch 2] 9 times, join with ss in top of beg ch-3.
Fasten off A. Join colour B with ss in top of beg ch-3 Round 6.

Round 7: Ch 2 (counts as first htr), 1 htr in each st and 2 htr in each ch-2 sp to the end of the round, join with ss in top of beg ch-2.

Round 8: Ss in each st to end of round.
Fasten off.

Colours:
- A
- B
- C

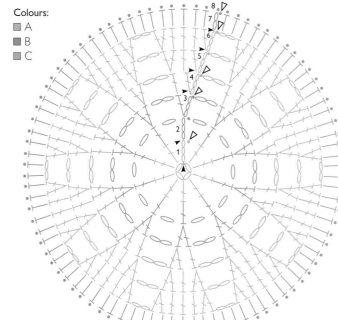

Extra large

13 TWO-TONE LAZY WHEEL

Foundation ring: Using A, ch 17, join with ss to eighth ch.

Row 1: Working in the ch-9 tail, 1 dc into the second ch from the hook, 1 htr in next ch, 1 tr in next ch, 2 trs in next ch, 1 tr in next ch, 2 dtr in next ch, 1 dtr in next ch, 2 trtrs in next ch, 1 trtr in next ch. Do not turn. (12 sts)

Row 2: Reverse dc in front loop only in each st, ss in centre ring. Do not turn.

Remove hook from working loop. Join B with ss to centre of ring.

Row 3: Working into the back loop only of each st 2 rows below (behind reverse dc row), 1 dc in next st, 1 htr in next st, 1 tr in next st, 2 trs in next st, 1 tr in next st, 2 dtr in next st, 1 dtr in next st, 2 trtrs in next st, 1 trtr in next st.

Repeat Rows 2 and 3 alternating colours A and B until 10 repeats have been completed.

Fasten off, leaving a 30cm (12in) tail. Sew first and tenth repeats together through back loops of sts in row 19.

Join B with ss to trtr at point of any repeat.

Round 1: Ch 1 (counts as first dc), dc in trtr at base of ch, ch 7, [1 dc in next trtr, ch 7] 9 times, join with ss in beg ch-1

Round 2: Ch 2 (counts as first htr), 1 htr in st at base of ch-2, 7 htr into ch-7 sp, [2 htr in next dc, 7 htr into ch-7 sp] 9 times, join with ss in beg ch-2.

Fasten off.

Colours:
- ☐ A
- ■ B

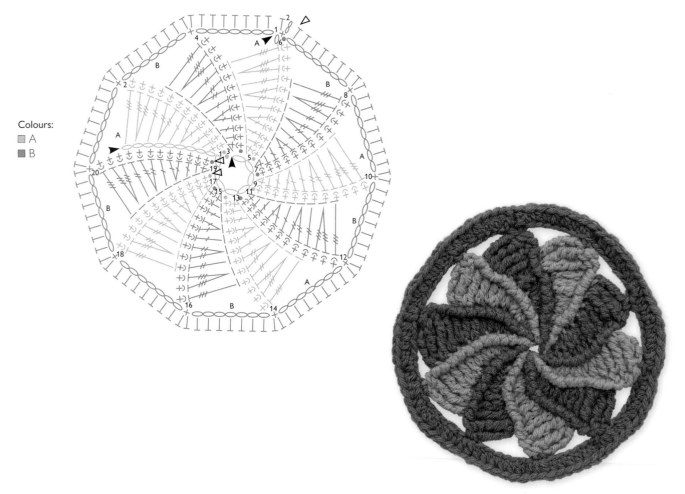

Large

14 BOBBLE SWIRL BLOCK

SPECIAL ABBREVIATION
FPpuff st (Front Post puff stitch): [Yrh, insert hook from front to back to front around post of indicated stitch, draw up loop] 4 times into same st, yrh, draw through all 9 loops on hook.

Foundation ring: Ch 6, join with ss to form a ring.
Round 1: 12 dc into ring, join with ss to first dc.
Round 2: Ch 4 (counts as first tr and ch 1) [1 tr in next dc, ch 1] 11 times, join with ss in third ch of beg ch-4.
Round 3: FPpuff st around beg ch-4 in Round 2, *[ch 1, 1 tr, ch 1, 1 tr] in next ch-1 sp, FPpuff st around next tr; rep from * 10 times more, [ch 1, 1 tr, ch 1, 1 tr] in next ch-1 sp, join with ss in first FPpuff st.
Round 4: *FPpuff st around the next FPpuff st, 1 tr between the 2 tr. Ch 1, 1 tr between the second tr and FPpuff st, ch 1; rep from * 11 times more, join with ss in first FPpuff st.
Rounds 5–7: Repeat Round 4. Fasten off.

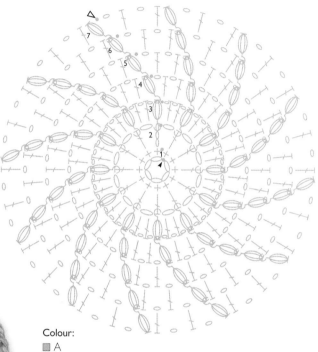

Colour:
■ A

Large

To make an appliqué flower

Mix and match: **14 + 143**   Mix and match: **14 + 134**

15 TWO-TONE PINWHEEL

Using A, cast on 15 stitches.
Row 1 (WS): Knit.
Row 2 (RS): K14, turn.
Row 3 (and all odd-numbered rows): Knit.
Row 4: K13, turn.
Row 6: K12, turn.
Row 8: K11, turn.
Row 10: K10, turn.
Row 12: K9, turn.
Row 14: K8, turn.
Row 16: K7, turn.
Row 18: K6, turn.
Row 19: Knit.

Change to B.
Row 20: Knit.
Repeat Rows 1–20, 7 times more, alternating yarns A and B after Row 19 of each repeat, ending with Row 19.
Cast off, leaving a long tail for sewing seam. Using a tapestry needle, sew cast-on edge to cast-off edge, then weave through centre stitches and gather.

Colours:
 A
■ B

Extra large

16 TRI-COLOUR BULLSEYE

Using A, cast on 6 stitches and divide evenly over 3 needles.
Join, taking care not to twist stitches.
Round 1: Knit.
Round 2: [K1, M1] 6 times. (12 sts)
Round 3: Knit.
Round 4: [K1, M1] 12 times. (24 sts)
Change to B.
Round 5: Knit.
Rounds 6–8: Purl.
Fasten off B. Change to A.
Round 9: Knit.
Round 10: [K1, M1] to end of the round. (48 sts)

Round 11: Knit.
Change to C.
Round 12: Knit.
Rounds 13–15: Purl.
Fasten off C. Change to A.
Round 16: Knit.
Round 17: [K1, M1] to the end of the round. (96 sts)
Round 18: Knit.
Fasten off A. Join B.
Round 19: Knit.
Rounds 20–22: Purl.
Cast off loosely knitwise.

Colours:
 A
■ B
■ C

Large

Mix and match: **16 + Rounds 1–4 of 16**

17 LACE SPIRAL

Cast on 8 stitches and divide evenly over 4 needles.

Join, taking care not to twist stitches.

Rounds 1 and 2: Knit.
Round 3: [Yo, k1] 8 times. (16 sts)
Round 4: Knit.
Round 5: [Yo, k1] 16 times. (32 sts)
Round 6: [K2, k2tog] 8 times. (24 sts)
Round 7: [Yo, k1, yo, k2tog] 8 times. (32 sts)
Round 8: Knit.
Round 9: [Yo, k1, yo, k1, yo, k2tog] 8 times. (48 sts)
Round 10: [K4, k2tog] 8 times. (40 sts)
Round 11: [(Yo, k1) 3 times, k2tog] 8 times. (56 sts)
Round 12: [K5, k2tog] 8 times. (48 sts)
Round 13: [Yo, k1, yo, k1, yo, k2, k2tog] 8 times. (64 sts)
Round 14: [K6, k2tog] 8 times. (56 sts)
Round 15: [Yo, k1, yo, k1, yo, k3, k2tog] 8 times. (72 sts)
Round 16: [K7, k2tog] 8 times. (64 sts)
Round 17: [Yo, k1, yo, k1, yo, k4, k2tog] 8 times. (80 sts)
Round 18: [K8, k2tog] 8 times. (72 sts)
Round 19: [Yo, k1, yo, k1, yo, k5, k2tog] 8 times. (88 sts)
Round 20: [K9, k2tog] 8 times. (80 sts)
Round 21: [Yo, k1, yo, k1, yo, k6, k2tog] 8 times. (96 sts)
Round 22: [K10, k2tog] 8 times. (88 sts)
Round 23: Purl.
Round 24: Knit.
Round 25: Purl.
Cast off loosely purlwise.

Colour:
■ A

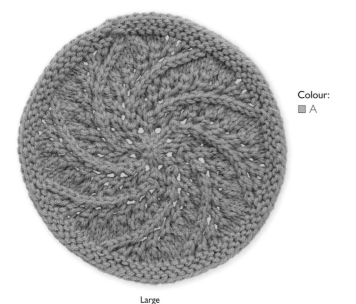

Large

18 TWO-TONE SUNBURST

Cast on 8 stitches and divide evenly over 4 needles.

Join, taking care not to twist stitches.

Round 1: Knit.
Round 2: [K1, M1] 8 times. (16 sts)
Rounds 3–5: Knit.
Round 6: [K1, M1] 16 times. (32 sts)
Rounds 7–11: Knit.
Round 12: [K1, M1] to end of round. (64 sts)

Fasten off A. Join B.
Rounds 13–19: Knit.
Round 20: [K2, M1] to end of round. (96 sts)
Round 21: Knit.
Rounds 22–25: [K1, p1] to end of round.
Cast off loosely in rib pattern.

Colours:
■ A
■ B

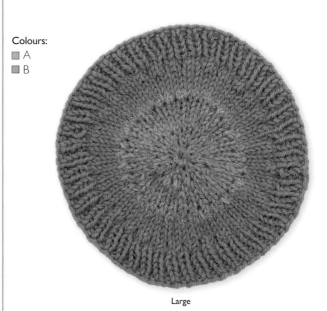

Large

Mix and match: **18 + 128**

19 LACE STAR MEDALLION

Cast on 6 stitches and divide evenly over 3 needles.

Join, taking care not to twist stitches.

Round 1: [K1f&b] 6 times. (12 sts)

Round 2 (and all even-numbered rounds): Knit all sts and yo; k and p into any double yo.

Round 3: * [K1, p1, k1] in next st, k1f&b in foll st; rep from * to end. (30 sts)

Round 5: [Sl 1, k1, psso, k1, k2tog, yo] 6 times. (24 sts)

Round 7: [Sl 1, k2tog, psso, yo, k1, yo] 6 times. (24 sts)

Round 9: [K1, yo, k3, yo] 6 times. (36 sts)

Round 11: [K1, yo, sl 1, k1, psso, k1, k2tog, yo] 6 times. (36 sts)

Round 13: [Yo, k1f&b, yo, k1, yo, sl 1, k2tog, psso, yo, k1] 6 times. (54 sts)

Round 15: [Sl 1, k1, psso, yo, sl 1, k1, psso, yo, k1f&b, yo, k2tog, yo, k2tog, yo] 6 times. (66 sts)

Round 17: [Sl 1, k1, psso, yo, sl 1, k2tog, psso, yo, sl 1, k2tog, psso, yo, k2tog, yo, k1, yo] 6 times. (60 sts)

Round 19: [Sl 1, k1, psso, yo, sl 1, k2tog, psso, yo, k2tog, (yo) twice, k3, (yo) twice] 6 times. (72 sts)

Round 21: [Sl 1, k1, psso, yo, k1, yo, k2tog, yo, k1, yo, sl 1, k1, psso, k1, k2tog, yo, k1, yo] 6 times. (84 sts)

Round 23: [Sl 1, k1, psso, k1f&b, k2tog, (yo) twice, k3, yo, sl 1, k2tog, psso, yo, k3, (yo) twice] 6 times. (102 sts)

Round 25: [Sl 1, k1, psso, yo, k2tog, yo, k1, yo, sl 1, k1, psso, k1, k2tog, yo, k1, yo, sl 1, k1, psso, k1, k2tog, yo, k1, yo] 6 times. (108 sts)

Round 27: [Yo, sl 1, k2tog, psso, yo, k3, yo, sl 1, k2tog, psso, yo, k3, yo, sl 1, k2tog, psso, yo, k3] 6 times.

Round 28: Purl.

Cast off loosely purlwise.

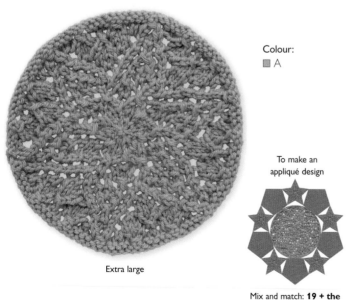

Extra large

Colour:

■ A

To make an appliqué design

Mix and match: 19 + the small version of 89 described on page 83 + 109

20 WHEEL WITH LACE SPOKES

Cast on 98 stitches loosely.

Row 1 (RS): Knit.

Row 2 (WS): P1, *k7, p1, yo, p2tog, k6; rep from * 5 times more, p1.

Row 3: K1, *p6, k1, yo, ssk, p7; rep from * 5 times more, k1.

Row 4: P1, *k7, p1, yo, p2tog, k6; rep from * 5 times more, p1.

Row 5: K1, p2tog, p4, *k1, yo, ssk, p5, p3tog, p5; rep from * 4 times more, k1, yo, ssk, p5, p2tog, k1. (86 sts)

Row 6: P1, *k6, p1, yo, p2tog, k5; rep from * 5 times more, p1.

Row 7: K1, p2tog, p3, *k1, yo, ssk, p4, sl 1, k2tog, psso, p4; rep from * 4 times more, k1, yo, ssk, p4, k2tog, k1. (74 sts)

Row 8: P2, k4, *p1, yo, p2tog, k4, p1, k4; rep from * 4 times more, p1, yo, p2tog, k4, p1.

Row 9: K1, p2tog, p2, *k1, yo, ssk, p3, sl 1, k2tog, psso, p3; rep from * 4 times more, k1, yo, ssk, p3, k2tog, k1. (62 sts)

Row 10: P2, k3, *p1, yo, p2tog, k3, p1, k3; rep from * 4 times more, p1, yo, p2tog, k3, p1.

Row 11: K1, p2tog, p1, *k1, yo, ssk, p2, sl 1, k2tog, psso, p2; rep from * 4 times more, k1, yo, ssk, p2, k2tog, k1. (50 sts)

Row 12: P2, k2, *p1, yo, p2tog, k2, p1, k2; rep from * 4 times more, p1, yo, p2tog, k2, p1.

Row 13: K1, p2tog, *k1, yo, ssk, p1, sl 1, k2tog, psso, p1; rep from * 4 times more, k1, yo, ssk, p1, k2tog, k1. (38 sts)

Row 14: P2, k1, *p1, yo, p2tog, k1, p1, k1; rep from * 4 times more, p1, yo, p2tog, k1, p1.

Row 15: K2tog, *k1, yo, ssk, sl 1, k2tog, psso; rep from * 5 times more. (25 sts)

Row 16: *P2, yo, p2tog; rep from * 5 times more, p1.

Row 17: K2, *yo, k1, sl 1, k2tog, psso, rep from * 4 times more, end yo, k3. (21 sts)

Row 18: Purl.

Row 19: [K2tog] 10 times, k1. (11 sts)

Row 20: Knit.

Row 21: [K2tog] 5 times, k1. (6 sts)

Cut yarn leaving a 25cm (10in) tail. Using a tapestry needle, weave the yarn through the remaining 6 stitches on the needle, gather and secure. Sew side seams together to form a circle block.

Colour:

■ A

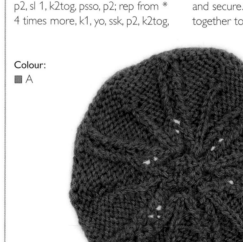

Large

21 MITRED DIAMOND

> **NOTE**
> Use a marker to indicate the centre single crochet stitch (centre dc of 3-dc group) and the right-side row.

Foundation chain: Ch 4.
Row 1 (RS): Insert hook into second ch from hook, 1 dc, 3 dc in next ch, 1 dc in next ch, turn. (5 sts)
Row 2: Ch 1, 1 blo dc in each dc to centre dc of 3-dc group, 3 dc in centre dc, 1 blo dc in each dc across to the end of the row, turn. Repeat Row 2, 15 times more. Fasten off.

Large

Colour:
■ A

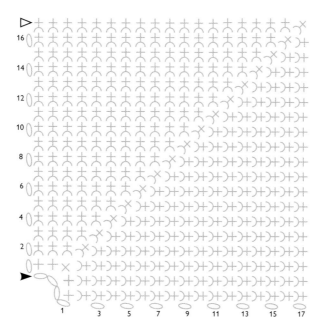

Same-block tessellation: **21**

Symbols and abbreviations
Turn to pages 140–141 for a full explanation of the symbols and abbreviations used.

22 GEOMETRIC DIAMOND

Foundation ring: Ch 4, join with ss to form a ring.

Round 1: Ch 1, [1 dc, 1 htr, 1 tr, 1 dtr, ch 3, 1 dtr, 1 tr, 1 htr] twice in ring, join with ss in top of beg ch-1.

Round 2: Ch 5 (counts first tr and ch 2), 1 tr in dc, 1 tr in each of next 3 sts, [3 tr, ch 4, 3 tr] into ch-3 sp, 1 tr in each of next 3 sts, [1 tr, ch 2, 1 tr] in next dc, 1 tr in each of next 3 sts, [3 tr, ch 4, 3 tr] into ch-3 sp, 1 tr in each of next 3 sts, join with ss in third ch of beg ch-5.

Round 3: Ch 3, (counts first tr), *[1 tr, ch 3, 1 tr] in ch-2 sp, 1 tr in next 2 tr, ch 1, skip next tr, 1 tr in each of next 3 tr, ch 1, skip next tr, [3 tr, ch 5, 3 tr] in ch-4 sp, ch 1, skip next tr, 1 tr in each of next 3 tr, ch 1, skip next tr, 1 tr in each of the next 2 tr; rep from * once more, skip the last tr at the end of last rep, join with ss into top of beg ch-3.

Fasten off.

Colour:
■ A

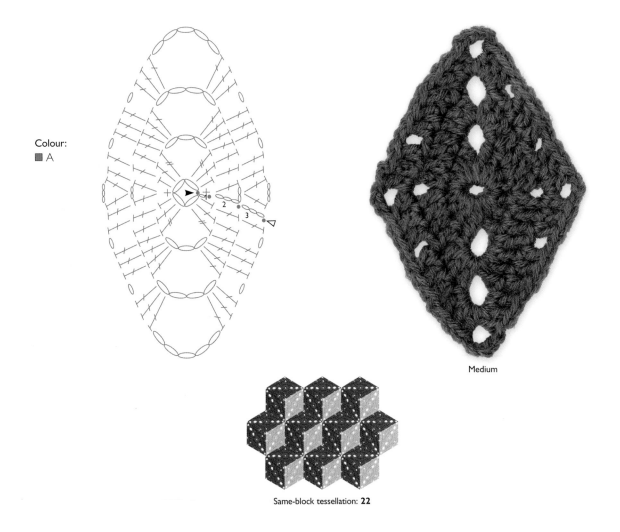

Medium

Same-block tessellation: **22**

23 BOBBLE DIAMOND

SPECIAL ABBREVIATIONS

beg popcorn: [1 dc, ch 2, 3 tr] into base of ch, remove hook, insert in second ch, catch working loop and pull through to close popcorn.

popcorn: 4 tr, remove hook from working loop, insert hook in first tr, catch working loop and pull through to close popcorn.

Foundation ring: Ch 8, join with ss to form a ring.

Round 1: Ch 1, work 16 dc into ring, ss into first dc.

Round 2: Ch 1, work beg popcorn, [ch 1, 1 dc in each of next 3 dc, 1 ch, popcorn in next dc] 3 times, ch 1, 1 dc into each of next 3 dc, ch 1, join with ss to top of beg popcorn.

Round 3: Ch 1, 1 ss in ch-1 sp before ss, ch 5 (counts as first tr and ch 3), [2 tr in next ch-1 sp, 1 tr into each of next 3 dc, 2 tr in ch-1 sp, ch 3] 3 times, 2 tr in next ch-1 sp, 1 tr in each of next 3 dc, 1 tr in first ch-1 sp, join with ss in second ch of beg ch-5.

Round 4: Ch 1, beg popcorn [1 tr, ch 3, 1 tr] in next ch-3 sp, [popcorn in next tr, 1 tr into each of next 2 tr] twice, popcorn in next tr [1 dtr, ch 3, 1 dtr] in next ch-3 sp, [popcorn in next tr, 1 tr into each of next 2 tr] twice, popcorn in next tr [1 tr, ch 3, 1 tr] in next ch-3 sp, [popcorn in next tr, 1 tr into each of next 2 tr] twice, popcorn in next tr. [1 dtr, ch 3, 1 dtr] in last ch-3 sp, [popcorn in next tr, 1 tr in each of next 2 tr] twice, join with ss to top of beg popcorn.

Round 5: Ss in first tr of Round 4, [ss , ch 1, 1 dc, ch 5 (counts as first tr and 3 ch), 2 tr] into next ch-3 sp, 1 tr in each of next 9 sts, [2 dtr, ch 3, 2 dtr] in next ch-3 sp, 1 tr in each of next 9 sts, [2 tr, ch 3, 2 tr] in next ch-3 sp, 1 tr in each of next 9 sts, [2 dtr, ch 3, 2 dtr] in next ch-3 sp, 1 tr in each of next 9 sts, 1 tr in first ch-3 sp, join with ss in second ch of beg ch-5.

Round 6: Ch 1, *3 dc in ch-3 sp, 1 dc in each of next 13 sts, 3 tr in next ch-3 sp, 1 dc in each of next 13 sts; rep from * once more, join with ss into first dc.

Fasten off.

Colour:
■ A

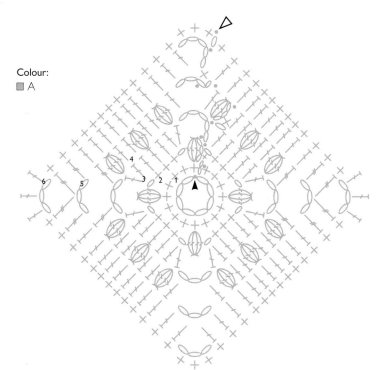

Large

24 TRI-COLOUR GRANNY

Foundation ring: Using A, ch 4, join with ss to form a ring.

Round 1: Ch 3 (counts as first tr), 2 tr in ring, ch 2, [3 tr in ring, ch 2] 3 times, join with ss in top of beg ch-3.

Fasten off A. Join B in any ch-2 sp.

Round 2: Ch 3, [2 tr, ch 2, 3 tr] in ch-2 sp at base of ch (right side corner made), ch 1, [2 tr, 1 dtr, ch 2, 1 dtr, 2 tr] in next ch-2 sp (top corner made), ch 1, [3 tr, ch 2, 3 tr] in next ch-2 sp (left side corner made), ch 1, [3 tr, 1 dtr, ch 2, 1 dtr, 2 tr] in next ch-2 sp (bottom corner made), ch 1, join with ss in top of beg ch-3.

Fasten off A. Join C with ss in ch-2 sp of right corner

Round 3: Ch 3, (2 tr, ch 2, 3 tr) in ch-2 sp at base of ch, ch 1, 3 tr in next ch-1 sp, ch 1, [2 tr, 1 dtr, ch 3, 1 dtr, 2 tr] in next ch-2 sp (top corner), ch 1, 3 tr in next ch-1 sp, ch 1, [3 tr, ch 2, 3 tr] in next ch-2 sp (left side), ch 1, 3 tr in next ch-1 sp, ch 1, (2 tr, 1 dtr, ch 3, 1 dtr, 2 tr) in next ch-2 sp (bottom corner), ch 1, 3 tr in next ch-1 sp, ch 1, join with ss in top of beg ch-3.

Fasten off.

Colours:
■ A
■ B
■ C

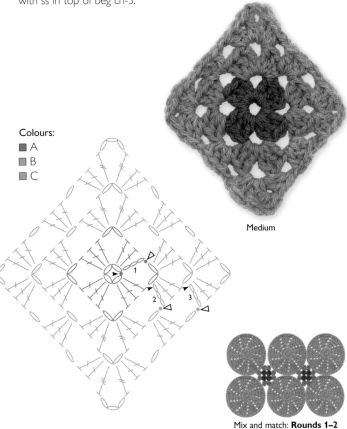

Medium

Mix and match: **Rounds 1–2 of 24 + 2**

25 STAR STITCH DIAMOND

> **SPECIAL ABBREVIATION:**
> **Star** = P3tog, do not slip sts off needle, yo, purl same 3 sts tog again, sl sts off needle.

Cast on 3 stitches.

Row 1: (RS): Knit.

Row 2: Purl.

Row 3: [K1, M1] twice, k1. (5 sts)

Row 4: Purl.

Row 5: K1, M1, k to the last st, M1, k1. (7 sts) The last row sets the position of the increases. Repeat the last row each alternate row until Row 25.

Row 6: P1, k1, star, k1, p1.

Row 8: P1, star, k1, star, p1.

Row 10: P3, k1, star, k1, p3.

Row 12: P2, [k1, star] twice, k1, p2.

Row 14: P1, [k1, star] 3 times, k1, p1.

Row 16: P1, [star, k1] 3 times, star, p1.

Row 18: P3, [k1 star] 3 times, k1, p3.

Row 20: P2, [k1, star] 4 times, k1, p2.

Row 22: P1 [k1, star] 5 times, k1, p1.

Row 24: P1, [star, k1] 5 times, star, p1.

Row 26: P3, (k1, star) 5 times, k1, p3.

Row 27: K1, M1, k25, M1, k1. (29 sts)

Row 28: P2, (k1, star) 6 times, k1, p2.

Row 29: K1, ssk, k to the last 3 sts, k2tog, k1. (27 sts)

The last row sets the position of the decreases. Repeat the last row each alternate row until Row 51.

Row 30: Rep Row 26.

Row 32: Rep Row 24.

Row 34: Rep Row 22.

Row 36: Rep Row 20.

Row 38: Rep Row 18.

Row 40: Rep Row 16.

Row 42: Rep Row 14.

Row 44: Rep Row 12.

Row 46: Rep Row 10.

Row 48: Rep Row 8.

Row 50: Rep Row 6.

Row 52: Purl.

Row 53: K1, sl1, k2tog, psso, k1. (3 sts)

Row 54: P3tog.

Fasten off.

Colour:
■ A

Medium

26 KNIT MITRED DIAMOND

Cast on 41 stitches.
Row 1 (RS): K20, sl1, k20.
Row 2: K20, p1, k20.
Row 3: K18, k2togtbl, sl1, k2tog, k18. (39 sts)
Row 4: Purl.
Row 5: K17, k2togtbl, sl1, k2tog, k17. (37 sts)
Row 6: Purl.
Row 7: K16, k2togtbl, sl1, k2tog, k16. (35 sts)
Row 8: K17, p1, k17.
Row 9: K15, k2togtbl, sl1, k2tog, k15. (33 sts)
Row 10: Purl.
Row 11: K14, k2togtbl, sl1, k2tog, k14. (31 sts)
Row 12: Purl.
Row 13: K13, k2togtbl, sl1, k2tog, k13. (29 sts)
Row 14: K14, p1, k14.
Continue in set patt, until 7 sts rem.
Row 36: Purl.
Row 37: K1, k2togtbl, sl1, k2tog, k1. (5 sts)
Row 38: K2, p1, k2.
Row 39: K2togtbl, sl1, k2tog. (3 sts)
Row 40: Purl.
Row 41: K3togtbl. (1 st)
Fasten off.

Colour:
◼ A

Large

To make a scarf

Same-block tessellation: **26**

27 KNIT GARTER DIAMOND

Cast on 4 stitches.
Row 1: Knit.
Row 2 (RS): K2, yo, k2. (5 sts)
Row 3: Knit.
Row 4: K2, yo, k1, yo, K2. (7 sts)
Row 5: Knit.
Row 6: K2, yo, k to last 2 sts, yo, k2. (9 sts)
Repeat the last 2 rows 9 more times. (27 sts)
Row 25: Knit.
Row 26: K1, k2tog, yo, k2tog, k17, ssk, yo, ssk, k1. (25 sts)
Row 27: Knit.
Rows 28: K1, k2tog, yo, k2tog, k to last 5 sts, ssk, yo, ssk, k1. (23 sts)
Repeat the last 2 rows 7 times more. (9 sts)
Row 43: Knit.
Row 44: K1, k2tog, yo, k3 tog, yo, ssk, k1. (7 sts)
Row 45: Knit.
Row 46: K1, K2tog, yo, k3tog, k1. (5 sts)
Row 47: Knit.
Row 48: K1, K3tog, k1. (3 sts)
Cast off.

Colour:
◼ A

Medium

28 KNIT RIBBED DIAMOND

Cast on 39 stitches.
Row 1 (RS): P18, p3tog, p18. (37 sts)
Rows 2 and 4: Knit
Row 3: K2, [yo, k2tog] 8 times, yo, k3tog, [yo, k2tog] 7 times, yo, k2.
Row 5: K2, yo, k2tog, [k2, p2] 3 times, k2, p1, [k2, p2] 3 times, k6.
Row 6: K2, yo, k2tog, [p2, k2] 3 times, p1, k3tog, p1, [k2, p2] 3 times, k4. (35 sts)
Row 7: K2, yo, k2tog, [k2, p2] 3 times, k3, [p2, k2] twice, p2, k6.
Row 8: K2, yo, k2tog, [p2, k2] 3 times, p3tog, [k2, p2] 3 times, k4. (33 sts)
Row 9: K2, yo, k2tog, [k2, p2] 3 times, k1, [p2, k2] twice, p2, k6.
Row 10: K2, yo, k2tog, [p2, k2] twice, p2, k1, k3tog, k1, [p2, k2] twice, p2, k4. (31 sts)
Row 11: K2, yo, k2tog, [k2, p2] twice, k2, p3, [k2, p2] twice, k6.
Row 12: K2, yo, k2tog, [p2, k2] twice, p2, k3tog,

[p2, k2] twice, p2, k4. (29 sts)
Row 13: K2, yo, k2tog, [k2, p2] twice, k2, p1, [k2, p2] twice, k6.
Row 14: K2, yo, k2tog, [p2, k2] twice, p1, p3tog, p1, [k2, p2] twice, k4. (27 sts)
Row 15: K2, yo, k2tog, [k2, p2] twice, k3, p2, k2, p2, k6.
Row 16: K2, yo, k2tog, [p2, k2] twice, p3tog, [k2, p2] twice, k4. (25 sts)
Row 17: K2, yo, k2tog, [k2, p2] twice, k1, p2, k2, p2, k6.
Row 18: K2, yo, k2tog, p2, k2, p2, k1, k3tog, k1, p2, k2, p2, k4. (23 sts)
Row 19: K2, yo, k2tog, k2, p2, k2, p3, k2, p2, k6.
Row 20: K2, yo, k2tog, p2, k2, p2, k3tog, p2, k2, p2, k4. (21 sts)
Row 21: K2, yo, k2tog, k2, p2, k2, p1, k2, p2, k6.
Row 22: K2, yo, k2tog, p2, k2, p1, p3tog, p1, k2, p2, k4. (19 sts)
Row 23: K2, yo, k2tog, k2, p2, k3, p2, k6.

Row 24: K2, yo, k2tog, p2, k2, p3tog, k2, p2, k4. (17 sts)
Row 25: K2, yo, k2tog, k2, p2, k1, p2, k6.
Row 26: K2, yo, k2tog, p2, k1, k3tog, k1, p2, k4. (15 sts)
Row 27: K2, yo, k2tog, k2, p3, k6.
Row 28: K2, yo, k2tog, p2, k3tog, p2, k4. (13 sts)
Row 29: K2, yo, k2tog, k2, p1, k6.
Row 30: K2, yo, k2tog, p1, p3tog, p1, k4. (11 sts)
Row 31: K2, yo, k2tog, k7.
Row 32: K2, yo, k2tog, p3tog, k4. (9 sts)
Row 33: K2, yo, k2tog, k5.
Row 34: K2, yo, k2tog, k1, k2tog, k2. (8 sts)
Row 35: K2, yo, k3tog, k3. (7 sts)
Row 36: K2, yo, k3tog, k2. (6 sts)
Row 37: K2, yo, k3tog, k1. (5 sts)
Row 38: K1, k3tog, k1. (3 sts)
Row 39: K3tog.
Fasten off.

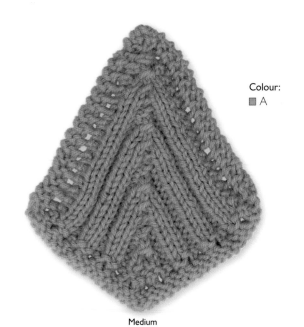

Medium

Colour:
■ A

Mix and match: **28 + 27**

SQUARES

29 COLOUR DOT SQUARE

Foundation ring: Using A, ch 4, join with ss to form a ring.

Round 1: Ch 3 (counts as first tr), 11 tr into ring, join with ss in top of beg ch-3. (12 sts)

Round 2: Ch 3 (counts as first tr), 1 tr in st at base of ch, 2 tr in each tr around, join with ss in top of beg ch-3. (24 sts) Fasten off A. Change to B.

Round 3: Ch 1, dc in st at base of ch, 1 dc in next st, 1 htr in next st, *3 tr in next st, 1 htr in next st, 1 dc in next 3 sts, 1 htr in next st; rep from * twice more, 3 tr in next st, 1 htr in next st, 1 dc in next st, join with ss in first dc. (32 sts)

Round 4: Ch 3, 1 tr in each of next 3 sts, *5 tr in next st, 1 tr in next 7 sts; rep from * twice more, 5 tr in next st, 1 tr in next 3 sts, join with ss in top of beg ch. (48 sts) Fasten off B. Change to C.

Round 5: Ch 2 (counts as first htr), 1 htr in each of the next 5 sts, *3 htr in next st, 1 htr in each of next 11 sts; rep from * twice more, 3 htr in next st, 1 htr in each of next 5 sts join with ss in top of beg ch. Fasten off.

Colours:
- A
- B
- C

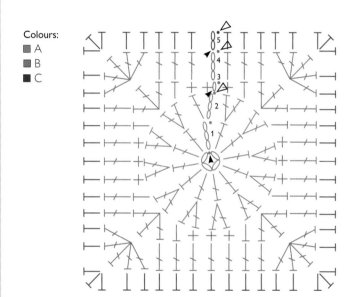

Medium

Mix and match: **29 + 30**

Symbols and abbreviations
Turn to pages 140–141 for a full explanation of the symbols and abbreviations used.

30 DOUBLE CROCHET SQUARE

Foundation ring: Ch 4, join with ss to form a ring.
Round 1: Ch 5 (counts as first tr and ch 2), [3 tr into ring, ch 2] 3 times, 2 tr into ring, join with ss to third ch of beg ch-5.
Round 2: Ss in next sp, ch 7 (counts as first tr and ch 4), 2 tr into sp at base of ch, *1 tr in each of the next 3 tr, [2 tr, ch 4, 2 tr] in the next sp; rep from * twice more, 1 tr in each of the next 3 tr, 1 tr in same sp as ch-7, join with ss to third ch of beg ch-7.

Round 3: Ss into next sp, ch 7 (counts as first tr and ch 4), 2 tr in sp at base of ch, *1 tr into each of the next 7 tr, [2 tr, ch 4, 2 tr] in the next sp; rep from * twice more, 1 tr into each of the next 7 tr, 1 tr in same sp as ch-7, join with ss to third ch of beg ch-7.

Round 4: Ss into next sp, ch 7 (counts as first tr and ch 4), 2 tr in sp at base of ch, *1 tr in each of the next 11 tr, [2 tr, ch 4, 2 tr] in the next sp; rep from * twice more, 1 tr into each of the next 11 tr, 1 tr in same sp as ch-7, join with ss to third ch of beg ch-7.
Fasten off.

Colour:
■ A

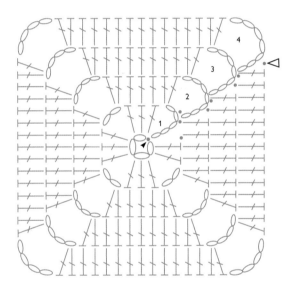

Medium

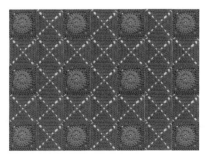

Mix and match: **30 + 29**

31 TRI-COLOUR GRANNY SQUARE

Foundation ring: Using A, ch 4, join with ss to form a ring.

Round 1: Ch 5 (counts as first tr and ch 2), [3 tr into ring, ch 2] 3 times, 2 tr in ring, join with ss to third ch of beg ch-5.

Fasten off A. Join B with ss to any ch-2 sp.

Round 2: Ch 5, (counts as first tr and ch 2), 3 tr into sp at base of ch, *ch 1, skip 3 tr [3 tr, ch 2, 3 tr] into next sp; rep from * twice more, ch 1, skip 3 sts, 2 tr in same sp as ch-5, join with ss to third ch of beg ch-5.

Round 3: Ss into next sp, ch 5, (counts as first tr and ch 2), 3 tr into sp at base of ch, *ch 1, skip 3 tr, 3 tr into next sp, ch 1, skip 3 tr; [3 tr, ch 2, 3 tr] into next sp; rep from * twice more, ch 1, skip 3 tr, 3 tr into next sp, ch 1, skip 3 tr, 2 tr into same sp as ch-5, join with ss to third ch of beg ch-5.

Fasten off B. Join C with ss to any ch-2 sp.

Round 4: Ch 5, (counts as first tr and ch 2), 3 tr into sp at base of ch, *[ch 1, skip 3 tr, 3 tr into next sp] twice, ch 1, skip 3 tr, [3 tr, ch 2, 3 tr] into next sp; rep from * twice more, [ch 1, skip 3 tr, 3 tr into next sp] twice, ch 1, skip 3 tr, 2tr into same sp as ch-5, join with ss to third ch of beg ch-5.

Fasten off.

Colours:
■ A
■ B
■ C

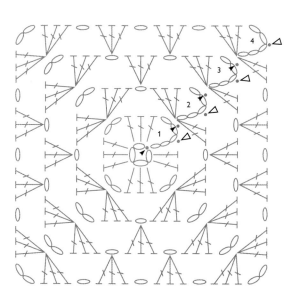

Small

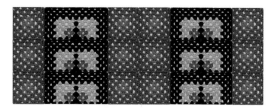

Mix and match: **31 + 35**

To make this block larger, continue to work in the pattern set. For this mix-and-match pattern work one more round in pattern set.

32 CIRCLES SQUARE

NOTE
Working from the inside of the block outwards, the first row creates the interior four quarters of the four inner circles. The first row is joined into a round, then the second round completes the inner four circles. The outer circles are worked in the same way. The third row attaches the inside portions of outer circles to the inner four circles and the final round completes the outer circles.

Colours:
■ A
■ B

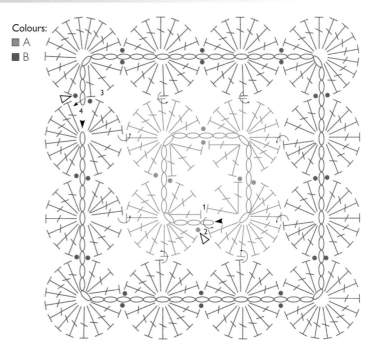

INTERIOR FOUR CIRCLES

Foundation chain: Using A, ch 22. This row creates the inside quarter of the interior circles.

Row 1: Starting in fourth ch from hook, *3 tr in the next ch, skip 2 ch, ss into next ch (one quarter circle), skip 2 ch; rep from * twice more, 3 tr in the next ch.
Remove hook from the working loop, insert hook in the last ch worked of the foundation chain, and catch the working loop and draw through the ch.
Continue to work along the other side of the foundation chain, inserting the hook into the same chains as worked on Row 1.

Round 2: Work 12 tr in the same ch as the last 3 tr of row 1, insert the hook through the chain and the last slip stich, work ss, * 11 tr in the ch at the base of the next 3-tr group, ss in the next ss; rep from * twice more, join with a ss in the last ch of the foundation ch.
Fasten off A.

OUTSIDE 12 CIRCLES

Foundation chain: Using B, ch 70.

Row 3: Starting in fourth ch from hook, *3 tr in the next ch, skip 2 ch, ss in next ch (one quarter circle), skip 2 ch, 3 tr in the next ch remove hook from working loop, insert hook in the fourth tr of the upper left circle of the second round, catch and draw the working loop though the tr st, 4 tr into the ch at the base of the last 3-tr group worked (one half circle) skip 2 ch, ss in the next ch, skip 2 ch, work another half-circle, joining it to the next circle, skip 2 st, ss, skip 2 st; rep from * 3 times more.
Remove hook from the working loop, insert hook in the last ch worked of the foundation chain, and catch the working loop and draw through the ch.
Continue to work along the other side of the foundation chain, inserting the hook into the same chains as worked on Row 3.

Round 4: Work 8 tr in the same ch as the last half shell of Row 3, insert the hook through the chain and the last slip stich, work ss, * 7 tr in the ch at the base of the next half shell, ss in the next ss, 11 tr in the ch at the base of the next 3-tr group, ss in the next ss, 7 tr in the ch at the base of the next 3-tr group, ss in the next ss, rep from * twice more, 7 tr in the ch at the base of the next half shell, ss in the next ss, 11 tr in the ch at the base of the next 3-tr group, join with a ss in the last ch of the foundation ch.
Fasten off B.

Large

Same-block tessellation: **32**

33 TRI-COLOUR WHEEL IN SQUARE

SPECIAL ABBREVIATION

St-sp: The space between the posts of 2 sts.

Foundation ring: Using A, ch 4, join with ss to form a ring.

Round 1: Ch 5 (counts as first tr, ch 2), [1 tr in ring, ch 2] 7 times, join with ss to third ch of beg ch-5: (8 tr and ch-2 sp).

Round 2: Ss in ch-2 sp, ch 3 (counts as first tr), 2 tr into sp at base of ch, ch 1, [3 tr in next ch-2 sp, ch 1] 7 times, join with ss to top of beg ch-3.

Fasten off A. Join B, and ss to next ch-1 sp.

Round 3: Ch 3 (counts as first tr), 2 tr into sp at base of ch, ch 1, 3 tr in next ch-1 sp, ch 5, [3 tr in next ch-1 sp, ch 1, 3 tr in next ch-1 sp, ch 5] 3 times, join with ss to top of beg ch 3.

Round 4: Ss between next 2 tr, ch 3 (counts as first tr), 1 tr in next st-sp, 3 tr in next ch-1 sp, 1 tr in the next 2 st-sp, [3 tr, ch 2, 3 tr] in next ch-5 sp, *1 tr in next 2 st-sp, 3 tr in next

ch-1 sp, 1 tr in next 2 st-sp, [3 tr; ch 2, 3 tr] in next ch-5 sp; rep from * twice more, join with ss to top of beg ch-3.

Round 5: Ss between last tr made and beg ch-3 of round 4, ch 3, 1 tr in next st-sp, skip 1 st-sp, 1 tr in each of next 2 st-sp, skip 1 st-sp, 1 tr in each of next 4 st-sp, *[3 tr; ch 2, 3 tr] in next ch-2 sp, 1 tr in each of next 4 st-sp, skip 1 st-sp, 1 tr in each of next 2 st-sp, skip 1 st-sp, 1 tr in each of the next 4 st-sp; rep from * twice more, [3 tr, ch 2, 3 tr] in next ch-2 sp, 1 tr in each of next 2 st-sp, join with ss to top of beg ch-3.

Fasten off B. Join C with ss.

Round 6: Ch 1, work 1 dc in each tr and 3 dc in each ch-2 sp, join with a ss to first dc.

Fasten off.

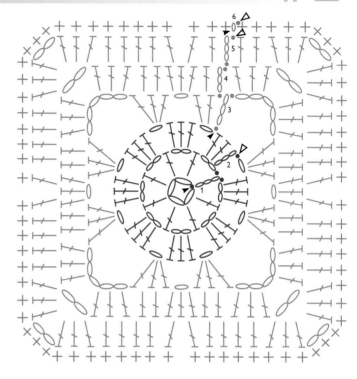

Large

Colours:
- ■ A
- ■ B
- ■ C

34 FLOWER SQUARE

SPECIAL ABBREVIATIONS

beg 2-dtr cl (2 double treble-crochet cluster): *Yrh twice, insert hook in st, yrh, pull loop through, [yrh, pull loop through 2 loops on hook] twice; rep from * once more working in same st, yrh and pull loop through all 3 loops on hook.

3-dtr cl (3 double treble-crochet cluster): *Yrh twice, insert hook in st, yrh, pull loop through, [yrh, pull loop through 2 loops on hook] twice; rep from * twice more working in same st, yrh and pull loop through all 4 loops on hook.

3-tr cl (3 treble-crochet cluster): [Yrh, insert hook in st, yrh, pull loop through, yrh, pull loop through 2 loops on hook] 3 times, yrh, pull through all 4 loops on hook

Colour:
☐ A

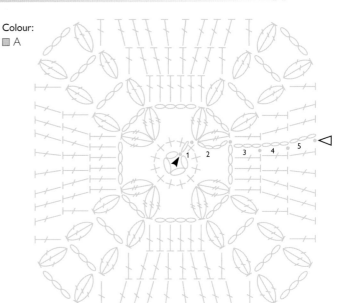

Foundation ring: Ch 4, join with ss to form a ring.

Round 1: Ch 1, 12 dc into ring, join with ss in top of beg dc.

Round 2: Ch 4, beg 2-dtr cl, ch 3, 3-dtr cl in the base of beg 2-dtr cl, *ch 4, skip next 2 sts, [3-dtr cl, ch 3, 3-dtr cl] in next st; rep from * twice more, ch 4, join with ss in top of beg 2-dtr cl.

Round 3: Ch 3 (counts as first tr) *1 tr in top of next cl, [3-tr cl, ch 3, 3-tr cl] in next ch-3 sp, 1 tr in top of next cl, 4 tr in next ch-4 sp; rep from * 3 times more, omitting last tr join with ss in top of beg ch-3.

Round 4: Ch 3, 1 tr in next tr, *1 tr in top of next cl, [3-tr cl, ch 3, 3-tr cl] in next ch-3 sp, 1 tr in top of next cl, 1 tr in each of next 6 sts; rep from * twice more, 1 tr in top of next cl, [3-tr cl, ch 3, 3-tr cl] in next ch-3 sp, 1 tr in top of next cl, 1 tr in each of next 4 sts, join with ss in top of beg ch-3.

Round 5: Ch 3, 1 tr in each of next 2 tr, *1 tr in top of next cl, [3-tr cl, ch 3, 3-tr cl] in next ch-3 sp, 1 tr in top of next cl, 1 tr in each of next 8 sts; rep from * twice more, 1 tr in top of next cl, [3-tr cl, ch 3, 3-tr cl] in next ch-3 sp, 1 tr in top of next cl, 1 tr in each of next 5 sts join with ss in top of beg ch-3.
Fasten off.

Extra large

35 OFF-CENTRED GRANNY

Foundation ring: Using A, ch 4, join with ss to form a ring.

Round 1 (RS): Ch 5 (counts as first tr and ch 2), [3 tr into ring, ch 2] 3 times, 2 tr in ring, join with ss to third ch of beg ch-5.

Only two sides of original round are worked until last round.

Fasten off A. Join B with ss to any ch-2 sp.

Row 2 (RS): Ch 2 (counts as first tr), 2 tr in ch-2 sp at base of ch, ch 1, [3 tr, ch 2, 3 tr] in next ch-2 sp, ch 1, 3 tr in next ch-2 sp, turn.

Row 3 (WS): Ch 3 (counts as first tr and ch 1), 3 tr in next ch-1 sp, ch 1, [3 tr, ch 2, 3 tr] in corner ch-2 sp, ch 1, 3 tr in next ch-1 sp, ch 1, 1 tr in last st of previous row, turn.

Row 4 (RS): Ch 2 (counts as first tr), 2 tr in first ch-1 sp, ch 1, 3 tr in next ch-1 sp, ch 1, [3 tr, ch 2, 3 tr] in corner ch-2 sp, [ch 1, 3 tr in next ch-1 sp] twice.

Fasten off B. Join C.

Row 5 (WS): Ch 3 (counts as first tr and ch 1), [3 tr in next ch-1 sp, ch 1] twice, [3 tr, ch 2, 3 tr] in next ch-2 sp, [ch 1, 3 tr in next ch-1 sp] twice, ch 1, 1 tr in last st of previous row, turn.

Row 6 (RS): Ch 2 (counts as first tr), 2 tr in first ch-1 sp, ch 1, [3 tr in next ch-1 sp, ch 1] twice, [3 tr, ch 2, 3 tr] in next ch-1 sp, [ch 1, 3 tr in next ch-1 sp] 3 times, turn.

Row 7(WS): Ch 3 (counts as first tr and ch 1), [3 tr in next ch-1 sp, ch 1] 3 times, [3 tr, ch 2, 3 tr] in next ch-1 sp, [ch 1, 3 tr in next ch-1 sp] 3 times, ch 1, 1 tr in last st of previous row, turn.

Round 8 (RS): Ch 2 (counts as first tr), 3 tr in next ch-1 sp, *[ch 1, 3 tr in next ch-1 sp] 3 times, ch 1, 7 tr in next ch-1 sp; rep from * once more, [ch 1, 3 tr in beg ch-3 at start of row] twice, ch 1, 3 tr in ch-2 sp Round 1, ch 1, 7 tr into next ch-2 sp, ch 1, 3 tr in next ch-2 sp, [ch 1, 3 tr around post of single tr st at the end of row] 3 times, join with ss to top of beg ch. Fasten off.

Colours:
■ A
□ B
■ C

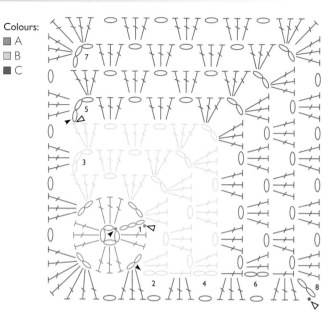

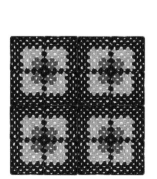

Same-block tessellation: **35**

Medium

36 POPCORN STITCH SQUARE

SPECIAL ABBREVIATIONS

beg popcorn: 4 tr in next st, remove hook from working loop, insert hook from front to back through top of beg ch-3, catch working loop, yrh, draw through loop and stitch.

popcorn: 5 tr in next st, remove hook from working loop, insert hook from front to back through first tr, catch working loop, yrh, draw through loop and stitch.

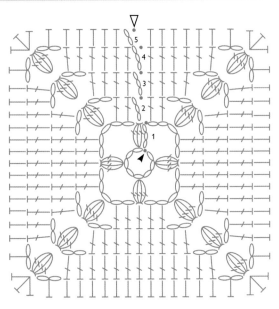

Colour:
■ A

Foundation ring: Ch 8, join with ss in first ch to form a ring.

Round 1: Ch 3, work beg popcorn, [ch 5, work popcorn into ring] 3 times, ch 5, join with ss to top of beg popcorn.

Round 2: Ch 3 (counts as first tr), *[2 tr, ch 2, popcorn, ch 2, 2 tr] in next ch-5 sp, 1 tr in next popcorn; rep from * twice more, [2 tr, ch 2, popcorn, ch 2, 2 tr] in next ch-5 sp, join with ss to top of beg ch-3.

Round 3: Ch 3 (counts as first tr), 1 tr in each of next 2 tr, *2 tr in next ch-2 sp, ch 2, popcorn in top of popcorn of previous round, ch 2, 2 tr in next ch-2 sp, 1 tr in each of next 5 tr; rep from * twice more, 2 tr into next ch-2 sp, ch 2, popcorn in top of popcorn of previous round, ch 2, 2 tr in next ch-2 sp, 1 tr in each of next 2 tr, join with ss to top of beg ch-3.

Round 4: Ch 3 (counts as first tr), 1 tr in each of next 4 tr, *2 tr in next ch-2 sp, ch 2, popcorn in top of popcorn of previous round, ch 2, 2 tr in next ch-2 sp, 1 tr in each of next 9 tr; rep from * twice more, 2 tr into next ch-2 sp, ch 2, popcorn in top of popcorn of previous round, ch 2, 2 tr in next ch-2 sp, 1 tr in each of next 4 tr, join with ss to top of beg ch-3.

Round 5: Ch 2 (counts as first htr) 1 htr in each of next 5 sts, *1 htr in next ch-2 sp, 3 htr in top of popcorn of previous round, 1 htr in next ch-2 sp, 1 htr in each of next 13 sts; rep from * twice more, 1 htr into ch-2 sp, 3 htr in top of popcorn of previous round, 1 htr in next ch-2 sp, 1 htr in each of next 6 sts, join with ss to top of beg ch-2. Fasten off.

Medium

Mix and match: **36 + 30**

37 MULTI-COLOURED QUATREFOIL

SPECIAL ABBREVIATIONS

beg 5-dtr cl (beginning 5 double treble-crochet cluster): Ch 4, *yrh twice, insert hook in next dtr; yrh and pull up a loop, [yrh and draw through 2 loops on hook] twice; rep from * 4 times more, yrh, draw through all 6 loops on hook.

6-dtr cl (6 double treble-crochet cluster): *Yrh twice, insert hook in next dtr; yrh and pull up a loop, [yrh and draw through 2 loops on hook] twice; rep from * 5 times more, yrh, draw through all 7 loops on hook.

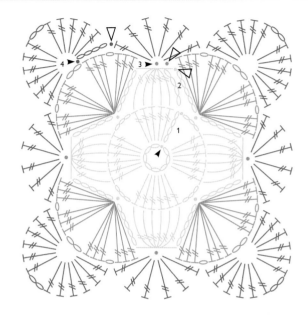

Foundation ring: Using A, ch 8, join with ss to form a ring.

Round 1 (RS): Ch 4 (counts as first dtr), 5 dtr into ring, ch 3, [6 dtr in ring, ch 3] 3 times, join with ss to top of beg ch-4. (24 dtr and 4 ch-3 sp)

Round 2: Work beg 5-dtr cl, ch 5, skip next ch, ss in next ch, ch 5, * work 6-dtr cl, ch 5, skip next ch, ss in next ch, ch 5; rep from * twice more, join with ss to top of beg 5-dtr. (4 cl)

Fasten off A. Join B with ss at top of any cluster.

Round 3: Working around next 2 ch-5 sp and next ss, [3 dtr, ch 1, 3 dtr, ch 2, 3 dtr, ch 1, 3 dtr] in next

ch-3 sp on Round 1, *ss in top of next cl on Round 2, working around next 2 ch-5 sp and next ss, [3 dtr, ch 1, 3 dtr, ch 2, 3 dtr, ch 1, 3 dtr] in next ch-3 sp on Round 1; rep from * twice more, join with ss to first ss. Fasten off B. Join C with ss to any corner ch-2 sp.

Round 4: Ch 4 (5 dtr, ch 2, 6 dtr) in sp at base of ch, skip next 6 dtr, 6 dtr in next ss, *skip next 6 dtr, [6 dtr, ch 2, 6 dtr] in next ch-2 sp, skip next 6 dtr, work 6 dtr in next ss; rep from * twice more, skip last 6 dtr; join with ss to beg ch-4. Fasten off.

Colours:
- ☐ A
- ■ B
- ■ C

Medium

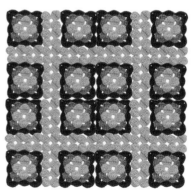

Mix and match: **37 + Rounds 1–2 of 37**

38 COLOUR SWIRL GRANNY

NOTE
Place working loops not in use onto a split ring-marker or safety pin.

Foundation chain: Using A, ch 2.
Round 1: Starting in second ch from hook [1 dc, 1 htr, 2 tr], remove hook from loop A, join B with dc in same ch, [1 htr, 2 tr] in same ch, remove hook from loop B, join C with dc in same ch, [1 htr, 2 tr] in same ch, remove hook from loop C, join D with dc in same ch, [1 htr, 2 tr] in same ch, remove hook from loop D, gently tighten chain into which sts have been worked.

Insert the hook into the working loops as required.
Round 2: Using A, *2 tr in next dc, 1 tr in next htr, 2 tr in next tr, 1 tr in next tr, remove hook from loop A; rep from * with colours B, C and D.
Round 3: Using A, *ch 2, 1 tr in next tr, skip 1 tr, 2 tr in each of next 2 tr, skip 1 tr, 1 tr, remove hook from loop A; rep from * with colours B, C and D.
Round 4: Using A, *[2 tr, ch 2, 2 tr] in next ch-2 sp, [ch 1, skip next tr, 2 tr in next tr] 3 times, remove hook from loop A; rep from * with colours B, C and D.

Round 5: Using A, *ch 1, [3 tr, ch 2, 3 tr] in next ch-2 sp, [ch 1, skip next 2 tr, 2 tr in next ch-1 sp] 3 times, remove hook from loop A; rep from * with colours B, C and D.
Round 6: Using A, *ch 1, 2 tr in ch-1 sp, ch 1, [3 tr, ch 1, 3 tr] in next ch-2 sp, skip 3 tr, ch 1, 2 tr in ch-1 sp, skip 2 tr, ch 1, [1 htr, 1 dc) in next ch-1 sp, skip 2 tr, ch 1, [1 dc, ss] in next ch-1 sp, fasten off A; rep from * with colours B, C and D.

Medium

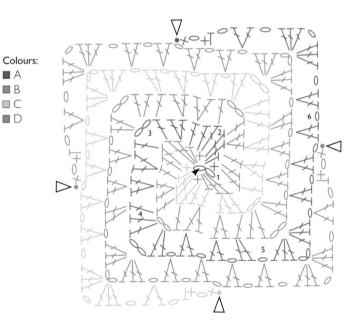

Colours:
■ A
■ B
□ C
■ D

39 MITERED GARTER SQUARE

> **NOTE**
> Mark the centre stitch with a detachable marker or safety pin and reposition as required.

Using A, cast on 49 stitches.

Row 1 (WS): Knit to centre st, wyf, sl next st knitwise, wyb, k to end. Change to B.

Row 2: Knit to 1 st before centre st, sl 2 sts, k1, p2sso, k to end. (47 sts)

Row 3: Knit to centre st, wyf, sl next st knitwise, wyb, k to end. Change to A.

Row 4 (RS): Knit to 1 st before centre st, sl 2 sts, k1, p2sso, k to end. (45 sts)

Row 5: Knit to centre st, wyf, sl next st knitwise, wyb, k to end. Change to B.

Repeat the last 4 rows and the yarn changes until 25 sts rem, ending with a WS row.

Fasten off A. Change to B.

Repeat Rows 4–5 until 3 sts rem ending with a RS row.

Next row (WS): K3tog. Fasten off.

Colours:

■ A
■ B

Medium

Same-block tessellation: **39**

40 CHEVRON SQUARE

Cast on 8 stitches and divide evenly over 4 needles.

Join, taking care not to twist stitches.

Round 1 (and all odd-numbered rounds): Knit.

Round 2: [Yo, k1] 8 times. (16 sts)

Round 4: [Yo, k3, yo, k1] 4 times. (24 sts)

Round 6: [Yo, k5, yo, k1] 4 times. (32 sts)

Round 8: [Yo, k7, yo, k1] 4 times. (40 sts)

Round 10: [Yo, k4, yo, ssk, k3, yo, k1] 4 times. (48 sts)

Round 12: [Yo, k3, k2tog, yo, k1, yo, ssk, k3, yo, k1] 4 times. (56 sts)

Round 14: [Yo, k3, k2tog, yo, k3, yo, ssk, k3, yo, k1] 4 times. (64 sts)

Round 16: [Yo, k3, k2tog, yo, k5, yo, ssk, k3, yo, k1] 4 times. (72 sts)

Round 18: [Yo, p18] 4 times. (76 sts)

Round 19: [K1, p18] 4 times.

Cast off loosely knitwise.

Colour:

■ A

Medium

41 EYELET SQUARE

Cast on 4 stitches and divide evenly over 4 needles.

Join, taking care not to twist stitches.

Round 1: [Yo, k1] 4 times. (8 sts)

Round 2: [K1, k1tbl] 4 times.

Round 3: [Yo, k1, yo, k1tbl] 4 times. (16 sts)

Round 4 (and all even-numbered rounds): [K to the last st on the needle, k1tbl] 4 times.

Round 5: [Yo, k3, yo, k1tbl] 4 times. (24 sts)

Round 7: [Yo, k5, yo, k1tbl] 4 times. (32 sts)

Round 9: [Yo, k7, yo, k1tbl] 4 times. (40 sts)

Round 11: [Yo, k3, yo, sl 1, k2tog, psso, yo, k3, yo, k1tbl] 4 times. (48 sts)

Round 13: [Yo, k2, k2tog, yo, k3, yo, ssk, k2, yo, k1tbl] 4 times. (56 sts)

Round 15: [Yo, k5, yo, sl 1, k2tog, psso, yo, k5, yo, k1tbl] 4 times. (64 sts)

Round 17: [Yo, k15, yo, k1tbl] 4 times. (72 sts)

Round 19: [Yo, k17, yo, k1tbl] 4 times. (80 sts)

Round 21: [Yo, ssk] to the end of the round.

Round 22: [Yo, p20] 4 times. (84 sts)

Using a larger size needle, cast off loosely purlwise.

Colour:
■ A

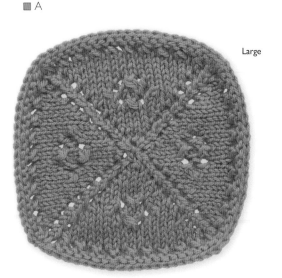

Large

42 TILTED SQUARE

Using A, cast on 8 stitches and divide evenly over 4 needles.

Join, taking care not to twist stitches.

Round 1: Knit.

Round 2: [K2, M1] 4 times. (12 sts)

Round 3: [K3, M1] 4 times. (16 sts)

Round 4: [K4, M1] 4 times. (20 sts)

Round 5: [P5, M1] 4 times. (24 sts)

Round 6: [P6, M1] 4 times. (28 sts)

Round 7: [P7, M1] 4 times. (32 sts)

Round 8: [P8, M1] 4 times. (36 sts) Fasten off A. Join B.

Round 9: [K9, M1] 4 times. (40 sts)

Round 10: [K10, M1] 4 times. (44 sts)

Round 11: [K11, M1] 4 times. (48 sts)

Round 12: [K12, M1] 4 times. (52 sts)

Round 13: [P13, M1] 4 times. (56 sts)

Round 14: [P14, M1] 4 times. (60 sts)

Round 15: [P15, M1] 4 times. (64 sts)

Round 16: [P16, M1] 4 times. (68 sts) Fasten off B. Join C.

Cont in increase patt as set and work 4 rounds of knit, 4 rounds of purl.

Cast off loosely knitwise.

Colours:
■ A
■ B
■ C

Medium

To see this design extrapolated into a blanket, see page 133

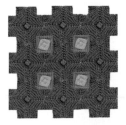

Mix and match: **Rounds 1–16 of 42 + 122**

43 FOUR-LEAF COUNTERPANE

Cast on 8 stitches and divide evenly over 4 needles.

Join, taking care not to twist stitches.

Round 1: [Yo, k1] 8 times. (16 sts)
Round 2: Knit.
Round 3: [Yo, k1] 16 times. (32 sts)
Round 4: [P1, k5, p1, k1] 4 times.
Round 5: [Yo, k3, yo, k1] 8 times. (48 sts)
Round 6: [P2, k7, p2, k1] 4 times.
Round 7: [Yo, k5, yo, k1] 8 times. (64 sts)
Round 8: [P3, k9, p3, k1] 4 times.
Round 9: [Yo, k7, yo, k1] 8 times. (80 sts)
Round 10: [P4, k11, p4, k1] 4 times.
Round 11: [Yo, k9, yo, k1] 8 times. (96 sts)
Round 12: [P5, k13, p5, k1] 4 times.
Round 13: [Yo, k11, yo, k1] 8 times. (112 sts)
Round 14: [P6, k15, p6, k1] 4 times.
Round 15: [Yo, k13, yo, k1] 8 times. (128 sts)
Round 16: [P7, k17, p7, k1] 4 times.
Round 17: [Yo, k7, ssk, k13, k2tog, k7, yo, k1] 4 times.
Round 18: [P8, k15, p8, k1] 4 times.

Round 19: [Yo, k8, ssk, k11, k2tog, k8, yo, k1] 4 times.
Round 20: [P9, k13, p9, k1] 4 times.
Round 21: [Yo, k9, ssk, k9, k2tog, k9, yo, k1] 4 times.
Round 22: [P10, k11, p10, k1] 4 times.
Round 23: [Yo, k10, ssk, k7, k2tog, k10, yo, k1] 4 times.
Round 24: [P11, k9, p11, k1] 4 times.
Round 25: [Yo, k11, ssk, k5, k2tog, k11, yo, k1] 4 times.
Round 26: [P12, k7, p12, k1] 4 times.
Round 27: [Yo, k12, ssk, k3, k2tog, k12, yo, k1] 4 times.
Round 28: [P13, k5, p13, k1] 4 times.
Round 29: [Yo, k13, ssk, k1, k2tog, k13, yo, k1] 4 times.
Round 30: [P14, k3, p14, k1] 4 times.
Round 31: [Yo, k14, k3tog, k14, yo, k1] 4 times.
Round 32: [P to the last st on the needle, k1] 4 times.
Round 33: [Yo, p to the last st on the needle, yo, k1] 4 times. (136 sts)
Using a larger size needle, cast off loosely.

44 TWO-COLOUR RIB

Using A, cast on 8 stitches and divide evenly on 4 needles.

Join, taking care not to twist stitches.

Round 1: [K1, yo, k1] 4 times. (12 sts)
Round 2: Knit.
Round 3: [K1, yo, k1, yo, k1] 4 times. (20 sts)
Round 4: Knit.
Round 5: [K1, yo, k3, yo, k1] 4 times. (28 sts)
Change to B.
Round 6: Knit.
Round 7: [K1, yo, p5, yo, k1] 4 times. (36 sts)
Round 8: [K1, p7, k1] 4 times.
Round 9: [K1, yo, p7, yo, k1] 4 times. (44 sts)
Round 10: [K1, p9, k1] 4 times.
Change to A.
Round 11: [K1, yo, k9, yo, k1] 4 times. (52 sts)
Round 12: Knit.
Round 13: [K1, yo, k11, yo, k1] 4 times. (60 sts)

Change to B.
Round 14: Knit.
Round 15: [K1, yo, p13, yo, k1] 4 times. (68 sts)
Round 16: [K1, p15, k1] 4 times.
Round 17: [K1, yo, p15, yo, k1] 4 times. (76 sts)
Round 18: [K1, p17, k1] 4 times.
Change to A.
Round 19: [K1, yo, k17, yo, k1] 4 times. (84 sts)
Round 20: Knit.
Round 21: [K1, yo, k19, yo, k1] 4 times. (92 sts)
Change to B.
Round 22: Knit.
Round 23: [K1, yo, k21, yo, k1] 4 times. (100 sts)
Round 24: [K1, p23, k1] 4 times.
Cast off loosely.

Colours:
■ A
■ B

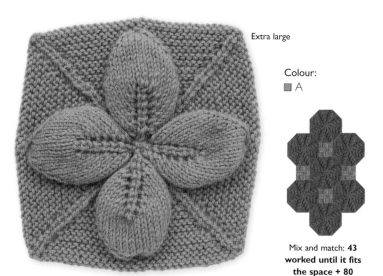

Extra large

Colour:
■ A

Medium

Mix and match: 43 worked until it fits the space + 80

45 FOUR SQUARE SWIRL

Cast on 8 stitches and divide evenly over 4 needles.

Join, taking care not to twist stitches.

Round 1: Knit.

Round 2: [Yo, k2] 4 times. (12 sts)

Round 3 (and all odd-numbered rounds): Knit.

Round 4: [Yo, k2tog, yo, k1] 4 times. (16 sts)

Round 6: [Yo, k2, yo, k2tog] 4 times. (20 sts)

Round 8: [Yo, k1, k2tog, yo, k2] 4 times. (24 sts)

Round 10: [Yo, k1, k2tog, yo, k1, yo, k2tog] 4 times. (28 sts)

Round 12: [Yo, k1, k2tog, yo, k1, yo, k1, k2tog] 4 times. (32 sts)

Round 14: [Yo, k1, k2tog, yo, k1, yo, k2, k2tog] 4 times. (36 sts)

Round 16: [Yo, k1, k2tog, yo, k1, yo, k1, k2tog, yo, k2tog] 4 times. (40 sts)

Round 18: [Yo, k1, k2tog, yo k1, yo, k1, k2tog, yo, k1, k2tog] 4 times. (44 sts)

Round 20: [Yo, k1, k2tog, yo, k1, yo, k1, k2tog, yo, k2, k2tog] 4 times. (48 sts)

Round 22: [Yo, k1, k2tog, yo, k1, yo, k1, k2tog, yo, k1, k2tog, yo, k2tog] 4 times. (52 sts)

Round 24: [Yo, k1, k2tog, yo, k1, yo, k1, k2tog, yo, k1, k2tog, yo, k1, k2tog] 4 times. (56 sts)

Round 26: [Yo, k1, k2tog, yo, k1, yo, k1, k2tog, yo, k1, k2tog, yo, k2, k2tog] 4 times. (60 sts)

Round 28: [Yo, p15] 4 times. (64 sts)

Round 29: [K1, p16] 4 times.

Using a larger size needle, cast off loosely.

Medium

Colour:
☐ A

46 LACE QUATREFOIL SQUARE

Cast on 8 stitches and divide evenly over 4 needles.

Join, taking care not to twist stitches.

Round 1: [K2, yo] 4 times. (12 sts)

Round 2 (and all even-numbered rounds): Knit all sts and yo; k and p into any double yo.

Round 3: [Yo, k2, yo, k1tbl] 4 times. (20 sts)

Round 5: [Yo, k1, yo, ssk, k1, yo k1 tbl] 4 times. (28 sts)

Round 7: [Yo, k3, yo, ssk, k1, yo, k1 tbl] 4 times. (36 sts)

Round 9: [Yo, k5, yo, ssk, k1, yo, k1tbl] 4 times. (44 sts)

Round 11: [Yo, k3, k2tog, yo, k2, yo, ssk, k1, yo, k1tbl] 4 times. (52 sts)

Round 13: [Yo, k3, k2tog, yo, k7, yo, k1tbl] 4 times. (60 sts)

Round 15: [(Yo) twice, ssk, k5, yo, ssk, k3, k2tog, (yo) twice, k1tbl] 4 times. (68 sts)

Round 17: [Yo, k2, yo, ssk, k5, yo, ssk, k1, k2tog, yo, k2, yo, k1tbl] 4 times. (76 sts)

Round 19: [Yo, k1, k2tog, yo, k1, yo, ssk, k1, k2tog, yo, k3, k2tog, yo, k1, yo, ssk, k1, yo, k1tbl] 4 times. (84 sts)

Round 21: [(Yo) twice, sl 1, k2tog, psso, yo, k1, k2tog, (yo) twice, ssk, k4, k2tog, (yo) twice, ssk, k1, yo, sl 1, k2tog, psso, (yo) twice, k1tbl] 4 times. (92 sts)

Round 23: [Yo, k2, yo, ssk, k2tog, yo, k2, yo, ssk, k2, k2tog, yo, k2, yo, ssk, k2tog, yo, k2, yo, k1tbl] 4 times. (100 sts)

Round 25: [Yo, k1, k2tog, (yo) twice, sl 1, k2tog, psso, yo, k1, k2tog, yo, k1, yo, ssk, k2tog, yo, k1, yo, ssk, k1, yo, sl 1, k2tog, psso, (yo) twice, ssk, k1, yo, k1tbl] 4 times. (108 sts)

Round 27: Purl.

Using a larger size needle, cast off loosely.

Extra large

Colour:
☐ A

TRIANGLES

47 GRANNY TRIANGLE

Foundation ring: Using A, ch 4, join with a ss to form a ring.

Round 1: Ch 5 (counts as first tr and ch 3), [3 tr in ring, ch 3] twice, 2 tr, join with ss in second ch of beg ch-5.

Round 2: Ss into first sp, ch 1 [1 dc, ch 5, 3 tr] in sp at base of ch, *ch 2, [3 tr, ch 3, 3 tr] in next ch-3 sp; rep from * once more, ch 2, 2 tr in first sp, join with ss in second ch of ch-5. Fasten off A. Join B with ss in first sp.

Round 3: Ch 1 [1 dc, ch 5, 3 tr] in sp at base of ch, *ch 2, 3 tr in next ch-2 sp, ch 2, [3 tr, ch 3, 3 tr] in next ch-3 sp; rep from * once more, ch 2, 3 tr in next ch-2 sp, ch 2, 2 tr in first sp, join with ss in second ch of ch-5.

Round 4: Ss into first sp, ch 1, [1 dc, ch 5, 3 tr] in sp at base of ch, *[ch 2, 3 tr in next ch-2 sp] twice, ch 2, [3 tr, ch 3, 3 tr] in next ch-3 sp; rep from * once more, [ch 2, 3 tr in next ch-2 sp] twice, ch 2, 2 tr in first sp, join with ss in second ch of ch-5. Fasten off.

Colours:
■ A
■ B

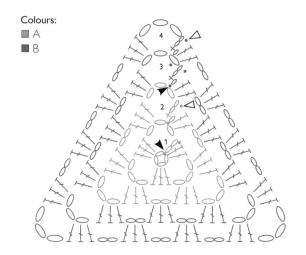

Medium

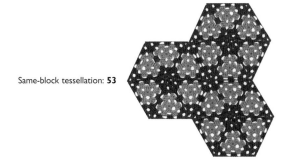

Same-block tessellation: **53**

Symbols and abbreviations
Turn to pages 140–141 for a full explanation of the symbols and abbreviations used.

48 SOLID GRANNY TRIANGLE

Foundation ring: Ch 4, join with ss to form a ring.

Round 1: 1 dc into ring, [ch 4, 1 dc into ring] twice, ch 4, join with ss to first dc.

Round 2: Ch 4 (counts as first tr and ch 1), *[2 tr; 1 dtr; ch 3, 1 dtr; 2 tr] in next ch-4 sp, ch 1, rep from * once more, [2 tr; 1 dtr; ch 3, 1 dtr; 1 tr] in next ch-4 sp, join with ss in third ch of beg ch-4.

Round 3: Ch 2 (counts as first htr), 1 htr into the ch-1 sp, 1 htr in each of the next 3 sts, *[1 htr; 1 tr; ch 3, 1 tr; 1 htr] in ch-3 sp, 1 htr in each of next 3 sts, 1 htr into next ch-1 sp, 1 htr in each of next 3 sts; rep from * once more, [1 htr; 1 tr; ch 3, 1 tr; 1 htr] in ch-3 sp, 1 htr in the next 2 sts, join with ss in top of beg ch-2. Fasten off.

Colour:
■ A

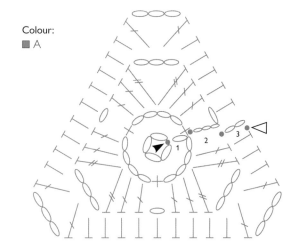

Small

Mix and match: **48 + 92**

49 TREBLE CROCHET TRIANGLE

Foundation ring: Ch 8, join with ss to form a ring.

Round 1: Ch 3 (counts as first tr), 2 tr into ring, ch 3, [3 tr; ch 3] twice, join with ss to top of beg ch-3. (9 tr and 3 ch-3 sp)

Round 2: Ch 3 (counts as first tr), 1 tr in each of next 2 sts, *[3 tr; ch 3, 3 tr] into next ch-3 sp, 1 tr in each of next 3 sts; rep from * once more, [3 tr; ch 3, 3 tr] into next ch-3 sp, join with ss to top of beg ch-3. (27 tr and 3 ch-3 sp)

Round 3: Ch 3 (counts as first tr), 1 tr in each of next 5 sts, *[3 tr; ch 3, 3 tr] into next ch-3 sp, tr in each of next 9 sts; rep from * once more, [3 tr; ch 3, 3 tr] in next ch-3 sp, 1 tr in each of next 3 sts, join with ss to top of beg ch-3. Fasten off.

Colour:
■ A

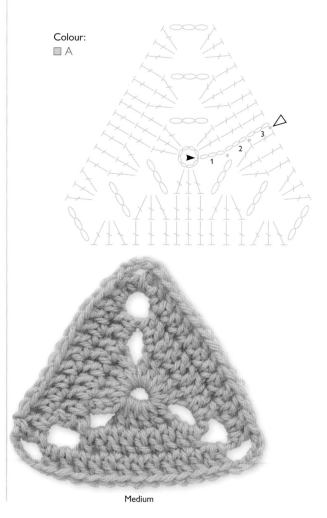

Medium

50 TWO-TONE TREFOIL

Foundation ring: With A, ch 4, join with ss to form a ring.

Round 1 (RS): Ch 1, 6 dc into ring, join with ss to beg dc. (6 dc)

Round 2: Ch 1, [1 dc, ch 7, 1 dc] in first dc, *1 dc in next dc, [1 dc, ch 7, 1 dc] in next dc; rep from * once more, 1 dc in next dc, join with ss to first dc. (9 sts, 3 ch-7 sp)

Round 3: Ch 1, skip first dc, [1 dc, 1 htr, 3 tr, 3 dtr, 3 tr, 1 htr, 1 dc] in next ch-7 sp (to create leaf),

*skip next dc, 1 dc in next dc, skip next dc [1 dc, 1 htr, 3 tr, 3 dtr, 3 tr, 1 htr, 1 dc) in next ch-7 sp; rep from * once more, skip next dc, 1 dc in next dc, join with ss to first dc. (42 sts)

Fasten off A. Join B to second tr of any leaf.

Round 4: Ch 1, 1 dc into base of ch, [ch 1, 1 dc in next st] 6 times, *ch 2, 1 tr in dc between leaves, ch 2, 1 dc in second tr of next leaf, [ch 1, 1 dc in next st] 6 times; rep from * once more, ch 2, 1 tr in dc between leaves, ch 2, join with ss to first dc.

Round 5: Ch 3 (counts as first tr), *[1 tr in next ch-1 sp, 1 tr in next dc] twice, 2 tr in the next (ch-1 sp, dc and ch-1 sp), [1 tr in next dc, 1 tr in next ch-1 sp] twice, tr in next dc, 2 tr into next ch-2 sp, 1 tr into next tr, 2 tr into next ch-2 sp, 1 tr in next dc; rep from * twice more, omitting last tr at the end of the last rep, join with ss to top of beg ch-3.

Fasten off.

Medium

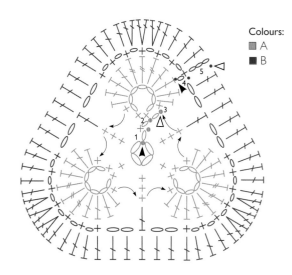

Colours:
■ A
■ B

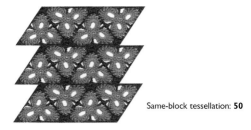

Same-block tessellation: **50**

51 DAINTY FLOWER TRIANGLE

SPECIAL ABBREVIATIONS

beg popcorn: Work 3 tr into ring, remove hook from working loop, and insert hook into top of ch-3, catch working loop with hook and draw the working loop through to close popcorn.

popcorn: Work 4 tr into ring, remove hook from working loop, and insert hook into top first tr, catch working loop with hook and draw the working loop through to close popcorn.

Foundation ring: Using A, ch 8, join with ss to form a ring.

Round 1: Ch 3 (counts as first tr), work beg popcorn, ch 3, [work popcorn, ch 3] 5 times, join with ss to top of beg ch-3. (6 clusters) Fasten off A. Join B in any ch-3 sp with ss.

Round 2: Ch 3 (counts as first tr), 8 tr into sp at base of ch-3, [ch 4, skip next ch-3 sp, 9 tr into next ch-3 sp] twice, ch 4, join with ss to top of beg ch-3.

Round 3: Ch 3, 1 tr into base of ch-3, *1 tr in each of next 3 tr, [1 tr, 1 dtr, ch 3, 1 dtr, 1 tr] in next tr, 1 tr in each of next 3 tr, 2 tr in next tr, dc in next ch-4 sp, 2 tr in next tr; rep from * once more, 1 tr in each of next 3 tr, [1 tr, 1 dtr, ch 3,

1 dtr, 1 tr] in next tr, 1 tr in each of next 3 tr, 2 tr in next tr, dc in next ch-4 sp, join with ss to top of beg ch-3.

Round 4: Ch 1, 1 dc into base of ch, 1 dc in next st, *1 htr in next st, 1 tr in each of next 4 sts, [3 tr, ch 3, 3 tr] in ch-3 sp, 1 tr in next 4 sts, 1 htr in next st, 1 dc in each of next 5 sts; rep from * once more, 1 htr in next st, 1 tr in each of next 4 sts, [3 tr, ch 3, 3 tr] in ch-3 sp, 1 tr in next 4 sts, 1 htr in next st, 1 dc in each of next 3 sts, join with ss to top of first dc.
Fasten off.

Colours:
■ A
□ B

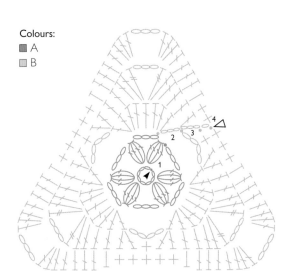

Large

Mix and match: **51 + 125**

52 POST STITCH TRIANGLE

SPECIAL ABBREVIATIONS

BPtr (Back Post treble crochet): Yrh, insert hook from back to front to back around post of the next stitch; yrh and draw up loop, [yrh and draw up through 2 loops on hook] twice.

FPtr (Front Post treble crochet): Yrh, insert hook from front to back to front around post of the next stitch; yrh and draw up loop, [yrh and draw up through 2 loops on hook] twice.

Foundation ring: Ch 8, join with ss to form a ring.

Round 1: Ch 3 (counts as first tr), 4 tr into ring, ch 3 [5 tr in ring, ch 3] twice, join with ss in top of beg ch-3.

Round 2: Ss in next tr, ch 3 (counts as first BPtr), FPtr, BPtr, FPtr, *[2 tr, ch 3, 2 tr] in next ch-3 sp, [FPtr, BPtr] twice, FPtr; rep from * once more, [2 tr, ch 3, 2 tr] in next ch-3 sp, FPtr, join with ss to beg ch-3. (9 sts each side)

Round 3: Ch 3 (counts as first BPtr), [FPtr, BPtr] twice, FPtr, *[2 tr, ch 3, 2 tr] in next ch-3 sp, [FPtr BPtr] 4 times, FPtr; rep from * once more, [2 tr, ch 3, 2 tr] in next ch-3 sp, FPtr, BPtr, FPtr, join with ss to beg ch-3. (13 sts each side)

Round 4: Ch 3 (counts as first BPtr), [FPtr, BPtr] 3 times, FPtr, *[2 tr, ch 3, 2 tr] in next ch-3 sp, [FPtr, BPtr] 6 times, FPtr; rep from * once more, [2 tr, ch 3, 2 tr] in next ch-3 sp, [FPtr, BPtr] twice, FPtr, join with a ss to beg ch-3. (17 sts each side)

Round 5: Ch 3 (counts as first BPtr), [FPtr, BPtr] 4 times, FPtr, *[2 tr, ch 3, 2 tr] in next ch-3 sp, [FPtr, BPtr] 8 times, FPtr; rep from * once more [2 tr, ch 3, 2 tr] in next ch-3 sp, [FPtr, BPtr] 3 times, FPtr, join with ss to beg ch-3. (21 sts each side)

Fasten off.

Colour:
■ A

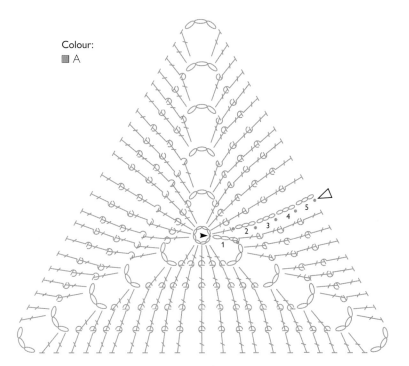

Large

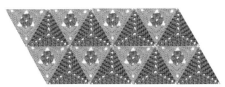

Mix and match: **52 + 51**

53 DOUBLE TRIANGLE

TURNING CORNERS ON SHAPED BLOCKS

Whether you are working a triangular, square, hexagonal or octagonal block, pay particular attention to turning the corners. After every round, also check that you have made the correct number of stitches along each side.

Foundation ring: Using A, ch 4, join with ss to form a ring.

Round 1 (RS): Ch 1, *[1 dc, 1 htr, 1 tr, 1 dtr, 1 tr, 1 htr] in ring; rep from * twice more, join with ss in first dc.

Fasten off A. Change to B.

Round 2: Ch 4 (counts as first dtr), 2 tr in next htr, 1 htr in next tr, 1 dc in next dtr, 1 htr in next tr, 2 tr in next htr, *1 dtr in next dc, 2 tr in next htr, 1 htr in next tr, 1 dc in next dtr, 1 htr in next tr, 2 tr in next htr; rep from * once more, join with ss in top of beg ch-4.

Fasten off B. Change to C.

Round 3: Ch 1, 1 dc in st at base of ch-1, *1 htr in next 2 tr, 2 tr in next htr, 3 dtr in next dc (point made), 2 tr in next htr, 1 htr in next 2 tr, 1 dc in next dtr; rep from * once more, 1 htr in next 2 tr, 2 tr in next htr, 3 dtr in next dc, 2 tr in next htr, 1 htr in next 2 tr, join with ss in first dc.

Fasten off.

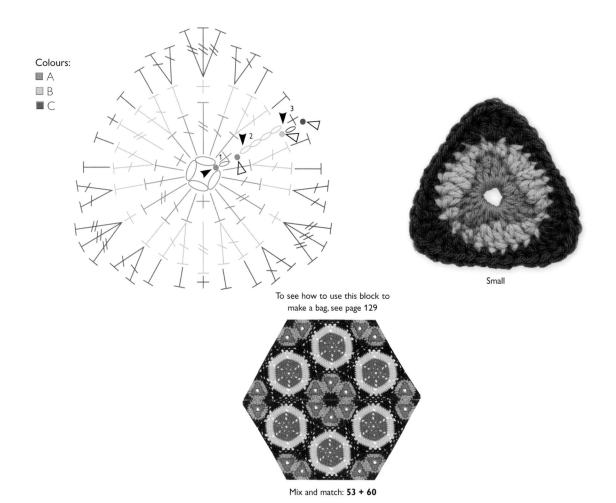

Colours:
- A
- B
- C

Small

To see how to use this block to make a bag, see page 129

Mix and match: **53 + 60**

54 OPEN TREFOIL

Foundation ring: [Ch 16, ss into first ch] 3 times, to create 3 base loops.

Round 1: In first loop, ch 1 (counts as first dc), work 23 dc into loop at base of ch, [24 dc in next loop] twice, join with ss to top of first dc.

Round 2: Ss in each of next 2 dc, ch 5 (counts as first tr and ch 2), skip next st, [1 tr in next st, ch 2, skip next st] 8 times 1 tr in next st, skip 5 sts, *[1 tr in next st, ch 2, skip next st] 9 times, rep from * once more, join with ss in third ch of beg ch-5.

Round 3: Ch 1, [3 dc in next ch-2 sp] 9 times, 2 dc in sp between the next 2 tr; rep from * twice more, join with ss to top of first dc.

Round 4: Ch 4 (counts as first htr and ch 2), skip first 2 sts, 1 htr in next st, *[ch 2, skip 1 st, 1 tr in next st] 10 times, ch 2, skip 1 st 1 htr in next st, ch 2, skip 3 dc, 1 dc between the sts before the next dc, skip 3 sts, 1 htr in next st; rep from * once more, *[ch 2, skip 1 st, 1 tr in next st] 10 times, ch 2, skip 1 st, 1 htr in next st, ch 2, join with ss to second ch of beg ch-4.

Round 5: Ch 1, work 3 dc in each ch-2 sp around, join with ss to beg ch-1.
Fasten off.

Colour:
■ A

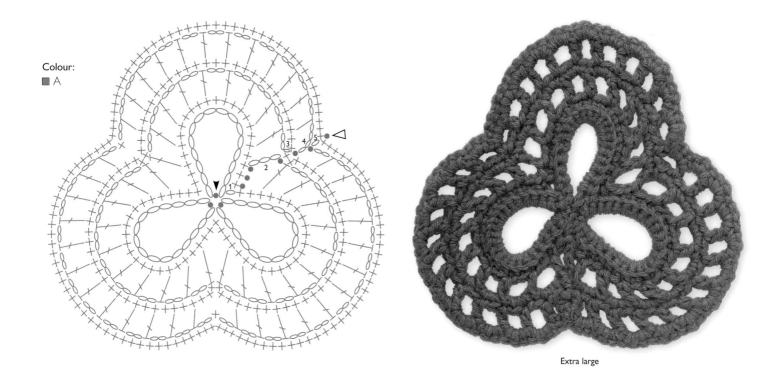

Extra large

55 KNIT BOBBLE TRIANGLE

SPECIAL ABBREVIATION

MB (Make Bobble): Into next st [k1, yo, k1, yo, k1, yo, k1], using left-hand needle, pass all stitches and yo, one at a time over stitch closest to tip of right-hand needle. Push bobble to the right side of work.

Cast on 3 stitches.
Row 1 (RS): Knit.
Row 2: Purl. Repeat the last row each even-numbered row until row 12 has been completed.
Row 3: K1, M1, k1, M1, k1. (5 sts)
Row 5: K1, M1, k3, M1, k1. (7 sts)
Row 7: K1, M1, k2, MB, k2, M1, k1. (9 sts)
Row 9: K1, M1, k2, MB, k1, MB, k2, M1, k1. (11 sts)
Row 11: K1, M1, k4, MB, k4, M1, k1. (13 sts)
Row 13: K1, M1, k11, M1, k1. (15 sts)
Row 14: Knit.
Row 15: P1, M1, p13, M1, p1. (17 sts)
Row 16: Purl.
Row 17: K1, M1, k15, M1, k1. (19 sts)
Row 18: Purl.
Row 19: P1, M1, p17, M1, p1. (21 sts)

Row 20: Knit.
Row 21: P1, M1, p19, M1, p1. (23 sts)
Row 22: Purl.
Row 23: K1, M1, k4, [MB, k3] 3 times, MB, k4, M1, k1. (25 sts)
Row 24: Purl.
Row 25: P1, M1, p23, M1, p1. (27 sts)
Row 26: Knit.
Row 27: P1, M1, p25, M1, p1. (29 sts)
Row 28: Purl.
Row 29: K1, M1, k27, M1, k1. (31 sts)
Row 30: Purl.
Row 31: P1, M1, p29, M1, p1 (33 sts)
Row 32: Knit.
Row 33: P1, M1, p31, M1, p1. (35 sts)
Cast off loosely knitwise.

Colour:
■ A

Large

56 EYELET TRIANGLE

Using 2 of the smaller dp needles, cast on 4 stitches.
Work backwards and forwards in rows until row 16 has been completed.
Row 1 (and all odd-numbered rows): Purl.
Row 2 (RS): [Yo, k1] 4 times. (8 sts)
Row 4: [Yo, k3, yo, k1] twice. (12 sts)
Row 6: [Yo, k5, yo, k1] twice. (16 sts)
Row 8: [Yo, k7, yo, k1] twice. (20 sts)
Row 10: [Yo, k4, yo, ssk, k3, yo, k1] twice. (24 sts)

Row 12: [Yo, k3, k2tog, yo, k1, yo, ssk, k3, yo, k1] twice. (28 sts)
Row 14: [Yo, k3, k2tog, yo, k3, yo, ssk, k3, yo, k1] twice. (32 sts)
Row 16: *Yo, k3, k2tog, yo, k5, yo, ssk, k3, yo, k1, with one dp needle; rep from * with a third dp needle. (18 sts on each needle)
Do not turn work.
With a fourth dp needle, pick up 18 sts evenly along bottom edge (18 sts on each needle)
Work in rounds.
Round 1: Purl.
Using a larger dp needle, cast off loosely.

Colour:
■ A

Small

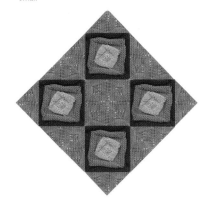

Mix and match: **56 + 42**

HEXAGONS

57 SOLID HEXAGON

Foundation ring: Ch 4, join with ss to form a ring.

Round 1: Ch 1 (counts as first dc), 11 dc into ring, join with ss in beg ch, turn. (12 sts)

Round 2: Ch 2 (counts as first htr), [3 htr in next dc, 1 htr in next dc] 5 times, 3 htr in next dc, join with ss in top of beg ch-2, turn. (24 sts)

Round 3: Ch 2 (counts as first htr), 1 htr in next htr; [3 htr in next htr, 1 htr into each of next 3 htr] 5 times, 3 htr in next htr, 1 htr in next htr, join with ss in top of beg ch-2, turn. (36 sts)

Round 4: Ch 2 (counts as first htr), 1 htr into each of next 2 htr, [3 htr in next htr, 1 htr into each of next 5 htr] 5 times, 3 htr in next htr, 1 htr into each of next 2 htr, join with ss in top of beg ch-2, turn. (48 sts)

Round 5: Ch 2 (counts as first htr), 1 htr into each of next 3 htr, [3 htr in next htr, 1 htr into each of next 7 htr] 5 times, 3 htr in next htr, 1 htr into each of next 3 htr, join with ss in top of beg ch-2, turn. (60 sts)

Round 6: Ch 2 (counts as htr), 1 htr into each of next 4 htr, [3 htr in next htr, 1 htr into each of next 9 htr] 5 times, 3 htr in next htr, 1 htr into each of next 4 htr; join with ss in top of beg ch-2. (72 sts)

Fasten off.

Colour:

■ A

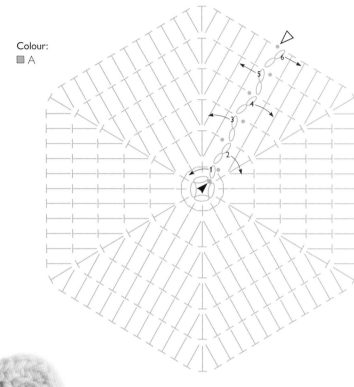

Medium

Mix and match: **57 + 62**

Symbols and abbreviations
Turn to pages 140–141 for a full explanation of the symbols and abbreviations used.

58 COLOUR DOT HEXAGON

Foundation ring: Using A, ch 4, join with ss to form a ring.
Round 1: Ch 1, 6 dc in ring, join with ss in first dc, turn.
Round 2: Ch 1, 2 dc in each dc, join with ss in first dc, turn. (12 dc)
Round 3: Ch 1, 1 dc in dc at the base of ch-1, 3 dc in next dc, [1 dc in next dc, 3 dc in next dc] 5 times, join with ss in first dc, turn. (24 dc)
Round 4: Ch 1, 1 dc in each dc around, join with ss in first dc, turn.
Round 5: Ch 1, 1 dc in dc at the base of ch-1, 1 dc in next dc, 3 dc in next dc, [1 dc in each of the next 3 dc, 3 dc in next dc] 5 times, 1 dc in last dc, join with ss in first dc, turn. (36 dc)
Round 6: Ch 1, 1 dc in each dc around, join with ss in first dc, turn.
Fasten off A. Join B.
Round 7: Ch 1, 1 dc into dc at the base of ch-1, 1 dc in each of next 2 dc, 3 dc in next dc, [1 dc in each of the next 5 dc, 3 dc in next dc] 5 times, 1 dc in each of the last 2 dc, join with ss in first dc, turn. (48 dc)
Round 8: Ch 1, 1 dc in each dc around, join with ss in first dc, turn.
Round 9: Ch 1, 1 dc in dc at the base of ch-1, 1 dc in each of next 3 dc, 3 dc in next dc, [1 dc in each of the next 7 dc, 3 dc in next dc] 5 times, 1 dc in each of the last 3 dc, join with ss in first dc, turn. (60 dc)
Round 10: Ch 1, 1 dc in each dc, join with ss in first dc, turn.
Round 11: Ch 1, 1 dc in each of the first 5 dc, 3 dc in next dc, *1 dc in each of the next 9 dc, 3 dc in next dc; rep from * 4 times more, 1 dc in each of the last 4 dc, join with ss in first dc, turn. (72 dc)
Round 12: Ch 1, 1 dc in each dc around, join with ss in first dc.
Fasten off.

Colours:
■ A
■ B

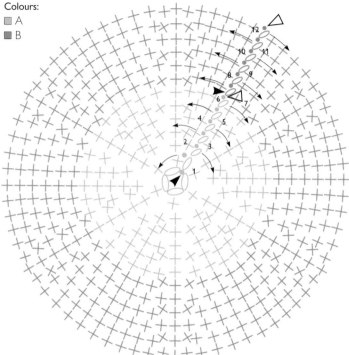

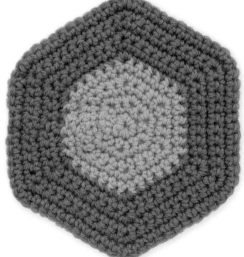

Large

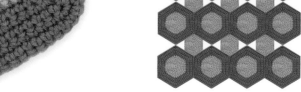

Mix and match: **58 + 58 worked until it fits the space**

59 GRANNY HEXAGON

Foundation ring: Using A, ch 6, join with ss to form ring.

Round 1: Ch 3 (counts as first tr), tr2tog into ring, [ch 3, tr3tog into ring] 5 times, ch 3, join with ss in top of beg ch-3. (6 ch-3 sp)

Round 2: Ss into ch-3 sp, ch 3 (counts as first tr), [tr2tog, ch 3, tr3tog] in sp at base of ch-3, [ch 3, (tr3tog, ch 3, tr3tog) in next ch-3 sp] 5 times, ch 3, join with ss in top of beg ch-3. (12 ch-3 sp)

Round 3: Ss into ch-3 sp, ch 3 (counts as first tr), [tr2tog, ch 3, tr3tog] in sp at base of ch-3, [ch 3, tr3tog in next ch-3 sp, ch 3, (tr3tog, ch 3, tr3tog) in next ch-3 sp] 5 times, ch 3, tr3tog in next ch-3 sp, ch 3, join with ss in top of beg ch-3. (18 ch-3 sp) Fasten off A. Join B with ss into last ch-3 sp of Round 3.

Round 4: Ch 3 (counts as first tr), 2 tr in sp at base of ch-3, [(3 tr, ch 2, 3 tr) in next ch-3 sp, (3 tr in next ch-3 sp) twice] 5 times, [3 tr, ch 2, 3 tr] in next ch-3 sp, 3 tr in last ch-3 sp, join with ss in top of beg ch-3. Fasten off.

Colours:
■ A
■ B

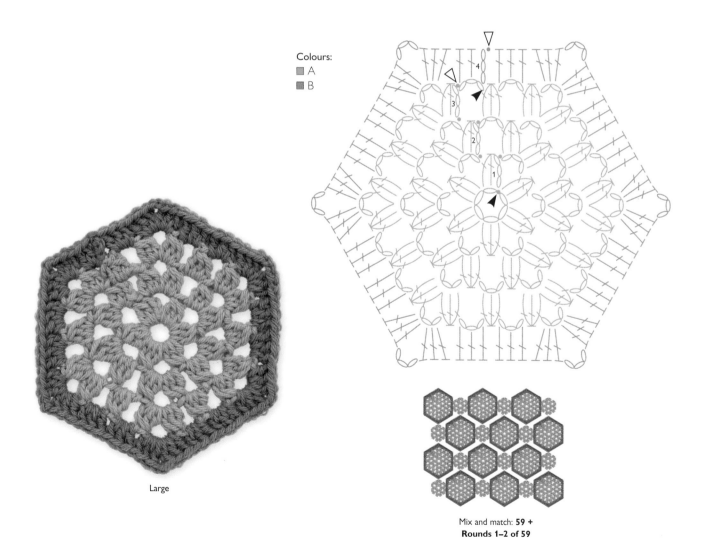

Large

Mix and match: **59 +**
Rounds 1–2 of 59

60 CLASSIC HEXAGON

Foundation ring: Using A, ch 6, join with ss to form a ring.

Round 1: Ch 4 (counts as first tr and ch 1), [1 tr in ring, ch 1] 11 times, join with ss to third of ch-4. (12 tr)

Round 2: Ch 3 (counts as first tr), 2 tr in next ch-1 sp, 1 tr in next tr, ch 2, [1 tr in next tr, 2 tr in next ch-1 sp, 1 tr in next tr, ch 2] 5 times, join with ss to top of beg ch-3.

Round 3: Ch 3 (counts as first tr), 1 tr in base of ch-3, 1 tr in each of next 2 tr, 2 tr in next tr, ch 2, [2 tr in next tr, 1 tr in each of next 2 tr, 2 tr in next tr, ch 2] 5 times, join with ss to top of beg ch-3. Fasten off A. Join B.

Round 4: Ch 3 (counts as first tr), 1 tr in base of ch-3, 1 tr in each of next 4 tr, 2 tr in next tr, ch 2, [2 tr in next tr, 1 tr in each of next 4 tr, 2 tr in next tr, ch 2] 5 times, join with ss to top of beg ch-3.

Round 5: Ch 3 (counts as first tr), 1 tr into each of next 7 tr, [ch 3, 1 dc into next ch-2 sp, ch 3, 1 tr in each of next 8 tr] 5 times, ch 3, 1 dc in next ch-2 sp, ch 3, join with ss to top of beg ch-3. Fasten off B. Join C.

Round 6: Ss into next tr, ch 3 (counts as first tr), 1 tr in each of next 5 tr, *ch 3, [1 dc in next ch-3 sp, ch 3] twice, skip next tr, 1 tr in each of next 6 tr; rep from * 4 times more, ch 3, [1 dc in next ch-3 sp, ch 3] twice, join with ss to top of beg ch-3.

Round 7: Ss into next tr, ch 3 (counts as first tr), 1 tr in each of next 3 tr, * ch 3, [1 dc in next ch-3 sp, ch 3] 3 times, skip next tr, 1 tr in each of next 4 tr; rep from * 4 times more, ch 3, [1 dc into next ch-3 sp, ch 3] 3 times, join with ss to top of ch-3.

Round 8: Ss into st-sp between second and third tr of group, ch 4 (counts as first tr and ch 1), 1 tr base of ch-4, *ch 3, [1 dc into next ch-3 sp, ch 3] 4 times, [1 tr, ch 1, 1 tr] into st-sp between second and third tr of nex 4-tr group; rep from * 4 times more, ch 3, [1 dc in ch-3 sp, ch 3] 4 times, join with ss to third ch of beg ch-4. Fasten off.

Colours:
- ■ A
- ■ B
- ■ C

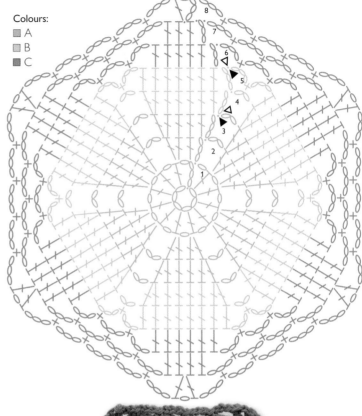

To see how to use this block to make a bag, see page 129

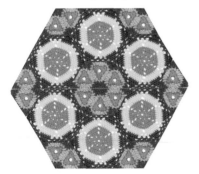

Mix and match: **60 + 53**

Extra large

61 SWIRL HEXAGON

NOTE
Mark the beginning of the round with a detachable marker or safety pin and move the marker up as you work.

STITCH ABBREVIATIONS
beg 2-tr cl (beginning 2 treble-crochet cluster): [Yrh, insert hook in ring, yrh, pull loop through, yrh, pull through 2 loops on hook] twice, yrh, pull through all 3 loops on hook.
3-tr cl (3 treble-crochet cluster): [Yrh, insert hook ring, yrh, pull loop through, yrh, pull through 2 loops on hook] 3 times, yrh, pull through all 4 loops on hook.

Colour:
■ A

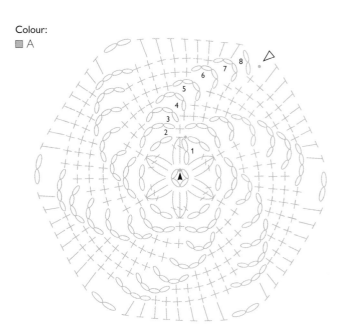

Foundation ring: Ch 4 and join with ss to form a ring.
Round 1 (RS): Ch 2, beg 2-tr cl, [ch 2, 3-tr cl] 5 times ch 2, join with ss in top of beg 2-tr cl. (6 clusters)
Round 2: [Ch 4, 1 dc in top of next cl] 6 times, ending in top of first cluster. (6 ch-4 sp)
Round 3: [Ch 4, 2 dc in next ch-4 sp, 1 dc in next dc] 6 times.
Round 4: [Ch 4, 2 dc in next ch-4 sp, 1 dc in each of the next 2 dc, skip 1 dc] 6 times.
Round 5: [Ch 4, 2 dc in next ch-4 sp, 1 dc in each of the next 3 dc, skip 1 dc] 6 times.

Round 6: [Ch 4, 2 dc in next ch-4 sp, 1 dc in each of the next 4 dc, skip 1 dc] 6 times.
Round 7: [Ch 4, 2 dc in next ch-4 sp, 1 dc in each of the next 5 dc, skip 1 dc] 6 times.
Round 8: [Ch 2, 2 htr in next ch-4 sp, 1 htr in each of the next 6 dc, skip 1 dc] 6 times, join with ss to beg ch-2.
Fasten off.

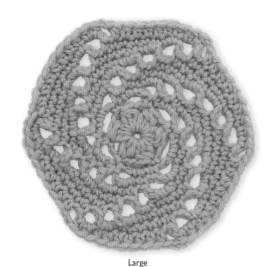
Large

62 WHEEL HEXAGON

Foundation ring: Ch 6, join with ss to form a ring.
Round 1: Ch 6 (counts as first dtr and ch-2), [1 dtr into ring, ch 2] 11 times, join with ss in fourth ch of beg ch-6. (12 ch-2 sp)
Round 2: Ss in next ch-2 sp, ch 3 (counts as first tr), [1 tr, ch 2, 2 tr] into the ch-2 sp at the base of the beg ch-3, [3 tr into next ch-2 sp,

(2 tr, ch 2, 2 tr) into next ch-2 sp] 5 times, 3 tr into next ch-2 sp, join with ss in top of beg ch-3.
Round 3: Ch 3 (counts as first tr), 1 tr in next tr, [(2 tr, ch 1, 2 tr) into next ch-2 sp, 1 tr in each of next 7 tr] 5 times, [2 tr, ch 1, 2 tr] into next ch-2 sp, 1 tr in each of next 5 tr; join with ss in top of beg ch-3.
Fasten off.

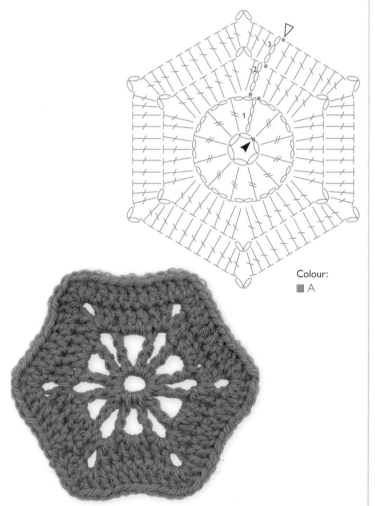

Colour:
■ A

Medium

63 COLOURWORK HEXAGON

Using A, cast on 80 stitches.
Row 1 (RS): Knit.
Row 2: Knit.
Row 3: K1, [k2tog, k9, ssk] 6 times, k1. (68 sts)
Row 4: Knit.
Row 5: K1, [k2tog, k7, ssk] 6 times, k1. (56 sts)
Row 6: Knit.
Change to B.
Row 7: Knit.
Row 8: Purl.
Join C. Use both B and C.
Row 9: K1 B, [k2tog B, k1 C, (k1 B, k1 C) twice, ssk B] 6 times, k1 B. (44 sts)
Change to B.
Row 10: Knit.
Row 11: K1, [k2tog, k3, ssk] 6 times, k1. (32 sts)
Fasten off B. Change to A.
Rows 12–14: Purl.
Using A and C.

Row 15: K1 A, [k2tog A, k1 C, ssk A] 6 times, k1 A. (20 sts)
Fasten off C. Continue with A.
Row 16: Purl.
Row 17: Knit.
Row 18: P1, [p3tog] 6 times, p1. (8 sts)
Cut yarn leaving a 40cm (15¾in) tail. Using a tapestry needle, weave the yarn through the remaining 8 stitches on the needle, gather and secure. Sew side seams together to form a hexagon block.

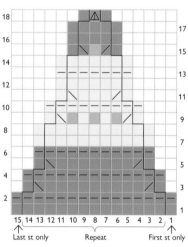

15 14 13 12 11 10 9 8 7 6 5 4 3 2 1
↑ Last st only   Repeat   First st only ↑

Colours:
■ A
□ B
■ C

Medium

64 STRIPED SWIRL HEXAGON

Using A, cast on 120 stitches and divide evenly over 3 needles, 40 sts oen.

Join, taking care not to twist stitches.

Round 1 (RS): Purl.
Round 2: Purl.
Round 3: [Sl 1, k2tog, psso, k17] 6 times. (108 sts)
Change to B.
Round 4: Knit.
Change to A.
Round 5: [Sl 1, k2tog, psso, k15] 6 times. (96 sts)
Round 6: Knit.
Round 7: [Sl 1, k2tog, psso, k13] 6 times. (84 sts)
Change to B.
Round 8: Knit.
Round 9: [Sl 1, k2tog, psso, k11] 6 times. (72 sts)
Change to A.
Round 10: Knit.

Round 11: [Sl 1, k2tog, psso, k9] 6 times. (60 sts)
Round 12: Knit.
Round 13: [Sl 1, k2tog, psso, k7] 6 times. (48 sts)
Change to B.
Round 14: Knit.
Round 15: [Sl 1, k2tog, psso, k5] 6 times. (36 sts)
Round 16: Knit.
Change to A.
Round 17: [Sl 1, k2tog, psso, k3] 6 times. (24 sts)
Round 18: Knit.
Round 19: [Sl 1, k2tog, psso, k1] 6 times. (12 sts)
Round 20: [Ssk] 6 times. (6 sts)
Cut yarn leaving a 25cm (10in) tail. Using a tapestry needle, weave the yarn through the remaining 6 stitches on the needle, gather and secure.

Colours:
■ A
■ B

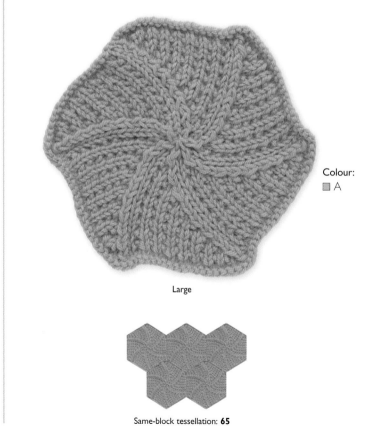

Large

65 BROKEN RIB HEXAGON

Cast on 122 stitches loosely.
Row 1 (RS): Knit.
Row 2 (and all even-numbered rows): Purl.
Row 3: K1, [sl 1, k2tog, psso, (k1, p1) 8 times, k1] 6 times, k1. (110 sts)
Row 5: K1, [sl 1, k2tog, psso, (k1, p1) 7 times, k1] 6 times, k1. (98 sts)
Row 7: K1, [sl 1, k2tog, psso, (k1, p1) 6 times, k1] 6 times, k1. (86 sts)
Row 9: K1, [sl 1, k2tog, psso, (k1, p1) 5 times, k1] 6 times, k1. (74 sts)
Row 11: K1, [sl 1, k2tog, psso, (k1, p1) 4 times, k1] 6 times, k1. (62 sts)
Row 13: K1, [sl 1, k2tog, psso, (k1, p1) 3 times, k1] 6 times, k1. (50 sts)

Row 15: K1, [sl 1, k2tog, psso, (k1, p1) 2 times, k1] 6 times, k1. (38 sts)
Row 17: K1, [sl 1, k2tog, psso, k1, p1, k1] 6 times, k1. (26 sts)
Row 19: K1, [sl 1, k2tog, psso, k1] 6 times, k1. (14 sts)
Row 20: [P2tog] 7 times. (7 sts)
Cut yarn leaving a 30cm (11¾in) tail. Using a tapestry needle, weave the yarn through the remaining 7 stitches on the needle, gather and secure. Sew side seams together to form a hexagon block.

Colour:
■ A

Large

Same-block tessellation: **65**

66 SEED STITCH SPIRAL HEXAGON

Cast on 114 stitches and divide evenly over 3 needles, 38 sts oen. Join, taking care not to twist stitches.

Round 1: Purl.
Round 2: [Ssk, (k1, p1) 8 times, k1] 6 times. (108 sts)
Round 3: [Ssk, (k1, p1) 8 times] 6 times. (102 sts)
Round 4: [Ssk, (k1, p1) 7 times, k1] 6 times. (96 sts)
Round 5: [Ssk, (k1, p1) 7 times] 6 times. (90 sts)
Round 6: [Ssk, (k1, p1) 6 times, k1] 6 times. (84 sts)
Round 7: [Ssk, (k1, p1) 6 times] 6 times. (78 sts)
Round 8: [Ssk, (k1, p1) 5 times, k1] 6 times. (72 sts)
Round 9: [Ssk, (k1, p1) 5 times] 6 times. (66 sts)
Round 10: [Ssk, (k1, p1) 4 times, k1] 6 times. (60 sts)
Round 11: [Ssk, (k1, p1) 4 times] 6 times. (54 sts)
Round 12: [Ssk, (k1, p1) 3 times, k1] 6 times. (48 sts)
Round 13: [Ssk, (k1, p1) 3 times] 6 times. (42 sts)
Round 14: [Ssk, (k1, p1) 2 times, k1] 6 times. (36 sts)
Round 15: [Ssk, (k1, p1) 2 times] 6 times. (30 sts)
Round 16: [Ssk, k1, p1, k1] 6 times. (24 sts)
Round 17: [Ssk, k1, p1] 6 times. (18 sts)
Round 18: [Ssk, k1] 6 times. (12 sts)
Round 19: [Ssk] 6 times. (6 sts)
Cut yarn leaving a 25cm (9¾in) tail. Using a tapestry needle, weave the yarn through the remaining 6 stitches on the needle, gather and secure.

Colour:
■ A

Large

67 LACE SWIRL HEXAGON

Cast on 119 stitches and divide over 3 needles: 40 sts on both needles 1 and 2; 39 sts on needle 3. Join, taking care not to twist stitches.

Round 1: Purl.
Round 2: Knit.
Round 3: [Yo, sl 1, k2tog, psso, k17] 5 times, yo, sl 1, k2tog, psso, k16. (113 sts)
Round 4: K1, [yo, sl 1, k2tog, psso, k16] 5 times, yo, sl 1, k2tog, psso, k14. (107 sts)
Round 5: K2, [yo, sl 1, k2tog, psso, k15] 5 times, yo, sl 1, k2tog, psso, k12. (101 sts)
Round 6: K3, [yo, sl 1, k2tog, psso, k14] 5 times, yo, sl 1, k2tog, psso, k10. (95 sts)
Round 7: K4, [yo, sl 1, k2tog, psso, k13] 5 times, yo, sl 1, k2tog, psso, k8. (89 sts)
Round 8: K5, [yo, sl 1, k2tog, psso, k12] 5 times, yo, sl 1, k2tog, psso, k6. (83 sts)
Round 9: K6, [yo, sl 1, k2tog, psso, k11] 5 times, yo, sl 1, k2tog, psso, k4. (77 sts)
Round 10: K7, [yo, sl 1, k2tog, psso, k10] 5 times, yo, sl 1, k2tog, psso, k2. (71 sts)
Round 11: K8, [yo, sl 1, k2tog, psso, k9] 5 times, yo, sl 1, k2tog, psso. (65 sts)
Round 12: K9, [yo, sl 1, k2tog, psso, k8] 5 times, sl next st onto foll needle to become first stitch of next round. (60 sts)
Round 13: Yo, sl 1, k2tog, psso, k8, [yo, sl 1, k2tog, psso, k7] 4 times, yo, sl 1, k2tog, psso, k6. (54 sts)
Round 14: K1, yo, sl 1, k2tog, psso, k7, [yo, sl 1, k2tog, psso, k6] 4 times, yo, sl 1, k2tog, psso, k4. (48 sts)
Round 15: K2, yo, sl 1, k2tog, psso, k6, [yo, sl 1, k2tog, psso, k5] 4 times, yo, sl 1, k2tog, psso, k2. (42 sts)
Round 16: K3, yo, sl 1, k2tog, psso, k5, [yo, sl 1, k2tog, psso, k4] 4 times, yo, sl 1, k2tog, psso. (36 sts)
Round 17: K4, yo, sl 1, k2tog, psso, k4, [yo, sl 1, k2tog, psso, k3] 4 times, sl last st onto next needle to become first stitch of next round. (31 sts)
Round 18: [Yo, sl 1, k2tog, psso, k3] twice, [yo, sl 1, k2tog, psso, k2] 3 times, yo, sl 1, k2tog, psso, k1. (25 sts)
Finish centre (do not count rounds for this part): K1 [yo, sl 1, k2tog, psso, k2] twice, [yo, sl 1, k2tog, psso, k1] 6 times, yo, [ssk, k1] 6 times. (12 sts)
Final round: [Ssk] 6 times. (6 sts)
Cut yarn leaving a 25cm (10in) tail. Using a tapestry needle, weave the yarn through the remaining 6 stitches on the needle, gather and secure.

Colour:
■ A

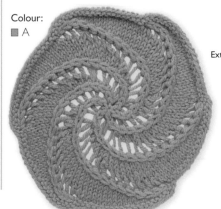

Extra large

68 GARTER EDGE TEXTURED HEXAGON

SPECIAL ABBREVIATION
MB (Make Bobble): [K1, p1, k1] into next st, turn, p3, turn, k3togtbl.

Cast on 114 stitches and divide evenly over 3 needles, 38 sts oen. Join, taking care not to twist stitches.
Round 1: Purl.
Round 2: [K7, ssk, k2tog, k8] 6 times. (102 sts)
Round 3: Purl.
Round 4: Knit.
Round 5: Purl.
Round 6: [K6, ssk, k2tog, k7] 6 times. (90 sts)
Round 7: Knit.
Round 8: [K5, ssk, k2tog, k6] 6 times. (78 sts)
Round 9: [MB, k1, MB, k6, (MB, k1) twice] 6 times.
Round 10: [K4, ssk, k2tog, k5] 6 times. (66 sts)
Round 11: [K1, MB, k6, MB, k1, MB] 6 times.

Round 12: [K3, ssk, k2tog, k4] 6 times. (54 sts)
Round 13: [MB, k6, MB, k1] 6 times.
Round 14: [K2, ssk, k2tog, k3] 6 times. (42 sts)
Round 15: [K6, MB] 6 times.
Round 16: [K1, ssk, k2tog, k2] 6 times. (30 sts)
Round 17: Knit.
Round 18: [Ssk, k2tog, k1] 6 times. (18 sts)
Round 19: Knit.
Round 20: [Sl 1, k2tog, psso] 6 times. (6 sts)
Cut yarn leaving a 25cm (9¾in) tail. Using a tapestry needle, weave the yarn through the remaining 6 stitches on the needle, gather and secure.

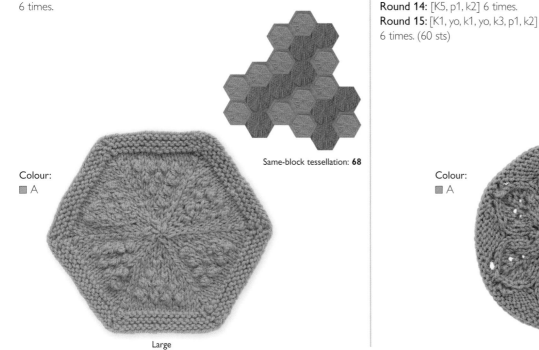

Same-block tessellation: **68**

Colour:
■ A

Large

69 LEAFY HEXAGON

Cast on 6 stitches and divide evenly over 3 needles, 2 sts oen. Join, taking care not to twist stitches.
Round 1 (RS): Knit.
Round 2: [Yo, k1] 6 times. (12 sts)
Round 3: [K1, (k1, yo, k1, yo, k1) into next st] 6 times.
Round 4: [Yo, k1, ssk, k1, k2tog] 6 times.
Round 5: [P2, sl 1, k2tog, psso] 6 times. (18 sts)
Round 6: Knit.
Round 7: [K1, yo, k1, yo, k1] 6 times. (30 sts)
Round 8: Knit.
Round 9: [K2, yo, p1, yo, k2] 6 times. (42 sts)
Round 10: [K3, p1, k3] 6 times.
Round 11: [Yo, k3, p1, k3] 6 times. (48 sts)
Round 12: [K4, p1, k3] 6 times.
Round 13: [Yo, k1, yo, k2tog, k1, p1, k1, ssk]. 6 times.
Round 14: [K5, p1, k2] 6 times.
Round 15: [K1, yo, k1, yo, k3, p1, k2] 6 times. (60 sts)

Round 16: [K7, p1, k2] 6 times.
Round 17: [K2, yo, k1, yo, k2, k2tog, M1P, p1, M1P, ssk] 6 times. (72 sts)
Round 18: [K8, p3, k1] 6 times.
The last ssk of following four rounds, will be worked into the last stitch of the round and first stitch of the next.
Round 19: K6, k2tog, M1P, p3, M1P, ssk, [k5, k2tog, M1P, p3, M1P, ssk] 5 times.
Round 20: K4, k2tog, M1P, p5, M1P, ssk, [k3, k2tog, M1P, p5, M1P, ssk] 5 times.
Round 21: K2, k2tog, yo, M1P, p7, M1P, yo, ssk, [k1, k2tog, yo, M1P, p7, M1P, yo, ssk] 5 times. (84 sts)
Round 22: K2tog, yo, p11, yo, sl 1, k2tog, psso, [yo, p11, yo, sl 1, k2tog, psso] 4 times, yo, p11, yo, ssk.
Round 23: Knit.
Round 24: Purl.
Using a larger-size needle, cast off loosely.

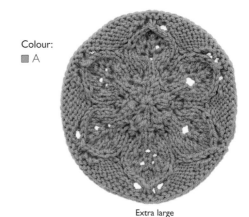

Colour:
■ A

Extra large

70   MULTI-COLOURED OCTAGON

Foundation ring: Using A, ch 4, join with ss to form a ring.

Round 1: Ch 3 (counts as first tr), 15 tr into ring, join B with ss in top of beg ch-3. (16 tr)
Fasten off A.

Round 2: Ch 3 (counts as first tr), 2 tr into the base of the ch-3, 1 tr in next tr, [3 tr in next tr, 1 tr in next tr] 7 times, join C with ss in top of beg ch-3. (32 tr)
Fasten off B.

Round 3: Ch 3 (counts as first tr), [3 tr in next tr, 1 tr in each of next 3 tr] 7 times, 3 tr in next tr, 1 tr in each of next 2 tr, join A with ss in top of beg ch-3. (48 tr)
Fasten off C.

Round 4: Ch 3, (counts as first tr) 1 tr in next tr, [3 tr in next tr, 1 tr in each of next 5 tr] 7 times, 3 tr in next tr, 1 tr in each of next 3 tr, join with ss in top of beg ch-3.
Fasten off.

Colours:
- ■ A
- ■ B
- ■ C

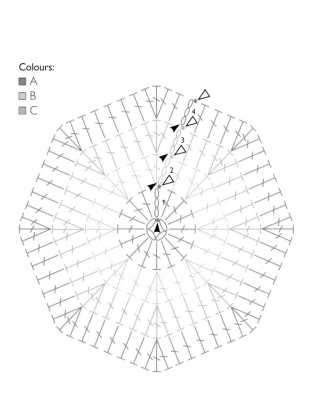

Medium

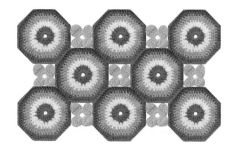

Mix and match: **70 + Rounds 1–2 of 37 (you may need to go down a hook size to make it fit)**

Symbols and abbreviations
Turn to pages 140–141 for a full explanation of the symbols and abbreviations used.

71 TWO-TONE BOBBLE OCTAGON

STITCH EXPLANATION

MB (Make Bobble): [Yrh, insert hook into st, yrh, draw yarn through, yrh draw through 2 loops] 5 times into the same st, yrh, draw through all 6 loops on hook.

Foundation ring: Using A, ch 4, join with ss to form a ring.

Round 1: Ch 5 (counts as first tr and ch 2), [1 tr into ring, ch 2] 7 times, join with ss into third ch of beg ch-5. (8 tr and ch-2 sps)

Round 2: Ch 3 (counts as first tr), 2 tr into the base of ch-3, ch 2 [3 tr into next tr, ch 2] 7 times, join with ss in top of beg ch-3.

Round 3: Ch 3 (counts as first tr), 1 tr into the base of ch-3, 1 tr in next tr, 2 tr into next tr, ch 2, [2 tr into next tr, 1 tr into next tr, 2 tr into next tr, ch 2) 7 times, join with ss in top of beg ch-3. Fasten off A. Join B to last stitch.

Round 4: Ch 5 (counts as first tr and ch 2), skip 1 tr, MB into next tr, ch 2, skip 1 tr, 1 tr into next tr, ch 2, [1 tr in next tr, ch 2, skip 1 tr, MB into next tr, ch 2, skip 1 tr, 1 tr into next tr, ch 2] 7 times, join with ss in top of beg ch-5. Fasten off B. Join A to last stitch.

Round 5: Ch 3, 1 tr into the base of ch-3, 2 tr into the first ch-2 sp, 1 tr into top of next bobble, 2 tr in next ch-2 sp, 2 tr in next tr, ch 1, [2 tr in next tr, 2 tr into next ch-2 sp, 1 tr into top of next bobble, 2 tr in next ch-2 sp, 2 tr in next tr, ch 1] 7 times, join with ss in top of beg ch-3. Fasten off.

Colours:
- ■ A
- ■ B

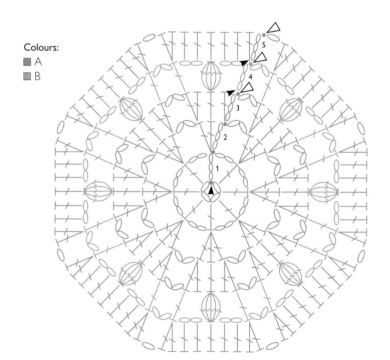

Large

72 DOUBLE CROCHET SPOKE OCTAGON

Foundation ring: Ch 4, join with ss to form ring.

Round 1: Ch 3 (counts as first tr), 23 tr into ring, join with ss in top of beg ch-3. (24 tr)

Round 2: Ch 3 (counts as first tr), 1 tr in each of next 2 tr, [ch 2, 1 tr in each of next 3 tr] 7 times, ch 2, join with ss in top of beg ch-3.

Round 3: Ch 3 (counts as first tr), 1 tr into the base of the ch-3, 1 tr in next tr, 2 tr in next tr, [ch 2, 2 tr in next tr, 1 tr in next tr, 2 tr in next tr] 7 times, ch 2, join with ss in top of beg ch-3.

Round 4: Ch 3 (counts as first tr), 1 tr into the base of the ch-3, 1 tr in each of next 3 tr, 2 tr in next tr, [ch 2, 2 tr in next tr, 1 tr in each of next 3 tr, 2 tr into next tr] 7 times, ch 2, join with ss in top of beg ch-3.

Round 5: Ch 3 (counts as first tr), 1 tr into the base of the ch-3, 1 tr in each of next 5 tr, 2 tr in next tr, [ch 2, 2 tr in next tr, 1 tr in each of next 5 tr, 2 tr in next tr] 7 times, ch 2, join with ss in top of beg ch-3.

Fasten off.

Colour:
■ A

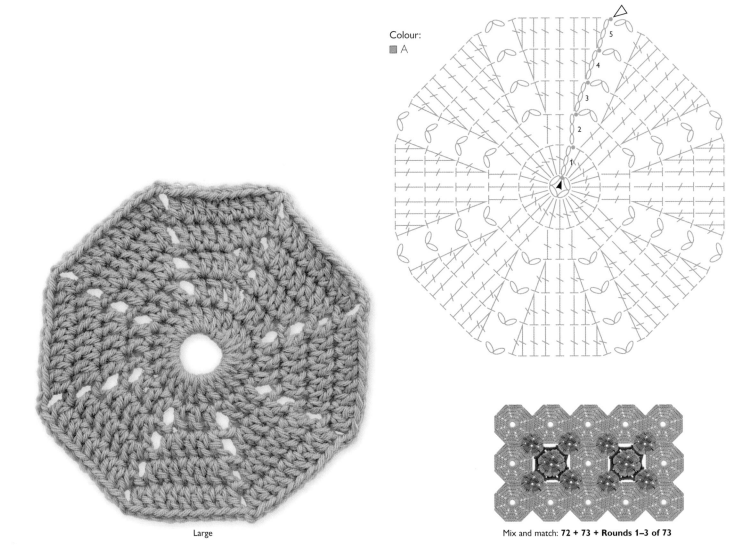

Large

Mix and match: **72 + 73 + Rounds 1–3 of 73**

73 CELTIC OCTAGON

Foundation ring: Using A, ch 6, join with ss to form a ring.

Round 1: [Ch 4, 3 dtr into ring, ch 4, 1 ss into ring] 4 times.

Fasten off A. Join B.

Round 2: Ch 6 (counts as the first tr and ch 3), skip [ch-4 sp, 3 dtr, ch-4 sp], *[1 tr, ch 3, 1 tr] into next ss, ch 3, skip [ch-4 sp, 3 dtr; ch-4 sp]; rep from * twice more, 1 tr into last ss, ch 3, join with ss to third ch of beg ch-6.

Round 3: Ch 5, *3 dtr into ch-3 sp, ch 4, 1 dc in next tr; ch 4; rep from * 6 times more, 3 dtr into ch-3 sp, ch 4, join with ss to the first ch of beg ch-5.

Fasten off B. Join C.

Round 4: Ch 5, *skip [ch-4 sp, 3 dtr; ch-4 sp], 1 dc in next dc, ch 4; rep from * 6 times more, skip [ch-4 sp, 3 dtr; ch-4 sp], join with ss to the first ch of beg ch-5.

Round 5: Ch 3 (counts as first tr), *[2 tr, ch 3, 2 tr] into ch-4 sp st base of beg ch-3, 1 tr in next dc; rep from * 6 times more, [2 tr; ch 3, 2 tr] into ch-4 sp, join with ss to top of beg ch-3.

Round 6: Ch 1, 1 dc into each of next 2 tr, *2 dc in ch-3 sp, ch 3, ss in last dc made, 1 dc in same ch-3 sp, 1 dc into each of next 5 tr; rep from * 6 times more, 2 dc in ch-3 sp, ch 3, ss in last dc made, 1 dc in same ch-3 sp, 1 dc in each of last 2 tr; join with ss to beg ch-1.

Fasten off.

Arrange petals of Round 3 in front of Round 4, and petals of Round 1 in front of Round 2.

Medium

Colours:
- ■ A
- ■ B
- ■ C

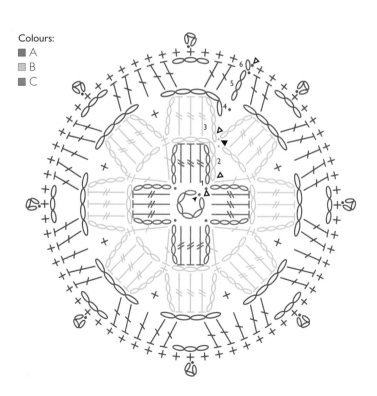

74 OCTAGON GRANNY

Foundation ring: Using A, ch 5, join with ss to form ring.

Round 1 (RS): Ch 3 (counts as first tr), 2 tr into ring, ch 1, [3 tr into ring, ch 1] 3 times, join with ss in third ch of beg ch-3. (4 3-tr groups and 4 ch-1 sp corners)

Fasten off A. Join B with ss in any ch-1 sp.

Round 2: Ch 3 (counts as first tr), [2 tr, ch 1, 3 tr] in sp at base of ch-3, ch 1, *[3 tr, ch 1, 3 tr] in next ch-1 sp, ch 1; rep from * twice more, join with ss in third ch of beg ch-3. (4 corners)

Round 3: Ss to and into next corner ch-1 sp, ch 3 (counts as first tr), [1 tr, ch 1, 2 tr] in sp at base of ch-3, ch 1, *[2 tr, ch 1, 2 tr] in next ch-1 sp, ch 1; rep from * 6 times more, join with ss in third ch of beg ch-3. (8 corners)

Fasten off B. Join C with ss in any ch-1 sp between 2 corner groups.

Round 4: Ch 3 (counts as first tr), [1 tr, ch 1, 2 tr] in sp at base of ch-3, ch 1 * 2 tr in next ch-1 sp ch 1, [2 tr, ch 1, 2 tr] in next ch-1 sp, ch 1; rep from * 7 times more, join with ss in third ch of beg ch-3.

Round 5: Ss to and into next corner ch-1 sp, ch 3 (counts as first tr), [1 tr, ch 1, 2 tr] in sp at base of ch-3, ch 1, [2 tr into next ch-1 sp, ch 1] twice, *[2 tr, ch 1, 2 tr] in next corner ch-1 sp, ch 1, [2 tr into next ch-1 sp, ch 1] twice; rep from * 6 times more, join with ss in third ch of beg ch-3.

Fasten off.

Colours:
- A
- B
- C

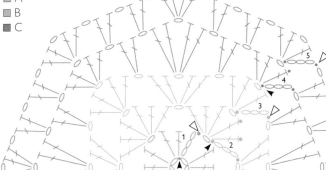

Large

Mix and match: **74 + Rounds 1–2 of 3**

75 OCTAGON WHEEL

Foundation ring: Using A, ch 7, join with ss to form ring.

Round 1 (RS): Ch 5 (counts as first dtr and ch 1), [1 dtr, ch 1] 15 times into ring, join with ss in fourth ch of beg ch-5. (16 ch-1 sp)

Fasten off A. Join B in any ch-1 sp.

Round 2: Ch 1, 1 dc in sp at base of ch, ch 2, [1 dc in next ch-1 sp, ch 2] 15 times, join with ss in top of first dc.

Fasten off B. Join C in any ch-2 sp.

Round 3: Ch 3 (counts as first tr), 1 tr in sp at base of ch, ch 1, [2 tr in next ch-2 sp, ch 1] 15 times, join with ss in top of beg ch-3.

Fasten off C. Join A in any ch-1 sp.

Round 4: Ch 3 (counts as first tr), 1 tr in sp at base of ch, ch 3, 2 tr in next ch-1 sp, ch 1, [2 tr in next ch-1 sp, ch 3, 2 tr in next ch-1 sp, ch 1] 7 times, join with ss in top of beg ch-3.

Fasten off.

Colours:
- A
- B
- C

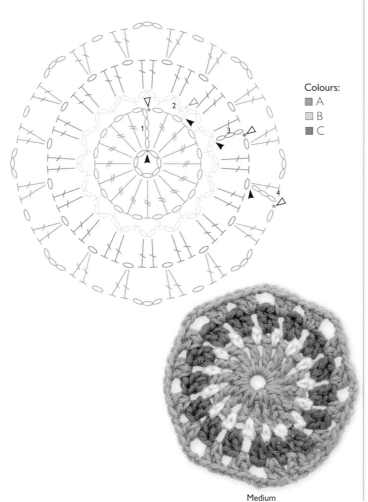

Medium

76 GARTER RIDGE OCTAGON

Cast on 96 stitches and divide evenly over 4 needles, 24 sts oen. Join, taking care not to twist stitches.

Round 1: Purl.
Round 2: Purl.
Round 3: [Ssk, k10] 8 times. (88 sts)
Round 4: [Ssk, k9] 8 times. (80 sts)
Round 5: Purl.
Round 6: Purl.
Round 7: [Ssk, k8] 8 times. (72 sts)
Round 8: [Ssk, k7] 8 times. (64 sts)
Round 9: Purl.
Round 10: Purl.
Round 11: [Ssk, k6] 8 times. (56 sts)
Round 12: [Ssk, k5] 8 times. (48 sts)
Round 13: Purl.
Round 14: Purl.
Round 15: [Ssk, k4] 8 times. (40 sts)
Round 16: [Ssk, k3] 8 times. (32 sts)
Round 17: Purl.
Round 18: Purl.
Round 19: [Ssk, k2] 8 times. (24 sts)
Round 20: [Ssk, k1] 8 times. (16 sts)
Round 21: Purl.
Round 22: Purl.
Round 23: [Ssk] 8 times. (8 sts)

Cut yarn leaving a 25cm (9¾in) tail. Using a tapestry needle, weave the yarn through the remaining 8 stitches on the needle, gather and secure.

Colour:
- A

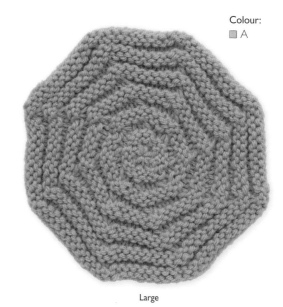

Large

77 SEED STITCH OCTAGON

Cast on 13 stitches.
Row 1: [K1, p1] 6 times, k1.
Row 2: K1f&b, [p1, k1] 5 times, p1, k1f&b. (15 sts)
Row 3: [P1, k1] 7 times, p1.
Row 4: K1f&b, [k1, p1] 6 times, k1, k1f&b. (17 sts)
Row 5: [K1, p1] 8 times, k1.
Row 6: K1f&b, [p1, k1] 7 times, p1, k1f&b. (19 sts)
Row 7: [P1, k1] 9 times, p1.
Row 8: K1f&b, [k1, p1] 8 times, k1, k1f&b. (21 sts)
Row 9: [K1, p1] 10 times, k1.
Row 10: K1f&b, [p1, k1] 9 times, p1, k1f&b. (23 sts)
Row 11: [P1, k1] 11 times, p1.
Row 12: K1f&b, [k1, p1] 10 times, k1, k1f&b. (25 sts)
Row 13: [K1, p1] 12 times, k1.
Row 14: K1f&b, [p1, k1] 11 times, p1, k1f&b. (27 sts)
Row 15: [P1, k1] 13 times, p1.
Row 16: K1f&b, [k1, p1] 12 times, k1, k1f&b. (29 sts)
Row 17: [K1, p1] 14 times, k1.
Row 18: K1f&b, [p1, k1] 13 times, p1, k1f&b. (31 sts)

Rows 19–33: [P1, k1] 15 times, p1.
Row 34: K2tog, [p1, k1] 13 times, p1, k2tog. (29 sts)
Row 35: [K1, p1] 14 times, k1.
Row 36: P2tog, [k1, p1] 12 times, k1, p2tog. (27 sts)
Row 37: [P1, k1] 13 times, p1.
Row 38: K2tog, [p1, k1] 11 times, p1, k2tog. (25 sts)
Row 39: [K1, p1] 12 times, k1.
Row 40: P2tog, [k1, p1] 10 times, k1, p2tog. (23 sts)
Row 41: [P1, k1] 11 times, p1.
Row 42: K2tog, [p1, k1] 9 times, p1, k2tog. (21 sts)
Row 43: [K1, p1] 10 times, k1.
Row 44: P2tog, [k1, p1] 8 times, k1, p2tog. (19 sts)
Row 45: [P1, k1] 9 times, p1.
Row 46: K2tog, [p1, k1] 7 times, p1, k2tog. (17 sts)
Row 47: [K1, p1] 8 times, k1.
Row 48: P2tog, [k1, p1] 6 times, k1, p2tog. (15 sts)
Row 49: [P1, k1] 7 times, p1.
Row 50: K2tog, [p1, k1] 5 times, p1, k2tog. (13 sts)
Cast off in set pattern.

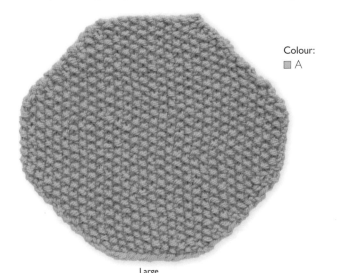

Colour:
■ A

Large

78 STAR OCTAGON

Cast on 8 stitches and divide evenly over 4 needles, 2 sts oen.
Join, taking care not to twist stitches.
Round 1 (and all odd-numbered rounds): Knit.
Round 2: [Yo, k1] 8 times. (16 sts)
Round 4: [Yo, k2] 8 times. (24 sts)
Round 6: [Yo, k3] 8 times. (32 sts)
Round 8: [Yo, k4] 8 times. (40 sts)
Round 10: [Yo, k5] 8 times. (48 sts)
Round 12: [Yo, k6] 8 times. (56 sts)

Round 14: [Yo, k1, yo, ssk, k4] 8 times. (64 sts)
Round 16: [Yo, k1, (yo, ssk) twice, k3] 8 times. (72 sts)
Round 18: [Yo, k1, (yo, ssk) 3 times, k2] 8 times. (80 sts)
Round 20: [Yo, k1, (yo, ssk) 4 times, k1] 8 times. (88 sts)
Round 22: [Yo, k1, (yo, ssk) 5 times] 8 times. (96 sts)
Cast off purlwise.

Colour:
■ A

Large

79 LACE LINE OCTAGON

Cast on 98 stitches.
Row 1: Purl.
Row 2: Knit.
Row 3: K1, [k5, yo, k2tog, k5] 8 times, k1.
Row 4: P1, [p5, yo, p2tog, p5] 8 times, p1.
Row 5: K1, [ssk, k3, yo, k2tog, k3, k2tog] 8 times, k1. (82 sts)
Row 6: P1, [p4, yo, p2tog, p4] 8 times, p1.
Row 7: K1, [k4, yo, k2tog, k4] 8 times, k1.
Row 8: P1, [p4, yo, p2tog, p4] 8 times, p1.
Row 9: K1, [ssk, k2, yo, k2tog, k2, k2tog] 8 times, k1. (66 sts)
Row 10: P1, [p3, yo, p2tog, p3] 8 times, p1.
Row 11: K1, [k3, yo, k2tog, k3] 8 times, k1.
Row 12: P1, [p3, yo, p2tog, p3] 8 times, p1.
Row 13: K1, [ssk, k1, yo, k2tog, k1, k2tog] 8 times, k1. (50 sts)

Row 14: P1, [p2, yo, p2tog, p2] 8 times, p1.
Row 15: K1, [k2, yo, k2tog, k2] 8 times, k1.
Row 16: P1, [p2, yo, p2tog, p2] 8 times, p1.
Row 17: K1, [ssk, yo, k2tog, k2tog] 8 times, k1. (34 sts)
Row 18: P1, [p1, yo, p2tog, p1] 8 times, p1.
Row 19: K2, [yo, k2tog, ssk] 8 times. (26 sts)
Row 20: P1, [yo, p2tog, p1] 8 times, p1.
Row 21: K1, [sl 2tog, k1, p2sso] 8 times, k1. (10 sts)
Cut yarn leaving a 25cm (9¾in) tail. Using a tapestry needle, weave the yarn through the remaining 10 stitches on the needle, gather and secure. Sew side seams together to form an octagon block.

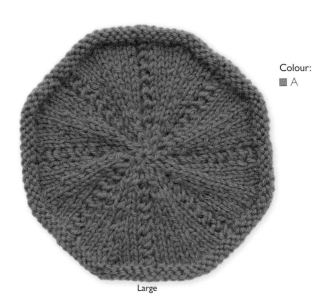

Large

Colour:
■ A

80 CABLED OCTAGON

SPECIAL ABBREVIATION

C3B dec: Slip 3 sts to cable needle and hold to back, from left-hand needle k2tog, k1, from cable needle, k2tog, k1.

Cast on 98 stitches.
Row 1: Purl
Row 2: Knit
Row 3: K1, [p3, C3B dec, p3] 8 times, k1. (82 sts)
Row 4: P1, [k3, p4, k3] 8 times, p1.
Row 5: K1, [p3, k4, p3] 8 times, k1.
Row 6: P1, [k3, p4, k3] 8 times, p1.
Row 7: K1, [p2, C3B dec, p2] 8 times, k1. (66 sts)
Row 8: P1, [k2, p4, k2] 8 times, p1.
Row 9: K1, [p2, k4, p2] 8 times, k1.
Row 10: P1, [k2, p4, k2] 8 times, p1.
Row 11: K1, [p1, C3B dec, p1] 8 times, k1. (50 sts)
Row 12: P1, [k1, p4, k1] 8 times, p1.

Row 13: K1, [p1, k4, p1] 8 times, k1.
Row 14: P1, [k1, p4, k1] 8 times, p1
Row 15: K1, [C3B dec] 8 times, k1. (34 sts)
Row 16: Purl.
Row 17: K1, [k2tog, k2] 8 times, k1. (26 sts)
Row 18: Purl.
Row 19: K1, [sl 1, k2tog, psso] 8 times, k1. (10 sts)
Cut yarn leaving a 25cm (9¾in) tail. Using a tapestry needle, weave the yarn through the remaining 10 stitches on the needle, gather and secure. Sew side seams together to form an octagon.

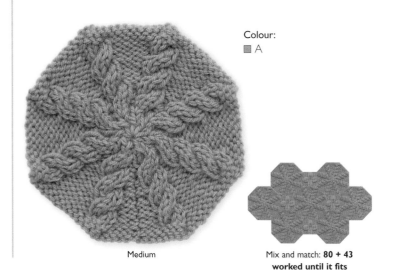

Medium

Colour:
■ A

Mix and match: **80 + 43 worked until it fits the space**

81 SPIRAL OCTAGON

Cast on 8 stitches and divide evenly over 4 needles, 2 sts oen.

Join, taking care not to twist stitches.

Round 1: Knit.

Round 2 (and all even-numbered rounds): Knit.

Round 3: (Yo, k1) 8 times. (16 sts)

Round 5: (Yo, k2) 8 times. (24 sts)

Round 7: (Yo, ssk, yo, k1) 8 times. (32 sts)

Round 9: (Yo, ssk, yo, k2) 8 times. (40 sts)

Round 11: (Yo, ssk, yo, k3) 8 times. (48 sts)

Round 13: (Yo, ssk, yo, k4) 8 times. (56 sts)

Round 15: (Yo, ssk, yo, k5) 8 times. (64 sts)

Round 17: (Yo, ssk, yo, k6) 8 times. (72 sts)

Round 19: (Yo, ssk, yo, k7) 8 times. (80 sts)

Round 21: (Yo, ssk, yo, k8) 8 times. (88 sts)

Rounds 22 and 23: Purl. Cast off knitwise.

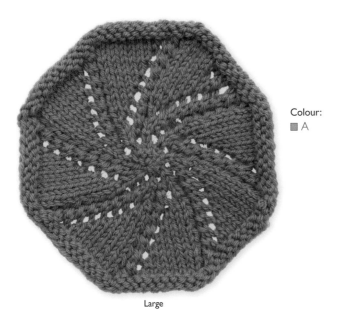

Large

Colour:
■ A

82 GARTER EYELET OCTAGON

Cast on 96 stitches and divide evenly over 4 needles, 24 sts oen.

Join, taking care not to twist stitches.

Round 1: Purl.

Round 2: [K5, ssk, k5] 8 times. (88 sts)

Round 3: Purl.

Round 4: Knit.

Round 5: Purl.

Round 6: [K4, ssk, k5] 8 times. (80 sts)

Round 7: [K2tog, yo] to end of round.

Round 8: [K4, ssk, k4] 8 times. (72 sts)

Round 9: Knit.

Round 10: [K3, ssk, k4] 8 times. (64 sts)

Round 11: Knit.

Round 12: [K3, ssk, k3] 8 times. (56 sts)

Round 13: Knit.

Round 14: [K2, ssk, k3] 8 times. (48 sts)

Round 15: Knit.

Round 16: [K2, ssk, k2] 8 times. (40 sts)

Round 17: [K2tog, yo] to end of round.

Round 18: [K1, ssk, k2] 8 times. (32 sts)

Round 19: Knit.

Round 20: [K1, ssk, k1] 8 times. (24 sts)

Round 21: Knit.

Round 22: [Ssk, k1] 8 times. (16 sts)

Round 23: [Ssk] 8 times. (8 sts)

Cut yarn leaving a 25cm (9¾in) tail. Using a tapestry needle, weave the yarn through the remaining 8 stitches on the needle, gather and secure.

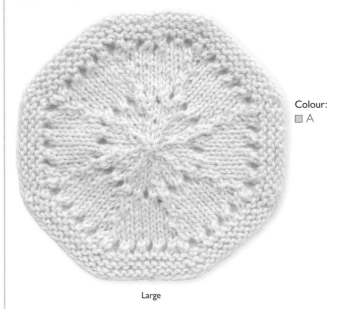

Large

Colour:
■ A

PENTAGONS

GRANNY PENTAGON

Foundation ring: With A, ch 5, join with ss in first ch.

Round 1: Ch 3 (counts as first tr), 1 tr into ring, [ch 1 (counts as corner), 2 tr into ring] 4 times, ch 1, join with ss in top of beg ch-3. (5 ch-1 sp)

Fasten off A. Join B to any ch-1 sp.

Round 2: Ch 3 (counts as first tr), [1 tr, ch 1, 2 tr] into ch-1 sp at base of ch-3, ch 1, *[2 tr, ch 1 (counts as corner), 2 tr] into next ch-1 sp, ch 1; rep from * 3 times more, join with ss in top of beg ch-3.

Fasten off B. Join C to the ch-1 sp of any corner.

Round 3: Ch 3 (counts as first tr), [1 tr, ch 1 (counts as corner), 2 tr] into ch-1 sp at base of ch-3, * ch 1, 2 tr in next ch-1 sp, ch 1, [2 tr, ch 1 (counts as corner), 2 tr] into next ch-1 sp; rep from * 3 times more, ch 1, 2 tr into next ch-1 sp, ch 1, join with ss in top of beg ch-3.

Fasten off C. Join A to the ch-1 sp of any corner.

Round 4: Ch 3 (counts as first tr), [1 tr, ch 1 (counts as corner), 2 tr] into ch-1 sp at base of ch-3, *[ch 1, 2 tr in next ch-1 sp] twice, ch 1, [2 tr, ch 1 (counts as corner), 2 tr] into next ch-1 sp; rep from * 3 times more, [ch 1, 2 tr in next ch-1 sp] twice, ch 1, join with ss in top of beg ch-3.

Fasten off.

Colours:
- ☐ A
- ☐ B
- ■ C

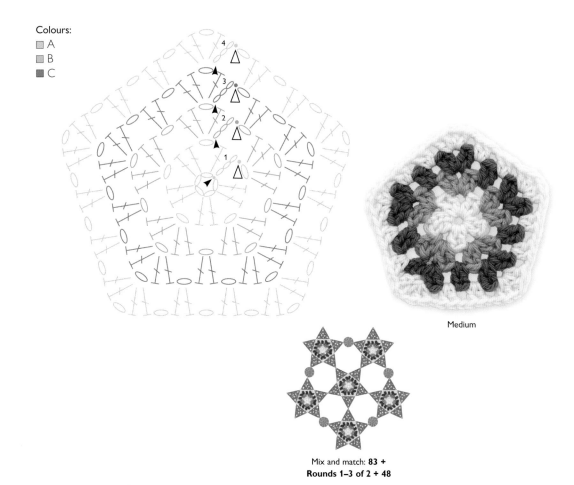

Medium

Mix and match: **83 +
Rounds 1–3 of 2 + 48**

Symbols and abbreviations
Turn to pages 140–141 for a full explanation of the symbols and abbreviations used.

84 TWO-TONE PENTAGON

DEALING WITH YARN ENDS

It is important to fasten off yarn ends securely so that they do not unravel during wear or laundering. Try to fasten off as neatly as possible so the darned ends do not show through the front of the work.

Foundation ring: Using A, ch 5, join with ss in first ch.

Round 1: Ch 2 (counts as first htr), 2 htr into ring, [ch 2, 3 htr into ring] 4 times, ch 2, join with ss in top of beg ch-2.

Round 2: Ss to next htr, ch 4 (counts as first tr and 1 ch), 1 tr in same st, [2 tr, ch 2, 2 tr] in next ch-2 sp, skip next htr, *[1 tr, ch 1, 1 tr] in next htr, [2 tr, ch 2, 2 tr] in next ch-2 sp, skip next htr; rep from * 4 times more, join with ss to third ch of beg ch-4.

Fasten off A. Join B in same st as ss.

Round 3: Ch 1 (count as first dc), 1 dc in next ch-1 sp, *1 dc in each of the next 3 sts, 3 dc into next ch-2 sp, 1 dc in each of the next 3 sts, 1 dc in next ch-1 sp; rep from * 4 times more, join with ss to beg ch-1.

Fasten off B. Join A in same st as ss.

Round 4: 1 dc in each st and 3 dc in the second dc of the 3-dc in each ch-2 sp of last round, join with ss to first dc.

Fasten off.

Colours:
■ A
■ B

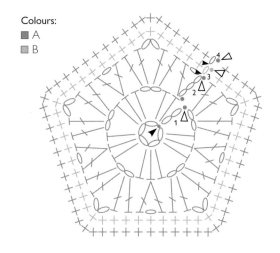

Small

For an edging

Mix and match: **84 +**
Rounds 1–2 of 48

85 GARTER PENTAGON

NOTE
Slip first stitch of each row as if to purl with yarn back.

Cast on 87 stitches.
Row 1 (WS): Sl 1, k7, p3, [k14, p3] 4 times, k7, p1.
Row 2: Sl 1, k7, sl 1, k2tog, psso, [k14, sl 1, k2tog, psso] 4 times, k7, p1. (77 sts)
Row 3: Sl 1, k6, p3, [k12, p3] 4 times, k6, p1.
Row 4: Sl 1, k6, k3tog, [k12, k3tog] 4 times, k6, p1. (67 sts)
Row 5: Sl 1, k5, p3, [k10, p3] 4 times, k5, p1.
Row 6: Sl 1, k5, sl 1, k2tog, psso, [k10, sl 1, k2tog, psso] 4 times, k5, p1. (57 sts)
Row 7: Sl 1, k4, p3, [k8, p3] 4 times, k4, p1.
Row 8: Sl 1, k4, k3tog, [k8, k3tog] 4 times, k4, p1. (47 sts)
Row 9: Sl 1, k3, p3, [k6, p3] 4 times, k3, p1.
Row 10: Sl 1, k3, sl 1, k2tog, psso, [k6, sl 1, k2tog, psso] 4 times, k3, p1. (37 sts)
Row 11: Sl 1, k2, p3, [k4, p3] 4 times, k2, p1.
Row 12: Sl 1, k2, k3tog, [k4, k3tog] 4 times, k2, p1. (27 sts)
Row 13: Sl 1, k1, p3, [k2, p3] 4 times, k1, p1.
Row 14: Sl 1, k1, sl 1, k2tog, psso, [k2, sl 1, k2tog, psso] 4 times, k1, p1. (17 sts)
Row 15: Sl 1, purl to end.
Row 16: Sl 1, [k3tog] 5 times, p1. (7 sts)
Row 17: Sl 1, purl to end.
Row 18: Sl 1, ssk, k1, ssk, p1. (5 sts)
Cut yarn leaving a 25cm (10in) tail. Using a tapestry needle, weave the yarn through the remaining 5 stitches on the needle, gather and secure. Sew side seams together to form a pentagon block.

Colour:
☐ A

To see this design extrapolated into a blanket, see page 128

Medium

Mix and match:
85 + 109

86 STRIPED PENTAGON

Using A, cast on 7 stitches.
Row 1: K1, [k1f&b] 5 times, k1. (12 sts)
Row 2: Purl.
Row 3: K1, [k1f&b, yo, k1] 5 times, k1. (22 sts)
Change to B.
Row 4: P1, k20, p1.
Row 5: K1, [k1f&b, k2, k1f&b] 5 times, k1. (32 sts)
Row 6: Purl.
Row 7: Knit.
Row 8: Purl.
Row 9: K1, [k1f&b, k4, k1f&b] 5 times, k1. (42 sts)
Change to A.
Row 10: P1, k40, p1.
Row 11: K1, [k1f&b, k6, k1f&b] 5 times, k1. (52 sts)
Change to B.
Row 12: Purl.
Row 13: K1, [k1f&b, k8, k1f&b] 5 times, k1. (62 sts)
Row 14: Purl.
Row 15: K1, [k1f&b, k10, k1f&b] 5 times, k1. (72 sts)
Row 16: Purl.
Row 17: Knit.
Change to A.
Row 18: Purl.
Row 19: K1, [k1f&b, k12, k1f&b] 5 times, k1. (82 sts)
Change to B.
Row 20: Purl.
Row 21: K1, p80, k1.
Cast off knitwise.
Sew side seams together to form a circle block.

Colours:
■ A
☐ B

Large

87 ACORN PENTAGON

Cast on 100 stitches and divide evenly over 4 needles, 25 sts oen. Join, taking care not to twist stitches.

Round 1: Purl.

Round 2: Purl.

Round 3: Knit.

Round 4: [(K1, yo, k1) into next st, p3, p2tog, p3, sl 2tog, k1, p2sso, p3, p2tog, p3] 5 times. (90 sts)

Round 5: [K1, yo, k1, yo, k1, p3, p2tog, p2, k1, p2, p2tog, p3] 5 times.

Round 6: [K5, p5, sl 2tog, k1, p2sso, p5] 5 times. (80 sts)

Round 7: [K5, p5, k1, p5] 5 times.

Round 8: [K5, p4, sl 2tog, k1, p2sso, p4] 5 times. (70 sts)

Round 9: [K5, p4, k1, p4] 5 times.

Round 10: [K5, p3, sl 2tog, k1, p2sso, p3] 5 times. (60 sts)

Round 11: [K5, p3, k1, p3] 5 times.

Round 12: [K5, p2, sl 2tog, k1, p2sso, p2] 5 times. (50 sts)

Round 13: [K5, p2, k1, p2] 5 times.

Round 14: [Ssk, k1, k2tog, p2, k1, p2] 5 times. (40 sts)

Round 15: [K3, p2, k1, p2] 5 times

Round 16: [Sl 2tog, k1, p2sso, p2, k1, p2] 5 times. (30 sts)

Round 17: [K1, p2] 10 times

Round 18: [Ssk, p1] 10 times. (20 sts)

Round 19: [K1, p1] 10 times

Round 20: [Ssk] 10 times. (10 sts)

Round 21: [Ssk] 5 times. (5 sts)

Cut yarn leaving a 25cm (9¾in) tail. Using a tapestry needle, weave the yarn through the remaining 5 stitches on the needle, gather and secure.

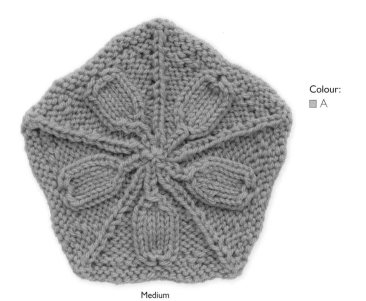

Colour:
■ A

Medium

88 GARTER BOBBLE PENTAGON

SPECIAL ABBREVIATION
MB (Make Bobble): [K1, p1, k1] into next st, turn, p3, turn, k3togtbl.

Cast on 100 stitches and divide evenly over 4 needles, 25 sts oen. Join, taking care not to twist stitches.

Round 1: Purl.

Round 2: [K8, sl 2tog, k1, psso, k9] 5 times. (90 sts)

Round 3: Purl.

Round 4: [K7, sl 2tog, k1, psso, k8] 5 times. (80 sts)

Round 5: Purl.

Round 6: [K6, sl 2tog, k1, psso, k7] 5 times. (70 sts)

Round 7: Knit.

Round 8: [K5, sl 2tog, k1, psso, k6] 5 times. (60 sts)

Round 9: [(K1, MB) twice, k3, (MB, k1) twice, MB] 5 times

Round 10: [K4, sl 2tog, k1, psso, k5] 5 times. (50 sts)

Round 11: Knit.

Round 12: [K3, sl 2tog, k1, psso, k4] 5 times. (40 sts)

Round 13: Knit.

Round 14: [K2, sl 2tog, k1, psso, k3] 5 times. (30 sts)

Round 15: [K5, MB] 5 times.

Round 16: [K1, sl 2tog, k1, psso, k2] 5 times. (20 sts)

Round 17: Knit.

Round 18: [Sl 2tog, k1, psso, k1] 5 times. (10 sts)

Round 19: [Ssk] 5 times. (5 sts)

Cut yarn leaving a 25cm (9¾in) tail. Using a tapestry needle, weave the yarn through the remaining 5 stitches on the needle, gather and secure.

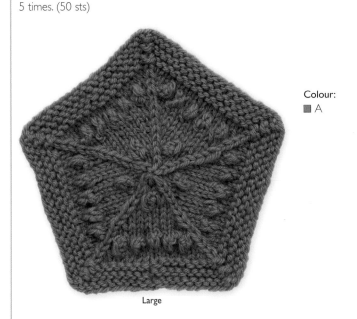

Colour:
■ A

Large

89 GARTER STITCH PENTAGON

Cast on 21 stitches.
Rows 1–3: Knit.
Row 4: K1f&b, k to last st, k1f&b. (23 sts).
Rows 5–8: Knit.
Repeat the last 5 rows until there are 33 sts.
Rows 30–33: Knit.

Row 34: K2tog, k to last 2 sts, k2tog. (31 sts)
Row 35: Knit.
Repeat the last 2 rows until there are 5 sts.
Row 62: K2tog, k1, k2tog. (3 sts)
Row 63: K3tog.
Fasten off.

To make this pentagon smaller, cast on the number of stitches required for one edge, calculate this number as a percentage of the cast on stated to the nearest odd number and apply the percentage to the number of stitches on Row 29. For this mix-and-match pattern cast on 13 stitches, work in the pattern and repeat Rows 5–8 until there are 21 stitches on the needle. Then continue to work and decrease stitches as stated in pattern.

To make an appliqué design

Mix and match: **89 + 19 + 109**

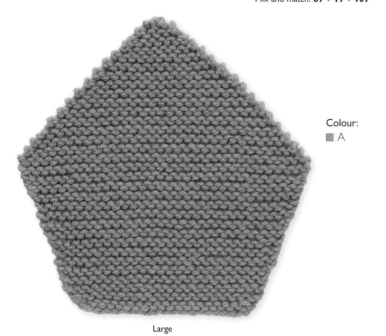

Large

Colour:
■ A

90 RIBBED PENTAGON

Cast on 102 stitches.
Row 1 (RS): Knit.
Row 2: Purl.
Row 3: K1, [sl 1, k2tog, psso, (k1, p1) 8 times, k1] 5 times, k1. (92 sts)
Row 4: P1, [(p1, k1) 8 times, p2] 5 times, p1.
Row 5: K1, [sl 1, k2tog, psso, (k1, p1) 7 times, k1] 5 times, k1. (82 sts)
Row 6: P1, [(p1, k1) 7 times, p2] 5 times, p1.
Row 7: K1, [sl 1, k2tog, psso, (k1, p1) 6 times, k1] 5 times, k1. (72 sts)
Row 8: P1, [(p1, k1) 6 times, p2] 5 times, p1.
Row 9: K1, [sl 1, k2tog, psso, (k1, p1) 5 times, k1] 5 times, k1. (62 sts)
Row 10: P1, [(p1, k1) 5 times, p2] 5 times, p1.
Row 11: K1, [sl 1, k2tog, psso, (k1, p1) 4 times, k1] 5 times, k1. (52 sts)
Row 12: P1, [(p1, k1) 4 times, p2] 5 times, p1.

Row 13: K1, [sl 1, k2tog, psso, (k1, p1) 3 times, k1] 5 times, k1. (42 sts)
Row 14: P1, [(p1, k1) 3 times, p2] 5 times, p1.
Row 15: K1, [sl 1, k2tog, psso, (k1, p1) 2 times, k1] 5 times, k1. (32 sts)
Row 16: P1, [(p1, k1) 2 times, p2] 5 times, p1.
Row 17: K1, [sl 1, k2tog, psso, k1, p1, k1] 5 times, k1. (22 sts)
Row 18: P1, [p1, k1, p2] 5 times, p1.
Row 19: K1, [sl 1, k2tog psso, k1] 5 times, k1. (12 sts)
Row 20: Purl.
Row 21: K1, [ssk] 5 times, k1. (7 sts)
Cut yarn leaving a 30cm (11¾in) tail. Using a tapestry needle, weave the yarn through the remaining 7 stitches on the needle, gather and secure. Sew side seams together to form a pentagon block.

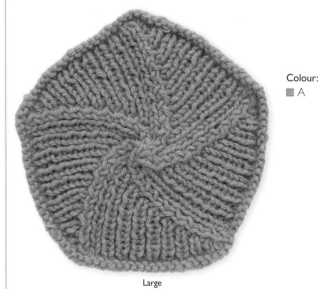

Large

Colour:
■ A

MAKING A NOTE OF PROJECT DETAILS
When you have finished making a knit or crochet project, store a small amount of leftover yarn in case you need to make future repairs. Punch a hole in a piece of cardboard and knot several lengths of yarn through the hole. Make a note of the type of yarn and colour, as well as details of the project, and attach one of the ball bands to remind you of the yarn composition and any special pressing or washing instructions. File the cards away in a closed box with a lid and store in a cool, dry place.

Foundation ring: Ch 9, join with ss to form a ring.
Round 1: Ch 8 (counts as first tr and ch 5), 3 tr into ring, [ch 5, 3 tr into ring] 4 times, ch 5, 2 tr into ring, join with ss to third ch of beg ch-8.
Round 2: Ss in each of next 2 ch, ch 7 (counts as first tr and ch 4), 4 tr into ch-5 sp at base of beg ch, *ch 1, [4 tr, ch 4, 4 tr] into next ch-5 sp; rep from * 4 times more, ch 1, 3 tr in beg ch-5 sp, join with ss to third ch of beg ch-7.
Round 3: Ss in each of next 2 ch, ch 6 (counts as first tr and ch 3), 3 tr into ch-4 sp at base of beg ch, *ch 3, [3 tr, ch 3, 3 tr] into next ch-4 sp; rep from * 4 times more, ch 3, 2 tr in beg ch-3 sp, join with ss to third ch of beg ch-6.
Round 4: Ss in each of next 2 ch, ch 8, ss in fourth ch from hook, ch 1, 2 tr into ch-3 sp at base of beg ch, ch 5, 1 dc into next ch-3 sp, *ch 5, [2 tr, ch 5, ss into fourth ch from hook, ch 1, 2 tr] into next ch-3 sp, ch 5, 1 dc in next ch-3 sp; rep from * 4 times more, ch 5, 1 tr in beg ch-3 sp, join with ss to third ch of beg ch-8.
Fasten off.

Colour:
■ A

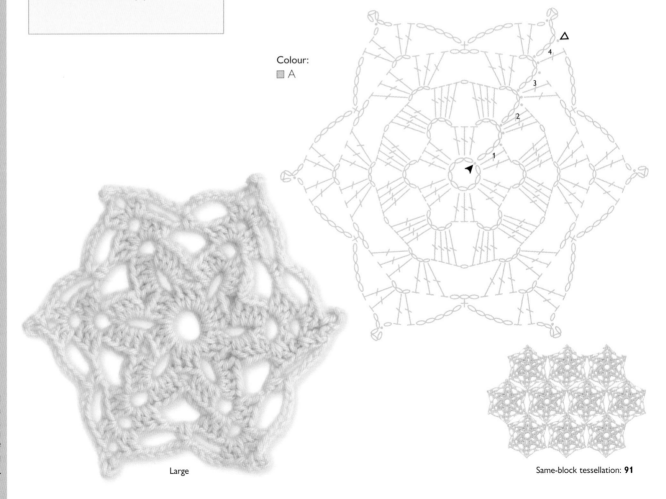

Large

Same-block tessellation: **91**

Symbols and abbreviations
Turn to pages 140–141 for a full explanation of the symbols and abbreviations used.

92 POINT SNOWFLAKE

Foundation ring: Ch 4, join with ss to form a ring.
Round 1 (RS): Work 6 dc into ring, join with ss to beg dc.
Round 2: Ch 5 (counts as first tr and ch 2), 1 tr in first dc, *[1 tr, ch 2, 1 tr] in next dc; rep from * 4 times more, join with ss in third ch of beg ch-5.
Round 3: Ss into ch-2 sp, ch 3 (counts as first tr), [1 tr, ch 3, 2 tr] in first ch-2 sp, *[2 tr, ch 3, 2 tr] in next ch-2 sp; rep from * 4 times more, join with ss in top of beg ch-3.
Round 4: Ss to and into ch-3 sp, ch 3 (counts as first tr), [2 tr, ch 3, 3 tr] in first ch-3 sp, *[3 tr, ch 3, 3 tr] in next ch-3 sp; repeat from * 4 times more, join with ss in top of beg ch-3.
Round 5: Ss to and into ch-3 sp, ch 3 (counts as first tr), [3 tr, ch 3, 4 tr] in first ch-3 sp, * 1 tr between 2 groups of tr [4 tr, ch 3, 4 tr] in next ch-3 sp; repeat from * 4 times more, 1 tr between 2 groups of tr, join with ss in top of beg ch-3.
Fasten off.

Colour:
☐ A

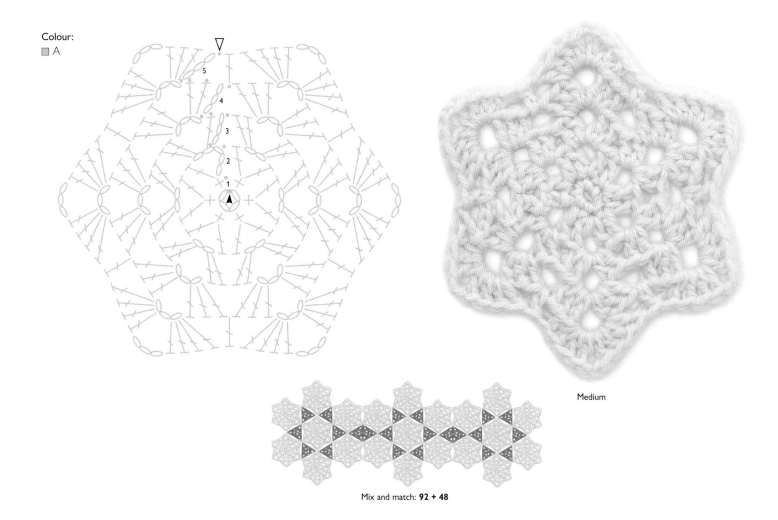

Medium

Mix and match: **92 + 48**

93 TWO-TONE CRYSTAL SNOWFLAKE

Foundation ring: Using A, ch 4, join with ss to form a ring.
Round 1 (RS): Ch 3 (counts as first tr), 1 tr into ring, ch 1, [2 tr into ring, ch 1] 5 times, join with ss in top of beg ch-3.
Fasten off A. Join B with ss to first ch-1 sp.
Round 2: Ch 3 (counts as first tr), [1 tr, ch 1, 2 tr] into first ch-1 sp, *[2 tr, ch 1, 2 tr] into next ch-1 sp; rep from * 4 times more, join with ss in top of beg ch-3.
Round 3: Ss in each st to and into first ch-1 sp, ch 3 (counts as first tr), [1 tr, ch 1, 2 tr] into first ch-1 sp,

1 tr in next tr, skip next 2 tr, tr in next tr, *[2 tr, ch 1, 2 tr) into next ch-1 sp, tr in next tr, skip next 2 tr, 1 tr in next tr; rep from * 4 times more, join with ss in top of beg ch-3.
Round 4: Ss in each st to and into first ch-1 sp, ch 3 (counts as first tr), [1 tr, ch 3, 2 tr] into first ch-1 sp, 1 tr in next 2 tr, skip next 2 tr, 1 tr in next 2 tr, *[2 tr, ch 3, 2 tr] into next ch-1 sp, 1 tr in next 2 tr, skip next 2 tr, 1 tr in next 2 tr; rep from * 4 times more join with ss in top of beg ch-3.
Fasten off.

Colours:
■ A
■ B

Medium

94 PETITE LACE SNOWFLAKE

Foundation ring: Ch 5, join with ss to form a ring.
Round 1 (RS): Ch 1, [2 dc in ring, ch 3] 6 times, join with ss in first dc. (6 ch-3 sp)
Round 2: Ss in next dc, ch 1, *[2 dc, ch 3, 2 dc) into next ch-3 sp; rep from * 5 times more, join with ss to first dc.

Round 3: Ch 1, *[1 dc, ch 3, 1 dc, ch 5, 1 dc, ch 3, 1 dc] into next ch-3 sp, ch 2; rep from * 5 times more, join with ss to first dc.
Fasten off.

Colour:
■ A

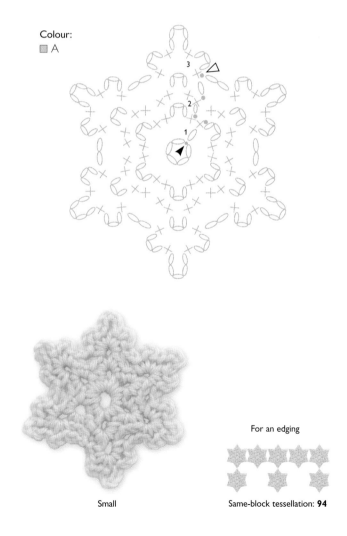

Small

For an edging

Same-block tessellation: 94

95 LARGE DOUBLE SNOWFLAKE

SPECIAL ABBREVIATION
Picot: Ch 5, then sl st into base of ch.

Colours:
■ A
■ B

Foundation ring: Using A, ch 6, join with ss to form a ring.

Round 1 (RS): Ch 3 (count as first tr), 1 tr into ring, [ch 2, 2 tr] 5 times in ring, ch 2, join with ss in top of beg ch-3.

Round 2: Ch 3 (counts as first tr), 1 tr into base of ch, 2 tr in next tr; *[1 tr, 1 dtr, picot, 1 tr] into ch-2 sp, 2 tr into each of next 2 tr; rep from * 4 times more, [1 tr, 1 dtr, picot, 1 tr] into last ch-2 sp, join with ss in top of beg ch-3.
Fasten off A. Join B with ss to top of last picot made in previous round,

Round 3: *Ch 5, ss into picot sp at base of ch, ch 9, ss into top of next picot; rep from * 5 times more, join with ss in base of beg ch-5.

Round 4: *Ss into ch-5 sp, ch 6, ss into sp at base of ch, work 9 dc in next ch-9 sp; rep from * 5 times more, join with ss into beg ch-5 sp.

Round 5: Ch 4 (counts as first dtr), 6 dtr into next ch-6 sp, picot, 6 dtr into same ch-6 sp, *skip 4 dc, ss into next dc, skip next 4 dc, work 7 dtr into next ch-6 sp, picot, 6 dtr into same ch-6 sp; rep from * 4 times more, skip 4 dc, ss into next dc, skip next 4 dc, join with ss in top of beg ch-4.
Fasten off.

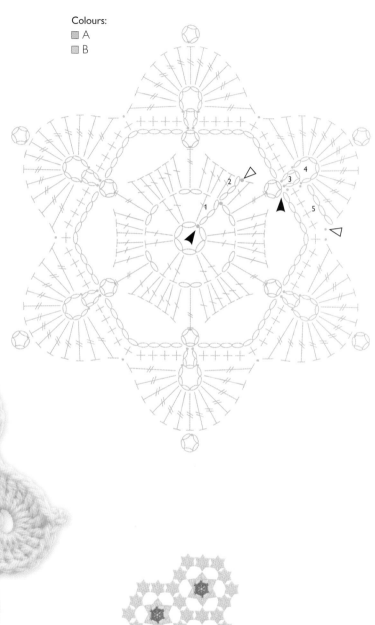

Extra large

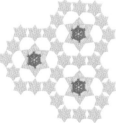

Mix and match: **95 + 94**

96 LACE TWELVE-SPOKE FLAKE

Cast on 102 stitches and divide evenly over 3 needles, 34 sts oen. Join, taking care not to twist stitches.

Round 1: Purl.

Round 2: [Ssk, k5, yo, sl 2tog, k1, p2sso, yo, k5, k2tog] 6 times. (90 sts)

Round 3: Purl.

Round 4: [K6, yo, sl 2tog, k1, p2sso, yo, k6] 6 times.

Round 5 (and all odd-numbered rounds): Knit.

Round 6: [Ssk, k4, yo, sl 2tog, k1, p2sso, yo, k4, k2tog] 6 times. (78 sts)

Round 8: [Ssk, k3, yo, sl 2tog, k1, p2sso, yo, k3, k2tog] 6 times. (66 sts)

Round 10: [Ssk, k2, yo, sl 2tog, k1, p2sso, yo, k2, k2tog] 6 times. (54 sts)

Round 12: [Ssk, k1, yo, sl 2tog, k1, p2sso, yo, k1, k2tog] 6 times. (42 sts)

Round 14: [Ssk, yo, sl 2tog, k1, p2sso, yo, k2tog] 6 times. (30 sts)

Round 16: [Ssk, k1, k2tog] 6 times. (18 sts)

Round 17: [Sl 2tog, k1, p2sso] 6 times. (6 sts)

Cut yarn leaving a 25cm (9¾in) tail. Using a tapestry needle, weave the yarn through the remaining 6 stitches on the needle, gather and secure.

Colour:
■ A

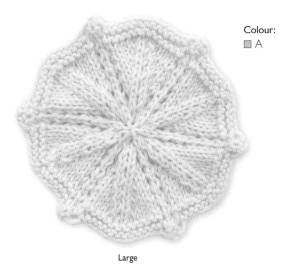

Large

97 TWO-NEEDLE LACE SNOWFLAKE

Cast on 110 stitches.

Row 1: Purl.

Row 2: Knit.

Row 3: K1, [k1, (ssk, yo) 3 times, k1, (yo, k2tog) 3 times, k1, (yo) twice, sl 2tog, k1, p2sso, (yo) twice] 6 times, k1. (122 sts)

Row 4 (and all even-numbered rows): Purl, dropping extra yo.

Row 5: K1, [K1, (ssk, yo) twice, ssk, k1, k2tog, (yo, k2tog) twice, k1, (yo) twice, sl 2tog, k1, p2sso, (yo) twice] 6 times, k1. (110 sts)

Row 7: K1, [k1, (ssk, yo) twice, sl 2tog, k1, p2sso, (yo, k2tog) twice, k1, (yo) twice, sl 2tog, k1, p2sso, (yo) twice] 6 times, k1. (98 sts)

Row 9: K1, [k1, ssk, yo, ssk, k1, k2tog, yo, k2tog, k1, (yo) twice, sl 2tog, k1, p2sso, (yo) twice] 6 times, k1. (86 sts)

Row 11: K1, [k1, ssk, yo, sl 2tog, k1, p2sso, yo, k2tog, k1, (yo) twice, sl 2tog, k1, p2sso, (yo) twice] 6 times, k1. (74 sts)

Row 13: K1, [k1, ssk, k1, k2tog, k1, (yo) twice, sl 2tog, k1, p2sso, (yo) twice) 6 times, k1. (62 sts)

Row 15: K1, [k1, sl 2tog, k1, p2sso, k1, (yo) twice, sl 2tog, k1, p2sso, (yo) twice] 6 times, k1. (50 sts)

Row 17: K1, [sl 2tog, k1, p2sso, (yo) twice, sl 2tog, k1, p2sso, (yo) twice] 6 times, k1. (38 sts)

Row 19: K1, [k1, sl 2tog, k1, p2sso] 6 times, k1. (14 sts)

Row 21: K1, [k2tog] 6 times, k1. (8 sts)

Cut yarn leaving a 25cm (9¾in) tail. Using a tapestry needle, weave the yarn through the remaining 8 stitches on the needle, gather and secure. Sew side seams together to form a snowflake block.

Colour:
■ A

Extra large

98 EMBOSSED SNOWFLAKE

Cast on 102 stitches and divide evenly over 3 needles, 34 sts oen. Join, taking care not to twist stitches.
Round 1: Purl.
Round 2: [K6, sl 2tog, k1, p2sso, k7] 6 times. (90 sts)
Round 3: Knit.
Round 4: [K6, sl 2tog, k1, p2sso, k6] 6 times. (78 sts)
Round 5: [K2, p9, k2] 6 times.
Round 6: [K5, sl 2tog, k1, p2sso, k5] 6 times. (66 sts)
Round 7: Knit.
Round 8: [K4, sl 2tog, k1, p2sso, k4] 6 times. (54 sts)
Round 9: [K2, p5, k2) 6 times.

Round 10: [K3, sl 2tog, k1, p2sso, k3] 6 times. (42 sts)
Round 11: Knit.
Round 12: [K2, sl 2tog, k1, p2sso, k2] 6 times. (30 sts)
Round 13: [K2, p1, k2) 6 times.
Round 14: [K1, sl 2tog, k1, p2sso, k1] 6 times. (18 sts)
Round 15: [Sl 2tog, k1, p2sso] 6 times. (6 sts)
Cut yarn leaving a 25cm (9¾in) tail. Using a tapestry needle, weave the yarn through the remaining 6 stitches on the needle, gather and secure.

Mix and match: **98 + 110**

Colour:
☐ A

Large

99 LACE SNOWFLAKE

Cast on 6 stitches and divide evenly over 3 needles, 2 sts oen. Join, taking care not to twist stitches.
Round 1: [K1, yo] to end of round. (12 sts)
Round 2: Knit.
Round 3: [K1, yo] to end of round. (24 sts)
Round 4: Knit.
Round 5: [K1, yo] to end of round. (48 sts)
Round 6: Purl.
Round 7: [K1, yo, k1, yo, k1, sl 2tog, k1, p2sso, k1, yo, k1, yo] 6 times. (60 sts)
Round 8: Knit.
Round 9: [K1, yo, k1, yo, k2, sl 2tog, k1, p2sso, k2, yo, k1, yo] 6 times. (72 sts)

Round 10: Purl.
Round 11: [K1, yo, k1, yo, k3, sl 2tog, k1, p2sso, k3, yo, k1, yo] 6 times. (84 sts)
Round 12: Knit.
Round 13: [K1, yo, k1, yo, k4, sl 2tog, k1, p2sso, k4, yo, k1, yo] 6 times. (96 sts)
Round 14: Knit.
Round 15: [K1, yo, k1, yo, k5, sl 2tog, k1, p2sso, k5, yo, k1, yo] 6 times. (108 sts)
Round 16: Purl.
Using a larger size needle, cast off loosely purlwise.

Colour:
☐ A

Large

100 STARFISH

DIFFERENT YARNS
Combine textured or metallic yarns to make striking and unique blocks (see Yarn Choices, page 137).

Round 1 (RS): Ch 2, work 5 dc into the second ch from the hook, join with ss in first dc. (5 dc)

Round 2: Ch 1, work 3 dc into each dc around, join with ss in first dc. (15 dc) Each point of the star is worked separately.

Round 3: Ch 1, dc into base of ch (base dc) *ch 6, ss into second ch from hook, 1 dc in next ch, 1 htr in next ch, 1 tr in next ch, 1 dtr in next ch, 1 dtr in base dc, skip 2 sts, dc in next dc (base dc); rep from 4 times more, skip last dc at end of last rep, join with ss in first dc.

Round 4: Ss into the outer edge of each ch and st around the star shape.
Fasten off.

Colour:
■ A

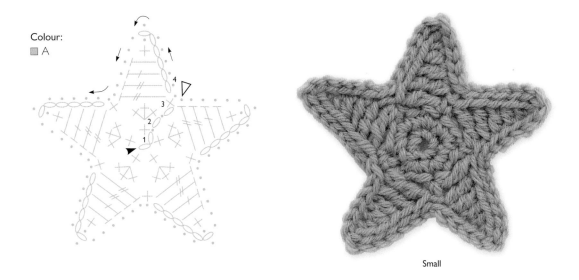

Small

Same-block tessellation: **100**

Symbols and abbreviations
Turn to pages 140–141 for a full explanation of the symbols and abbreviations used.

101 LARGE FIVE-POINTED STAR

STITCH ABBREVIATIONS
tr2tog: Treble crochet 2 together.
tr4tog: Treble crochet 4 together.
dc3tog: Double crochet 3 together.

Foundation ring: Using A, ch 4, join with ss to form a ring.
Round 1: Ch 3 (counts as first tr), 14 tr into the ring, join with ss to third ch of beg ch-3.
Round 2: Ch 3 (counts as first tr), [2 tr in next tr, 2 htr in next tr, 2 tr in next tr] 5 times, ending

1 tr into base of beg ch-3, join with ss to third ch of beg ch-3. (30 sts)

FIRST POINT
Row 3: Ch 3 (counts as first tr), skip first tr, 1 tr in next tr, tr2tog over the next 2 htr, 1 tr in each of next 2 tr, turn.
Row 4: Ch 2 (counts as first tr), skip first tr, tr4tog over next 3 sts and third ch of beg ch-3, ch 1. Fasten off.

SECOND POINT
With right side facing, rejoin A to next unworked tr of round 2.

Work as for first point.
Work 3 more points in the same way.
Join B to any point.

Last round: Ch 3, 1 dc into base of beg ch-3, *4 dc down side edge of point, dc3tog at inner corner, 4 dc up side edge of next point, [1 dc, 2 ch, 1 dc] at outer point; rep from * 4 times more, 4 dc down side edge of point, dc3tog at inner corner, 5 dc up side edge of next point, join with ss to first ch of beg ch-3. Fasten off.

Colours:
■ A
■ B

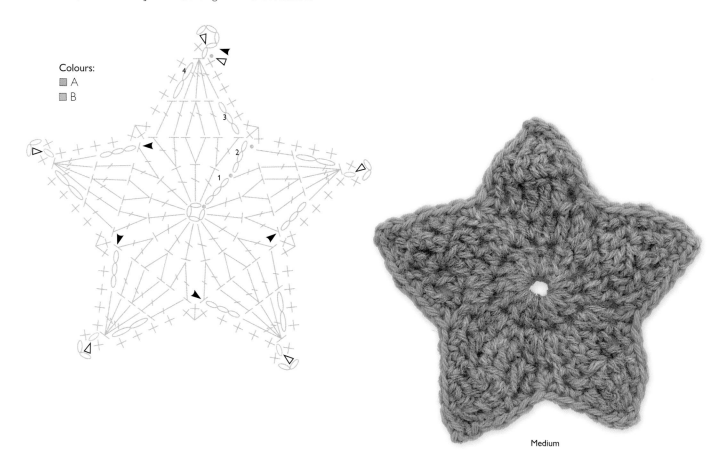

Medium

102 LACE STAR

Foundation ring: Ch 3, join with ss to form a ring.
Round 1 (RS): Ch 2 (counts as first htr) work 9 htr into ring, join with ss in top of beg ch-2, turn.
Round 2 WS): Ch 1, *[2 htr, ch 2, 2 htr] in next htr, skip next htr; rep from * 4 times more, join with ss in top of first htr, turn.
Round 3 (RS): Ch 1, skip next htr, *1 dc in next htr, [2 dc, ch 2, 2 dc] in next ch-2 sp, 1 dc in next htr; skip 2 htr; rep from * to end of round, join with ss in top of first dc, turn.

Round 4 (WS): Ch 1, skip next dc, *1 htr in each of next 2 dc, [2 htr, ch 2, 2htr] in next ch-2 sp, 1 htr in next 2 dc, skip next 2 dc; rep from * to end of round, join with ss in top of first htr, turn.

Round 5 (RS): Ch 2, 1 htr in each of next 4 htr; *[2 htr, ch 2, 2htr] in next ch-2 sp, 1 htr in each of next 8 htr; rep from * 3 times more, [2 htr, ch 2, 2 htr] in next ch-2 sp, 1 htr in each of next 3 htr; join with ss in top of first htr.
Fasten off.

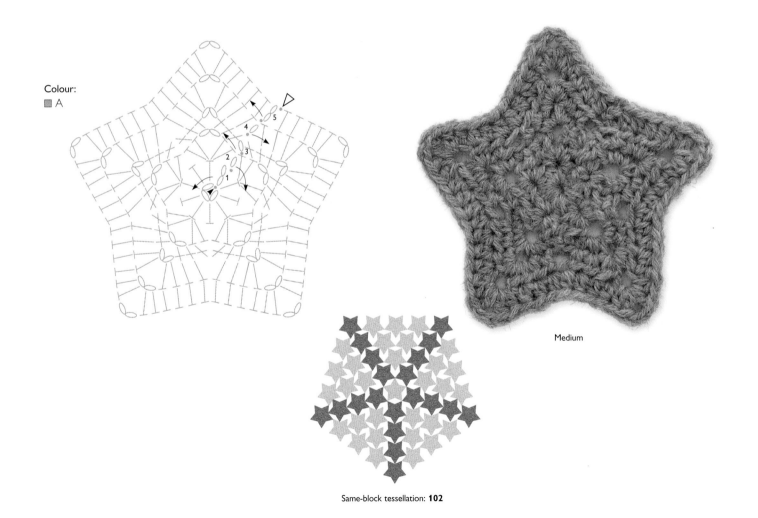

Colour:
■ A

Same-block tessellation: **102**

Medium

103 TWO-TONE DOUBLE CROCHET STAR

STITCH ABBREVIATIONS

beg 2-tr cl (beginning 2 treble-crochet cluster): [Yrh, insert hook in ring, yrh, pull loop through, yrh, pull through 2 loops on hook] twice, yrh, pull through all 3 loops on hook.

3-tr cl (3 treble-crochet cluster): [Yrh, insert hook ring, yrh, pull loop through, yrh, pull through 2 loops on hook] 3 times, yrh, pull through all 4 loops on hook.

Foundation ring: Ch 5, join with ss to form a ring.

Round 1 (RS): Ch 2, beg 2-tr cl into ring, ch 3, [3-tr cl into ring, ch 3] 4 times, join with ss in top of beg 2-tr cl.

Round 2: Ss into next ch-3 sp, ch 3, [2 tr, ch 2, 3 tr] in ch-3 sp, *[3 tr, ch 2, 3 tr] in next ch-3 sp; rep from * 3 times more, join with ss in top of beg ch-3.

Round 3: Ss into next st, ch 3, 1 tr in next st, [3 tr, ch 2, 3 tr] into next ch-2 sp, 1 tr in each of next 2 sts, skip next 2 sts, *1 tr in each of next 2 sts, [3 tr, ch 2, 3 tr] in next ch-2 sp, 1 tr in each of next 2 sts, skip next 2 sts; rep from * 3 times more, join with ss in top of beg ch-3.

Round 4: Ss into next st, ch 3, 1 tr in each of next 3 sts, [3 tr, ch 2, 3 tr] in next ch-2 sp, 1 tr in each of next 4 sts, skip next 2 sts, *1 tr in each of next 4 sts, [3 tr, ch 2, 3 tr] in next ch-2 sp, 1 tr in each of next 4 sts, skip next 2 sts; rep from * 3 times more, join with ss in top of beg ch-3. Fasten off.

Colour:
☐ A

Medium

104 SIX-POINTED STAR

SPECIAL ABBREVIATIONS

xdc (extended double crochet): Insert the hook into the base of the last st, yrh, draw yarn through fabric, yrh, draw yarn through 1 loop on the hook, yrh, draw yarn through both loops on the hook.

dc2tog: Double crochet 2 together.

Foundation chain: Using A, ch 2.

Row 1: 1 Dc in second ch from hook, turn. (1 dc)

Row 2: Ch 1, 2 dc in dc, turn. (2 dc)

Row 3: Ch 1, 2 dc in next dc, 1 dc in next dc, turn. (3 dc)

Row 4: Ch 1, 2 dc in next dc, 1 dc into each of next 2 dc, turn. (4 dc)

Row 5: Ch 5, dc2tog over second and third chs from hook, 1 dc in each of next 2 ch, 1 dc into each of next 4 dc, 4 xdc, turn. (11 sts)

Row 6: Ch 1, dc2tog over first and second xdc, 1 dc in each st to end, turn. (10 sts)

Repeat Row 6, twice. (8 sts)

Row 9: Ch 1, 2 dc in first dc, 1 dc in each dc to end, turn. (9 sts)

Repeat Row 9, 3 times more. (12 sts)

Row 13: Ch 1, ss in each of next 5 dc, ch 1, 1 dc into base of beg ch-1, 1 dc into each of next 3 dc, turn leaving last 4 dc unworked.

Row 14: Ch 1, dc2tog over first and second dc, 1 dc in each of next 2 dc, turn.

Row 15: Ch 1, dc2tog over first and second dc, 1 dc in last dc, turn.

Row 16: Ch 1, dc2tog over remaining 2 sts, turn. Fasten off A. Join B to any point.

Last round: Ch 4, 1 dc into base of beg ch-4, *2 dc down side edge of point, dc2tog at inner corner, 2 dc up side edge of next point, [1 dc, ch 3, 1 dc] at outer point; rep from * 4 times more, 2 dc down side edge of point, dc2tog at inner corner, 2 dc up side edge of next point, 1 dc, join with ss to first ch of beg ch-4. Fasten off.

Colours:

■ A

■ B

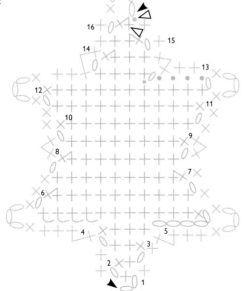

Small

Same-block tessellation: **104**

105 GARTER STAR

Cast on 95 stitches and divide evenly over 5 needles, 19 sts oen. Join, taking care not to twist stitches.
Round 1: Purl.
Round 2: [K8, sl 2tog, k1, p2sso, k8] 5 times. (85 sts)
Round 3: [P7, k3, p7] 5 times.
Round 4: [K7, sl 2tog, k1, p2sso, k7] 5 times. (75 sts)
Round 5: [P6, k3, p6] 5 times.
Round 6: [K6, sl 2tog, k1, p2sso, k6] 5 times. (65 sts)
Round 7: [P5, k3, p5] 5 times.
Round 8: [K5, sl 2tog, k1, p2sso, k5] 5 times. (55 sts)
Round 9: [P4, k3, p4] 5 times.
Round 10: [K4, sl 2tog, k1, p2sso, k4] 5 times. (45 sts)
Round 11: [P3, k3, p3] 5 times.

Round 12: [K3, sl 2tog, k1, p2sso, k3] 5 times. (35 sts)
Round 13: [P2, k3, p2] 5 times.
Round 14: [K2, sl 2tog, k1, p2sso, k2] 5 times. (25 sts)
Round 15: [P1, k3, p1] 5 times.
Round 16: [K1, sl 2tog, k1, p2sso, k1] 5 times. (15 sts)
Round 17: Knit.
Round 18: [Sl 2tog, k1, p2sso] 5 times. (5 sts)
Cut yarn leaving a 25cm (9¾in) tail. Using a tapestry needle, weave the yarn through the remaining 5 stitches on the needle, gather and secure.

Colour:
☐ A

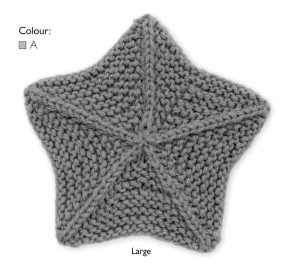

Large

106 HALF GARTER STAR

Cast on 21 stitches.
Preparation row (WS): Purl.
Row 1: Sl 1, p8, sl 1, k2tog, psso, k9. (19 sts)
Rows 2: Sl 1, purl to end.
Repeat the last row each even-numbered row until row 18 has been completed.
Row 3: Sl 1, p7, sl 1, k2tog, psso, k8. (17 sts)
Row 5: Sl 1, p6, sl 1, k2tog, psso, k7. (15 sts)
Row 7: Sl 1, p5, sl 1, k2tog, psso, k6. (13 sts)
Row 9: Sl 1, p4, sl 1, k2tog, psso, k5. (11 sts)
Row 11: Sl 1, p3, sl 1, k2tog, psso, k4. (9 sts)
Row 13: Sl 1, p2, sl 1, k2tog, psso, k3. (7 sts)
Row 15: Sl 1, p1, sl 1, k2tog, psso, k2. (5 sts)
Row 17: Sl 1, sl 1, k2tog, psso, k1. (3 sts)
Row 19: Sl 1, k2tog, psso. (1 st)
**With right side facing, pick up 10 sts along left edge of previous star point, and then cast on 21 sts.
Row 20: P20, p2tog, turn.

Row 21: Sl 1, p8, sl 1, k2tog, psso, k9.
Row 22: Sl 1, p17, p2tog.
Row 23: Sl 1, p7, sl 1, k2tog, psso, k8.
Row 24: Sl 1, p15, p2tog.
Row 25: Sl 1, p6, sl 1, k2tog, psso, k7.
Row 26: Sl 1, p13, p2tog.
Row 27: Sl 1, p5, sl 1, k2tog, psso, k6.
Row 28: Sl 1, p11, p2tog.
Row 29: Sl 1, p4, sl 1, k2tog, psso, k5.
Row 30: Sl 1, p9, p2tog.
Row 31: Sl 1, p3, sl 1, k2tog, psso, k4.
Row 32: Sl 1, p7, p2tog.
Row 33: Sl 1, p2, sl 1, k2tog, psso, k3.
Row 34: Sl 1, p5, p2tog.
Row 35: Sl 1, p1, sl 1, k2tog, psso, k2.
Row 36: Sl 1, p3, p2tog.
Row 37: Sl 1, sl 1, k2tog, psso, k1.
Row 38: Sl 1, p1, p2tog.
Row 39: Sl 1, k2tog, psso. **
Repeat from ** to ** 3 times more. There will be 5 sts on needle and 5 star points.
Cut yarn leaving a 25cm (9¾in) tail. Using a tapestry needle, weave the yarn through the remaining 5 stitches on the needle, gather and secure. Sew side seams together to form a star block..

Colour:
☐ A

Large

107 RADIANT STAR

Cast on 102 stitches.
Row 1: Purl.
Row 2: Knit.
Row 3: K1, [sl1 wyb, p8, sl 2tog, k1, p2sso, p8] 5 times, k1. (92 sts)
Row 4: P1, [k8, p1, k8, sl1 wyf] 5 times, p1.
Row 5: K1, [sl1 wyb, p7, sl 2tog, k1, p2sso, p7] 5 times, k1. (82 sts)
Row 6: P1, [k7, p1] 10 times, p1.
Row 7: K1, [sl1 wyb, p6, sl 2tog, k1, p2sso, p6] 5 times, k1. (72 sts)
Row 8: P1, [k6, p1, k6, sl1 wyf] 5 times, p1.
Row 9: K1, [sl1 wyb, p5, sl 2tog, k1, p2sso, p5] 5 times, k1. (62 sts)
Row 10: P1, [k5, p1] 10 times, p1.
Row 11: K1, [sl1 wyb, p4, sl 2tog, k1, p2sso, p4] 5 times, k1. (52 sts)
Row 12: P1, [k4, p1, k4, sl1 wyf] 5 times, p1.
Row 13: K1, [sl1 wyb, p3, sl 2tog, k1, p2sso, p3] 5 times, k1. (42 sts)

Row 14: P1, [k3, p1] 10 times, p1.
Row 15: K1, [sl1 wyb, p2, sl 2tog, k1, p2sso, p2] 5 times, k1. (32 sts)
Row 16: P1, [k2, p1, k2, sl1 wyf] 5 times, p1.
Row 17: K1, [sl1 wyb, p1, sl 2tog, k1, p2sso, p1] 5 times, k1. (22 sts)
Row 18: P1, [p1, k2, sl1 wyf] 5 times, p1.
Row 19: K1, [sl1 wyb, sl 2tog, k1, p2sso] 5 times, k1. (12 sts)
Row 20: Purl.
Row 21: K1, [k2tog] 5 times, k1. (7 sts)
Cut yarn leaving a 25cm (9¾in) tail. Using a tapestry needle, weave the yarn through the remaining 7 stitches on the needle, gather and secure. Sew side seams together to form a star block.

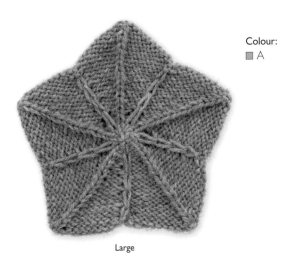

Large

Colour:
■ A

108 BOBBLE AND LACE STAR

SPECIAL ABBREVIATION

MB (Make Bobble): [K1, p1, k1] into next st, turn, p3, turn, k3togtbl.

Cast on 87 stitches.
Row 1: Knit.
Row 2: K1, [k8, yo, k1, yo, k8] 5 times, k1. (97 sts)
Row 3: K1, [k9, yo, k1, yo, k9] 5 times, k1. (107 sts)
Row 4 (and all even-numbered rows): Purl.
Row 5: K1, [k9, sl 2tog, k1, p2sso, k9] 5 times, k1. (97 sts)
Row 7: K1, [k1, (yo, k2tog) 3 times, k1, sl 2tog, k1, p2sso, k1, (ssk, yo) 3 times, k1] 5 times, k1. (87 sts)
Row 9: K1, [k1, (yo, k2tog) 3 times, sl 2tog, k1, p2sso, (ssk, yo) 3 times, k1] 5 times, k1. (77 sts)
Row 11: K1, [k1, (yo, k2tog) twice, k1, sl 2tog, k1, p2sso, k1, (ssk, yo) twice, k1] 5 times, k1. (67 sts)
Row 13: K1, [k1, (MB, k1) twice, sl 2tog, k1, p2sso, (k1, MB) twice, k1] 5 times, k1. (57 sts)

Row 15: K1, [yo, k2tog, yo, k2, sl 2tog, k1, p2sso, k2, yo, ssk] 5 times, k1. (52 sts)
Row 17: K1, k2tog, yo, k2, [sl 2tog, k1, p2sso, k2, yo, sl 2tog, k1, p2sso, yo, k2] 4 times, sl 2tog, k1, p2sso, k2, yo, k2tog. (42 sts)
Row 19: K1, [MB, k2, sl 2tog, k1, p2sso, k2] 5 times, k1. (32 sts)
Row 21: K1, [k2, sl 2tog, k1, p2sso, k1] 5 times, k1. (22 sts)
Row 23: K1, [k1, sl 2tog, k1, p2sso] 5 times, k1. (12 sts)
Row 24: P2tog 6 times. (6 sts)
Cut yarn leaving a 25cm (9¾in) tail. Using a tapestry needle, weave the yarn through the remaining 6 stitches on the needle, gather and secure. Sew side seams together to form a star block.

Extra large

Colour:
■ A

109 RIBBED STARFISH

Cast on 5 stitches and divide evenly over 5 needles (reserving an extra, sixth needle).

Join, taking care not to twist stitches.

Round 1: [K1f&b] 5 times. (10 sts)

Round 2: Knit.

Round 3: [(K1, yo, k1) all into next st, k1] 5 times. (20 sts)

Round 4: [P1, k1] 10 times.

Round 5: [P1, [k1, yo, k1] all in next st, p1, k1] 5 times. (30 sts)

Round 6: [P1, k3, p1, k1] 5 times.

Round 7: [P1, k1, [k1, yo, k1] all in next st, k1, p1, k1] 5 times. (40 sts)

Round 8: [P1, k1] 20 times.

Round 9: [P1, k1, p1, [k1, yo, k1] all in next st, [p1, k1] twice] 5 times. (50 sts)

Round 10: [P1, k1, p1, k3, [p1, k1] twice] 5 times.

POINTS

Preparation row: With RS facing (p1, k1) twice, and working on the next 10 sts only, work in rows as follows:

Row 1: K2, [p1, k1] 3 times, p1, k1f&b, turn. (11 sts)

Row 2: P2, [k1, p1] 3 times, k1, p2.

Row 3: K2, p1, k1, sl 2tog, k1, p2sso, k1, p1, k2. (9 sts)

Row 4: P2, k1, p3, k1, p2.

Row 5: K2, p1, sl 2tog, k1, p2sso, p1, k2. (7 sts)

Row 6: P2, k1, p1, k1, p2.

Row 7: K2, sl 2tog, k1, p2sso, k2. (5 sts)

Row 8: Purl.

Row 9: K1, sl 2tog, k1, p2sso, k1. (3 sts)

Row 10: P3tog.

Fasten off.

Reattach yarn to remaining sts and repeat Rows 1–10 four times more.

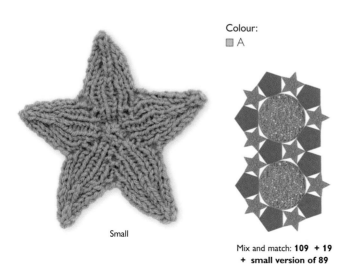

Small

Colour:
■ A

Mix and match: **109 + 19 + small version of 89 described on page 83**

110 TWO-TONE GARTER STAR

With A. cast on 9 stitches, leaving a 30cm (11¾in) tail.

Rows 1: Knit.

Rows 2: K1f&b, k to last 2 sts, k2tog. (9 sts)

Repeat the last 2 rows 4 more times.

Row 11: Knit.

Cast off all sts except last st.

Do not turn work. Leaving last st on needle, continue with A to pick up 8 sts along the left edge. (9 sts)

Do not cut yarn. Change to B.

Repeat Rows 1–11 and cast off as before.

Do not cut yarn. Change to A.

Repeat sequence, alternating yarns, until 6 segments have been completed, ending with a segment worked in B.

Cast off.

Cut yarn leaving a 25cm (9¾in) tail. Sew seam to join last segment to first segment worked.

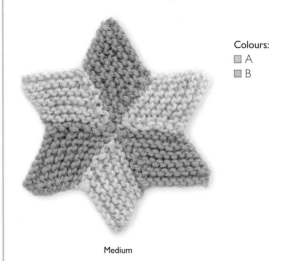

Medium

Colours:
■ A
■ B

111 CABLED STAR

Cast on 5 stitches and divide evenly over 5 needles (reserving an extra, sixth needle).

Join, taking care not to twist stitches.

Round 1: [K1, yo] 5 times. (10 sts)
Round 2: Knit.
Round 3: [K2, yo] 5 times. (15 sts)
Round 4: [K2, yo, k1, yo] 5 times. (25 sts)
Round 5: Knit.
Round 6: [K3, yo, k1, yo, k1] 5 times. (35 sts)
Round 7: Knit.
Round 8: [K4, yo, k1, yo, k2] 5 times. (45 sts)
Round 9: Knit, to last st, sl next st onto foll needle to become first stitch of next round.
Round 10: [C4B, k2, yo, k1, yo, k2] 5 times. (55 sts)
Round 11: Knit.
Round 12: [K7, yo, k1, yo, k3] 5 times. (65 sts)
Round 13: Knit.
Round 14: [C4B, k4, yo, k1, yo, k4] 5 times. (75 sts)
Round 15: Knit.
Round 16: [K9, yo, k1, yo, k5] 5 times. (85 sts)
Round 17: Knit.
Round 18: [C4B, k6, yo, k1, yo, k6] 5 times. (95 sts)
Round 19: [K11, yo, k1, yo, k7] 5 times. (105 sts)
Round 20: Purl.
Round 21: Purl.
Cast off knitwise.

Colour:
■ A

Extra large

112 LACE STAR

Cast on 5 stitches and divide evenly over 5 needles (reserving an extra, sixth needle).

Join, taking care not to twist stitches.

Round 1: [K1, yo] 5 times. (10 sts)
Round 2: Knit.
Round 3: [Yo, k1, yo, k1] 5 times. (20 sts)
Rounds 4: Knit all sts and yo; knit front and back into any double yo. Repeat the last row each even-numbered row until Row 18 has been completed.
Round 5: [K2, (yo) twice, k2] 5 times. (30 sts)
Round 7: [K3, (yo) twice, k3] 5 times. (40 sts)
Round 9: [K1, yo, ssk, k1, (yo) twice, k1, k2tog, yo, k1] 5 times. (50 sts)
Round 11: [K2, yo, ssk, k1, (yo) twice, k1, k2tog, yo, k2] 5 times. (60 sts)
Round 13: [K3, yo, ssk, k1, (yo) twice, k1, k2tog, yo, k3] 5 times. (70 sts)
Round 15: [K4, yo, ssk, k1, (yo) twice, k1, k2tog, yo, k4] 5 times. (80 sts)
Round 17: [K5, yo, ssk, k1, (yo) twice, k1, k2tog, yo, k5] 5 times. (90 sts)
Round 19: [P9, (yo) twice, p9] 5 times. (100 sts)
Round 20: Purl, dropping the second yo. (95 sts)
Round 21: [K9, yo, k1, yo, k9] 5 times. (105 sts)
Cast off purlwise.

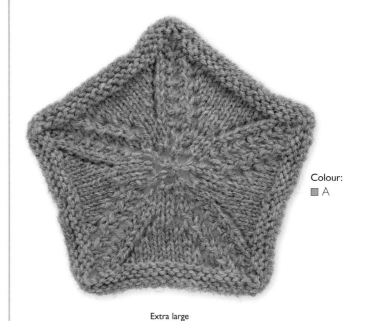

Colour:
■ A

Extra large

113 MINI GARTER STAR

Cast on 57 stitches loosely.
Row 1 (WS): Sl 1, knit 5, purl 1, [k10, p1] 4 times, k5, p1.
Row 2: Sl 1, k4, sl 2tog, k1, p2sso, [k8, sl 2tog, k1, p2sso] 4 times, k4, p1. (47 sts)
Row 3: Sl 1, k4, p1, [k8, p1] 4 times, k4, p1.
Row 4: Sl 1, k3, sl 2tog, k1, p2sso, [k6, sl 2tog, k1, p2sso] 4 times, k3, p1. (37 sts)
Row 5: Sl 1, k3, p1, [k6, p1] 4 times, k3, p1.
Row 6: Sl 1, k2, sl 2tog, k1, p2sso, [k4, sl 2tog, k1, p2sso] 4 times, k2, p1. (27 sts)
Row 7: Sl 1, k2, p1, [k4, p1] 4 times, k2, p1.

Row 8: Sl1, k1, sl 2tog, k1, p2sso, [k2, sl 2tog, k1, p2sso] 4 times, k1, p1. (17 sts)
Row 9: Sl 1, k1, p1, [k2, p1] 4 times, k1, p1.
Row 10: Sl 1, [sl 2tog, k1, p2sso] 5 times, p1. (7 sts)
Row 11: Sl 1, p1, k1, p1, k1, p2.
Row 12: Sl 2tog, k1, p2sso, k1, sl 2tog, k1, p2sso. (3 sts)
Row 13: Sl 1 purlwise, p2.
Row 14: Sl 2tog, k1, p2sso.
Cut yarn leaving a 25cm (9¾in) tail. Fasten off. Sew side seams together to form a star block.

STANDARD BED AND BLANKET SIZES
Making a blanket will always be a big project, requiring a lot of time and a lot of yarn. However, if you complete only one block each day, then even the largest project will take less than eight months, and if the blocks are interesting and varied, it won't be a chore.

There are few certainties in making a blanket, and the following figures are only a guide. Always double check that the bed is, in fact, a standard size, calculate the yarn carefully (see page 138), and buy slightly more yarn than you need.

Bed	Mattress size	Quilt size
A Cot	58 × 117cm (23 × 46in)	90 × 135cm (36 × 54in)
B Twin	99 × 190cm (39 × 75in)	135 × 210cm (54 × 84in)
C Double	135 × 190cm (54 × 75in)	165 × 210cm (66 × 84in)
D Queen	150 × 200cm (60 × 80in)	180 × 225cm (72 × 90in)
E King	193 × 200cm (76 × 80in)	225 × 225cm (90 × 90in)

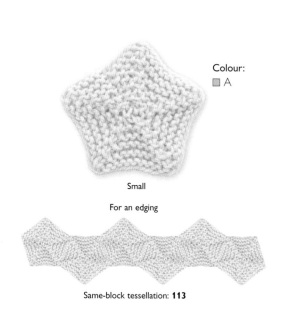

Colour:
■ A

Small

For an edging

Same-block tessellation: **113**

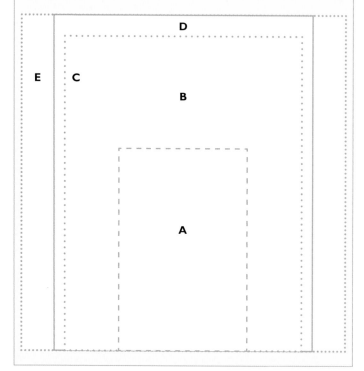

COLOUR TIPS

- Neutral colours get a new lease on life when combined with small amounts of colour from another palette.
- Colours that go with almost anything include black, dark loden green, very dark purple, navy and chocolate brown.
- Turquoise and aqua look good against most skin tones.
- Baby garments can be worked in colours other than pastels so long as the yarn is suitable for delicate skin.
- When you have narrowed down your choices, place skeins of each colour together in natural daylight to see how well they blend together.
- When in doubt – swatch, swatch, swatch!
- Colours can change when placed next to each other. A blue-green, for example, will appear greener when placed next to blue yarn and bluer when placed next to green yarn.

Foundation ring: Ch 6, join with ss to form a ring.

Round 1: Ch 3 (counts as first tr), 1 tr into ring, [ch 6, 3 tr into ring] 5 times, ch 6, 1 tr into ring, join with ss to top of beg ch-3.

Round 2: *Ch 1, [1 dc, 1 htr, 7 tr, 1 htr, 1 dc] into next ch-6 sp, ch 1, skip next tr, ss into next tr; rep from * 4 times more, ch 1, [1 dc, 1 htr, 7 tr, 1 htr, 1 dc] into next ch-6 sp, ch 1, skip next tr; join with ss to base of beg ch-1.

Fasten off.

Colour:
■ A

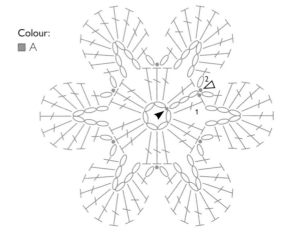

Small

To see how to use this block to make a scarf, see page 129

Same-block tessellation: **114**

Symbols and abbreviations
Turn to pages 140–141 for a full explanation of the symbols and abbreviations used.

115 PRIMROSE

Foundation ring: With A, ch 6, join with a ss to form a ring.

Round 1: Ch 6 (counts as first tr and ch 3), [1 tr in ring, ch 3] 6 times, join with ss to third ch of beg ch-6. (7 tr and 7 ch-3 sps)

Round 2: [(1 dc, ch 4, 1 dc) in next ch-3 sp (ss, ch 3, ss) in next tr] 6 times, [1 dc, ch 4, 1 dc] in next ch-3 sp (ss, ch 3, ss) into third ch of beg ch 6 of round 1. (7 ch-4 sps and 7 picots made)
Fasten off A. Join B with ss in any ch-4 sp.

Round 3: Ch 3 (count as first tr), [2 tr; ch 2, 3 tr] in sp at base of beg ch-3, *[3 tr, ch 2, 3 tr] into next ch-4 sp: rep from * 5 times more, join with ss in top of beg ch-3.

Round 4: Ss in next tr (centre tr of 3-tr group), ch 3 (counts as first tr), 1 tr in next tr. *[2 tr, ch 2, 2 tr] in next ch-2 sp, 1 tr in each of next 2 tr, skip next 2 tr, 1 tr in each of next 2 tr; rep from * 5 times more, [2 tr, ch 2, 2 tr] in last ch-2 sp, 1 tr in each of next 2 tr, skip last tr, join with ss to top of beg ch-3.

Round 5: Ss in next tr, ch 3 (counts as first tr), 1 tr in each of next 2 tr. *[2 tr, ch 2, 2 tr] in next ch-2 sp, 1 tr in each of next 3 tr, skip 2 tr, 1 tr in next 3 tr; rep from * 5 times more, [2 tr, ch 2, 2 tr] in last ch-2 sp, 1 tr in each of next 3 tr, skip last tr, join with ss to top of beg ch-3.

Round 6: Ch 1, 1 dc in st at base of beg ch-1, *skip next tr, 5 tr in next tr (to make shell), skip next tr, 1 dc in next tr, 1 dc in ch-2 sp, 1 dc in next tr, skip next tr, 5 tr in next tr, skip next tr, 1 dc in each of next 2 tr; rep from * 5 times more skip next tr, 5 tr in next tr, skip next tr, 1 dc in next tr, 1 dc in ch-2 sp, 1 dc in next tr, skip next tr, 5 tr in next tr, skip next tr, 1 dc in last tr, join with ss in first dc made.
Fasten off.

Colours:
■ A
■ B

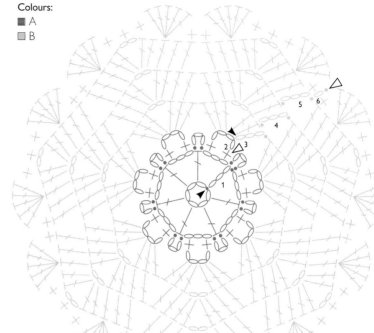

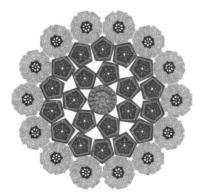

Mix and match: **115 + 8 + 84**

Extra large

116 STARBURST FLOWER

SPECIAL ABBREVIATION

Dtr4tog (double treble 4 stitches together):
[(Yrh) twice, insert hook in next st and draw up a loop, (yrh and draw through 2 loops) twice] 4 times, yrh and draw through all 5 loops on hook.

Foundation ring: Using A, ch 6, join with ss to form a ring.

Round 1: Ch 3 (counts as first tr), 15 tr into ring, join with ss in top of beg ch-3.
Fasten off A. Join B with ss.

Round 2: Ch 3 (counts as first tr), 2 tr in next tr; [1 tr in next tr, 2 tr in next tr] 7 times, join with ss to top of beg ch-3. (24 tr)
Fasten off B. Join C with ss.

Round 3: Ch 3 (counts as first tr), 1 tr into st at base of beg ch-3, 2 tr in each of the next 23 tr, join with ss in top of beg ch-3. (48 tr)

Round 4: *Ch 4, dtr4tog, ch 4, ss into next tr (6 dtr petal made), ss into next tr; rep from * 6 times more, ch 4, dtr4tog, ch 4, ss into next tr.
Fasten off.

Colours:
- ◼ A
- ◼ B
- ◻ C

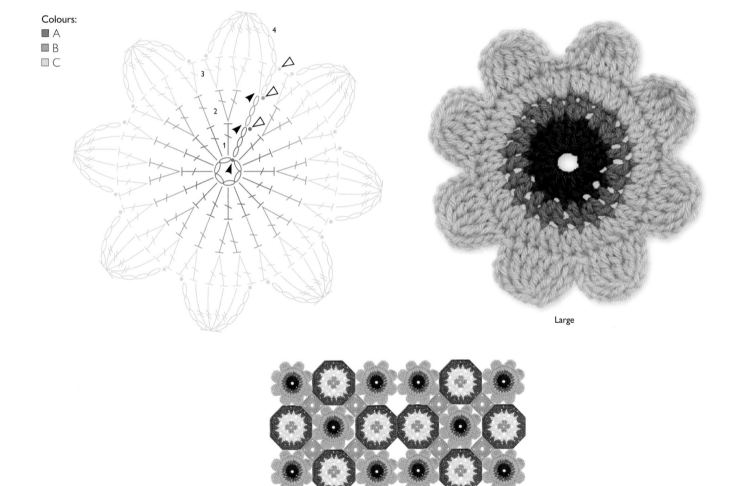

Large

Mix and match: **116 + 74 + 145**

117 SUNFLOWER

SPECIAL ABBREVIATIONS

blo trtr4tog (back loops only, triple treble 4 stitches together): *[Yrh] 3 times, insert the hook into the next st, yrh, draw loop through fabric, [yrh draw loop through 2 loops on the hook] 3 times; rep from * 3 times more, yrh, draw the loop through the 5 loops remaining on the hook.

blo trtr5tog (back loops only, triple treble 5 stitches together): Working in blo of sts, [yrh] 3 times, insert the hook into the same st as the last st of the previous cluster, yrh, draw loop through fabric, [yrh draw loop through 2 loops on the hook] 3 times, * [yrh] 3 times, insert the hook into the next st, yrh, draw loop through fabric, [yrh draw loop through 2 loops on the hook] 3 times; rep from * 3 times more, yrh, draw the loop through the 6 loops on the remaining hook.

Foundation ring: Using A, ch 5, join with ss to form a ring.
Round 1: Ch 3 (counts as first tr), 15 tr into ring, join with B and ss to third ch of beg ch-3. Fasten off A.
Round 2: Ch 1, 2 dc in st-sp between ch-3 and first tr; [2 dc in st-sp before next tr] 14 times, 2 dc in st-sp before ch-3, join with C and ss to beg ch-1.
Fasten off B.

Round 3: Ch 5, skip first dc, blo trtr4tog over next 4 dc, [ch 9, blo trtr5tog] 7 times, ch 9, join with ss to top of beg trtr4tog.
Round 4: Ch 1, 9 dc into next ch-9 sp, [skip trtr5tog, 9 dc into next ch-9 sp] 7 times, join with ss to beg ch-1.
Fasten off.

Colours:
- ☐ A
- ■ B
- ☐ C

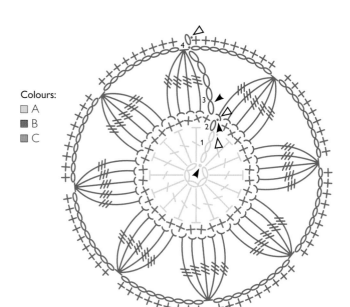

Medium

118 TWO-TONE ANEMONE FLOWER

Foundation ring: Using A, ch 6, join with ss to form a ring.

Round 1: Ch 1, 24 dc into ring, join with ss to beg dc.

Round 2: Ch 5, (counts as first tr and ch 2), 1 tr into next dc, [ch 1, skip next dc, 1 tr into next dc, ch 2, 1 tr into next dc] 7 times, ch 1, skip next dc, join with ss to third ch of beg ch-5.
Fasten off A. Join B with ss into first ch-2 sp.

Round 3: Ch 2 (counts as first htr), [1 htr, ch 2, 2 htr] into ch-2 sp at base of beg ch-2, 1 dc into next ch-1 sp, *[2 htr, ch 2, 2 htr] into next ch-2 sp, 1 dc into next ch-1 sp; rep from * 6 times more, join with ss to top of beg ch-2.

Round 4: Ss into next tr and into next ch-2 sp, ch 3 (counts as first tr), [2 tr, ch 1, 3 tr] into same ch-2 sp at base of beg ch-2, 1 dc into st-sp before the next dc, 1 dc into st-sp after the next dc, *[3 tr, ch 1, 3 tr] into next ch-2 sp, 1 dc into st-sp before the next dc, 1 dc into st-sp after the next dc; rep from * 6 times more, join with ss to top of beg ch-3.
Fasten off.

Colours:
- ■ A
- ■ B

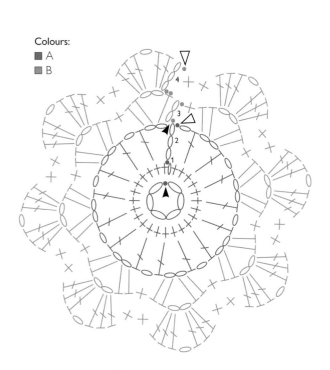

Medium

Mix and match: **118 + 134**

119 DOGWOOD

Foundation ring: Work a finger wrap.

Round 1: Ch 1, 7 dc into wrap, join with ss to beg ch-1.

Round 2: Ch 5, [skip 1 dc, 1 dc in next dc, ch 4] 3 times, join with ss to first ch of beg ch-5.

Round 3: Ss in next ch, ch 3 (counts as first tr), 6 tr into ch sp at base of beg ch-3, ch 2, skip 1 dc, [7 tr in next ch-4 sp, ch 2, skip 1 dc] 3 times, join with ss to top of beg ch-3.

Round 4: Ch 1, 1 dc into base of beg ch-1, [1 dc in each of next 2 tr, 2 dc in next tr] twice, skip 2 ch, *2 dc in next tr; [1 dc in each of next 2 tr, 2 dc in next tr] twice, skip 2 ch; rep from * twice more, join with ss to beg ch-1.
Complete the first petal in rows.

Row 5: Ch 3 (count as first tr), 1 tr into base of beg ch-3, [1 tr in next dc, 2 tr in next dc] twice, 2 tr in next dc, [1 tr in next dc, 2 tr in next dc] twice, turn. (16 tr)

Row 6: Ch 1, skip first tr, 1 dc in each of 14 tr, 1 dc in third ch of beg ch-3, turn.

Row 7: Ch 1, skip first dc, 1 htr in next dc, 1 tr in each of next 4 dc, 1 dc in next dc, 1 ss in each of next 2 dc, 1 dc in next dc, 1 tr in each of next 4 dc, 1 htr in last dc, ch 1, 1 ss in beg ch-1 of Row 6, 2 ss in side edge of tr below, 1 ss in side edge of dc below tr, 1 ss in next dc of Round 4.

Repeat Rows 5–7, 3 times, to complete each remaining petal.
Fasten off.

Colour:
■ A

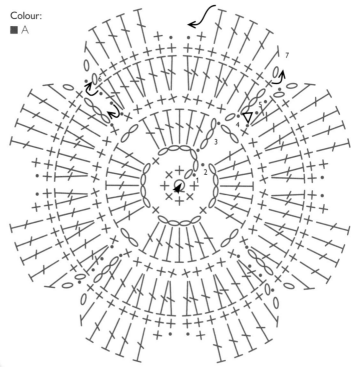

Medium

Mix and match: **119 + 118 + Rounds 1–2 of 118**

To make an appliqué flower

Mix and match: **119 + 118 + 135**

120 LACE EIGHT-PETAL FLOWER

Cast on 8 stitches and divide evenly over 4 needles, 2 sts oen.

Join, taking care not to twist stitches.

Rounds 1–2: Knit.

Round 3: [K1f&b] 8 times. (16 sts)

Round 4: Knit.

Round 5: [K2, (yo) twice] 8 times. (32 sts)

Round 6: [K2, (k1, yo, k1) into double yo] 8 times. (40 sts)

Rounds 7–10: Knit.

Round 11: [K5, yo] 8 times. (48 sts)

Round 12: Knit.

Round 13: [Ssk, k1, k2tog, yo, k1, yo] 8 times. (48 sts)

Round 14: Knit.

Round 15: [Sl 1, k2tog, psso, yo, (k1, yo) 3 times] 8 times. (64 sts)

Round 16: [Sl 1, k7] 8 times.

Round 17: [K1, yo, ssk, yo, k3, yo, k2tog, yo] 8 times. (80 sts)

Round 18: Knit.

Round 19: Purl.

Cast off purlwise.

Colour:
■ A

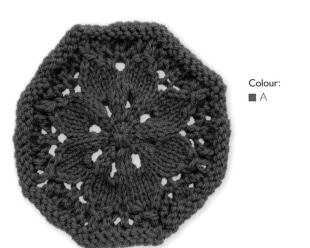

Medium

Mix and match: **120 +**
Rounds 1–10 of 44 + 138

121 ROUND POSY WITH BUTTON

> **NOTE**
> All stitches are slipped with the yarn in front.

Cast on 5 stitches and divide over 3 needles.

Join, taking care not to twist stitches.

Round 1: Knit into front and back (k1f&b) of next 5 sts. (10 sts)

Round 2: (K1f&b, k1) 5 times. (15 sts)

Round 3: Knit.

Round 4: (K1, k1f&b, k1) 5 times. (20 sts)

Round 5: (K1, M1, sl 1, k1, sl 1, M1) 5 times. (30 sts)

Round 6: (K3, sl 1, k2) 5 times.

Round 7: (K2, M1, sl 1, k1, sl 1, M1, k1) 5 times. (40 sts)

Round 8: (K4, sl 1, k3) 5 times.

Round 9: (K3, M1, sl 1, k1, sl 1, M1, k2) 5 times. (50 sts)

Round 10: (K5, sl 1, k4) 5 times.

Round 11: (K4, M1, sl 1, k1, sl 1, M1, k3) 5 times. (60 sts)

Round 12: (K6, sl 1, k5) 5 times.

Round 13: (K5, M1, sl 1, k1, sl 1, M1, k4) 5 times. (70 sts)

Round 14: (K7, sl 1, k6) 5 times.

Round 15: (K6, M1, sl 1, k1, sl 1, M1, k5) 5 times. (80 sts)

Round 16: (K8, sl 1, k7) 5 times.

Round 17: (K7, M1, sl 1, k1, sl 1, M1, k6) 5 times. (90 sts)

Round 18: (K9, sl 1, k8) 5 times.

Round 19: (K8, sl 1, k1, sl 1, k7) 5 times.

Round 20: (P8, k1, sl 1, k1, p7) 5 times.

Round 21: (P8, sl 1, k1, sl 1, p7) 5 times.

Cast off all sts purlwise.

Colour:
■ A

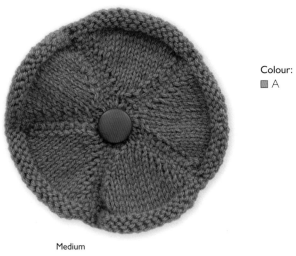

Medium

122 FOLK FLOWER WITH BUTTON

Using A, cast on 8 stitches and divide evenly over 4 needles.
Join, taking care not to twist stitches.
Round 1: [K1f&b] 8 times. (16 sts)
Rounds 2: Purl.
Repeat the last round for all even-numbered rounds until Round 14 has been completed.
Round 3: [K1, k1f&b, k1f&b, k1] 4 times. (24 sts)
Round 5: [K2, k1f&b, k1f&b, k2] 4 times. (32 sts)
Round 7: [K3, k1f&b, k1f&b, k3] 4 times. (40 sts)
Round 9: [K4, k1f&b, k1f&b, k4] 4 times. (48 sts)
Round 11: [K5, k1f&b, k1f&b, k5] 4 times. (56 sts)

Round 13: [K6, k1f&b, k1f&b, k6] 4 times. (64 sts)
Fasten off A. Join B.
Work backwards and forwards in rows.
**Row 1(RS): K1, k2tog, k5, turn.
Work on these 7 sts only.
Row 2: K1, k2tog, k4. (6 sts)
Row 3: K1, k2tog, k3. (5 sts)
Row 4: K1, k2tog, k2. (4 sts)
Row 5: K1, k2tog, k1. (3 sts)
Row 6: K1, k2tog. (2 sts)
Row 7: K2tog. (1 st)
Fasten off.
With RS facing, rejoin yarn to work the next 8 sts.
Repeat from ****** 7 times more.

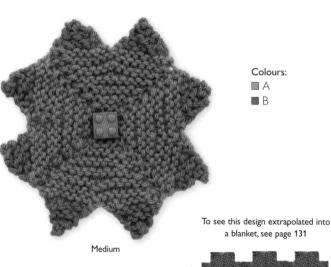

Medium

Colours:
■ A
■ B

To see this design extrapolated into a blanket, see page 131

Mix and match: **122 +
Rounds 1–16 of 42**

123 BOBBLE FLOWER

SPECIAL ABBREVIATION
MB (Make Bobble): [K1, p1, k1] into next st, turn, p3, turn, k3togtbl.

NOTE
All stitches are slipped with the yarn in front.

Cast on 6 stitches and divide evenly over 3 needles, 2 sts oen.
Join, taking case not to twist stitches.
Round 1: [K1f&b] 6 times. (12 sts)
Round 2: Knit.
Round 3: [K1f&b, k1] 6 times. (18 sts)
Round 4: [MB, k2] 6 times.
Round 5: [K1, k1f&b, k1] 6 times. (24 sts)
Round 6: [K1, M1, sl 1, k1, sl 1, M1] 6 times. (36 sts)
Round 7: [K1, MB, k3, MB] 6 times.
Round 8: [K2, M1, sl 1, k1, sl 1, M1, k1] 6 times. (48 sts)
Round 9: [MB, k1, MB, k3, MB, k1] 6 times.
Round 10: [K3, M1, sl 1, k1, sl 1, M1, k2] 6 times. (60 sts)

Round 11: [(K1, MB) twice, k3, MB, k1, MB] 6 times.
Round 12: [K4, M1, sl 1, k1, sl 1, M1, k3] 6 times. (72 sts)
Round 13: [(MB, k1) twice, MB, k3, (MB, k1) twice] 6 times.
Round 14: [K5, M1, sl 1, k1, sl 1, M1, k4) 6 times. (84 sts)
Round 15: [(K1, MB) twice, k7, MB, k1, MB] 6 times.
Round 16: [K6, M1, sl 1, k1, sl 1, M1, k5) 6 times. (96 sts)
Round 17: [MB, k1, MB, k11, MB, k1] 6 times.
Round 18: [K7, M1, sl 1, k1, sl 1, M1, k6) 6 times. (108 sts)
Round 19: Purl.
Round 20: Purl.
Cast off stitches knitwise.

Large

Colour:
■ A

STITCH EXPLANATIONS:

Htr2tog (half treble crochet two stitches together): [Yrh, insert hook into next st, yrh, draw up a loop] twice, yrh, draw through all 5 loops on the hook.

Foundation chain: Ch 3.
Row 1 (RS): 2 Htr into third ch from hook, turn. (2 sts)
Row 2: Ch 2 (does not count as a st here and throughout), 2 htr in each st, turn. (4 sts)
Row 3: Ch 2, 2 htr into the st at the base of beg ch-2, 1 htr in each st across to last st, 2 htr in last st, turn. (6 sts)
Repeat the last row 5 times more. (16 sts)
FIRST SIDE
Row 9: Ch 2, 1 htr in st at base of beg ch-2, 1 htr in each of next 5 sts, htr2tog, turn, leave remaining sts unworked. (7 sts)

Rows 10: Ch 2, 1 htr in st at base of beg ch-2, 1 htr in each st to last 2 sts, htr2tog, turn.
Repeat the last row twice more. (4 sts)
Fasten off.
SECOND SIDE
With right side facing, join yarn to next unworked st Row 9.
Row 9: Ch 2, htr2tog into the st at the base of beg ch-2 and the next st, 1 htr in each st to the end of the row, turn. (7 sts)
Repeat the last row 3 times more. (4 sts)
Fasten off.

Colour:
■ A

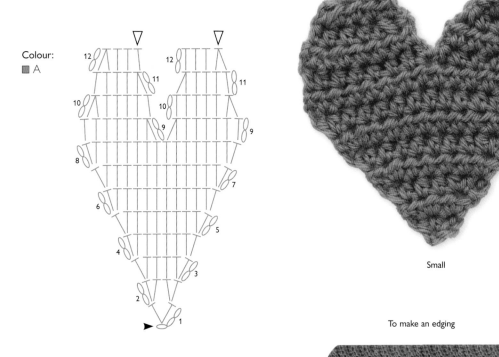

Small

To make an edging

Same-block tessellation: **124**

Symbols and abbreviations
Turn to pages 140–141 for a full explanation of the symbols and abbreviations used.

125 SIMPLE HEART

Foundation chain: Using A, ch 3.

Row 1 (WS): 1 dc into second ch from hook, 1 dc in next ch, turn. (2 dc)

Row 2: Ch 1, 2 dc in st at base of ch-1, 1 dc in next dc, turn. (3 dc)

Row 3: Ch 1, 2 dc in st at base of ch-1, 1 dc in next dc, 2 dc in last dc, turn. (5 dc)

Row 4: Ch 1, 2 dc in st at base of ch-1, 1 dc in next 3 dc, 2 dc in last dc, turn. (7 dc.)

Row 5: Skip first dc, 5 tr in next dc (shell made), skip next dc, ss in next dc, skip next dc, 5 tr in next dc, skip last dc, join with ss in beg ch-1 of Row 4. (2 shells made)

Turn, work in rounds.

Round 6: Ch 2 (does not count as a st), 2 tr in each of next 3 tr, 1 dc in next tr, ss in next tr, skip next ss, ss in next tr, 1 dc in next tr, 2 tr in each of next 3 tr, working in the ends of rows, work 6 tr evenly spaced along side of heart, working across the opposite side of foundation chain, 3 tr in space between 2 dc at base of heart, working in the ends of rows, work 6 tr evenly spaced up side of heart, join with ss in top of beg ch-1. Fasten off A. Join B with ss.

Round 7: Ch 2, 2 tr in each of next 6 tr, 1 dc in next dc, ss between next 2 ss, 1 dc in next dc, 2 tr in each of next 6 tr, 1 tr in next 7 tr, 3 tr in next tr (point), 1 tr in next 7 tr; join with ss in top of beg ch-2.

Fasten off.

Colours:
☐ A
■ B

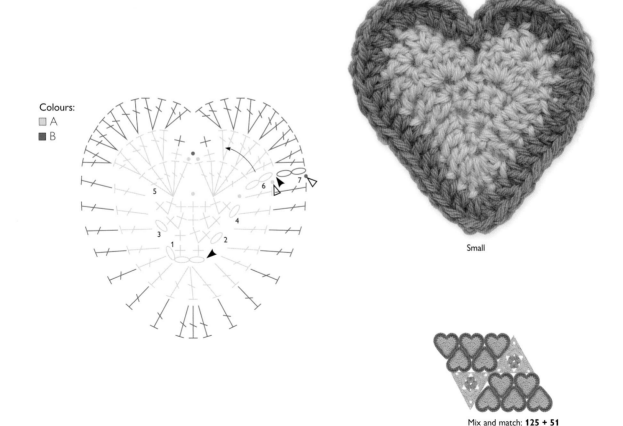

Small

Mix and match: **125 + 51**

126 SWEET HEART

Foundation chain: Using A, ch 17.

Round 1: 3 htr into second ch from the hook, 1 htr in each of next 6 ch, skip next 2 ch, 1 htr in each of next 6 ch, 3 htr in next ch, work each ch loop on opposite side of the foundation chain, 1 htr in next 6 ch, [1 htr; ch 2, 1 htr] into next ch-2 sp, 1 htr in each of the last 6 ch, do not join. (32 sts)

Round 2: 2 htr in each of the next 3 sts, 1 htr in each of next 5 sts, skip next 2 sts, 1 htr in each of next 5 sts, 2 htr in each of the next 3 sts, 1 htr in each of next 7 sts, [1 htr; ch 2, 1 htr] into next ch-2 sp, 1 htr in each of last 7 sts. (38 sts)

Round 3: [2 htr in next sts, 1 htr in next st] 3 times, 1 htr in each of next 4 sts, skip next 2 sts, 1 htr in each of next 4 sts, [2 htr in next sts, 1 htr in next st] 3 times, 1 htr in each of next 8 sts, [1 htr; ch 2, 1 htr] into next ch-2 sp, 1 htr in each of last 8 sts. (44 sts)

Round 4: 1 htr in next st, [2 htr in next st, 1 htr in each of next 2 sts] 3 times, 1 htr in each of next 2 sts, skip next 2 sts, 1 htr in each of next 4 sts, [2htr in next st, 1 htr in each of next 2 sts] 3 times, 1 htr in each of next 8 sts, [1 htr; ch 2, 1 htr] into next ch-2 sp, 1 htr in each of last 9 sts. (50 sts)

Round 5: 1 htr in each of next 2 sts, [2 htr in next st, 1 htr in each of next 3 sts] 3 times, skip next 2 sts, 1 htr in each of next 3 sts, [2 htr in next st, 1 htr in each of next 3 sts] 3 times, 1 htr in each of next 9 sts, [1 htr; ch 2, 1 htr] into next ch-2 sp, 1 htr in each of last 10 sts, join with ss to beg of last round.
Fasten off.

Colour:
☐ A

Medium

Mix and match: **126 + 118**

127 REVERSE STOCKING HEART

Cast on 2 stitches.
Row 1 (RS): K1, yo, k1. (3 sts)
Row 2: Purl.
Row 3: K1, M1, p1, M1, k1. (5 sts)
Row 4: P2, M1, k1, M1, p2. (7 sts)
Row 5: K2, purl to the last 2 sts, k2.
Repeat the last row for each odd-numbered row until Row 17 has been completed.
Row 6: P2, M1, k3, M1, p2. (9 sts)
Row 8: P2, M1, k5, M1, p2. (11 sts)
Row 10: P2, M1, k7, M1, p2. (13 sts)
Row 12: P2, M1, k9, M1, p2. (15 sts)
Row 14: P2, M1, k11, M1, p2. (17 sts)
Row 16: P2, M1, k13, M1, p2. (19 sts)
Row 18: P2, M1, k15, M1, p2. (21 sts)
Row 19: K2, p8, k1f&b, p8, k2. (22 sts)
Row 20: P2, k8, p2, k8, p2.

Row 21: K2, p8, M1, k2, M1, p8, k2. (24 sts)
Row 22: P2, k8, p4, k8, p2.
Row 23: K2, p8, k4, p8, k2.
Row 24: P2, k8, p2, turn.
Work on these 12 sts only, place remaining sts onto a stitch holder
Row 25: K1, ssk, p6, k2tog, k1. (10 sts)
Row 26: P2, k6, p2.
Row 27: K1, ssk, p4, k2tog, k1. (8 sts)
Row 28: P2, k4, p2.
Row 29: K1, sk2p, k3tog, k1. (4 sts)
Row 30: P2tog, p2togtbl, pass first st over the second stitch.
Fasten off.
With WS facing, rejoin yarn to work the remaining 12 sts.
Row 24: P2, k8, p2.
Repeat Rows 25–30.
Fasten off.

Colour:
■ A

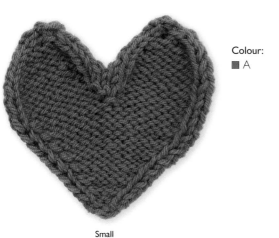

Small

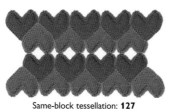

Same-block tessellation: **127**

128 EYELET BORDER HEART

Cast on 4 stitches.
Row 1: K2, yo, k to end of row. (5 sts)
Repeat Row 1, until there are 36 sts.
SHAPE TOP OF HEART:
Row 33: K2, yo, [k2tog] twice, k12, turn.
Work on these 17 sts only, place any remaining sts onto a stitch holder.
Row 34: K2, yo, [k2tog] twice, k to end. (16 sts)
Repeat Row 34 until 9 sts remain.

Row 42: [K2tog] twice, k1, [k2tog] twice. (5 sts)
Bind off.
Starting from the centre of the heart, rejoin yarn to work the remaining 18 sts.
Row 33: K2, yo, [K2tog] twice, k12.
Repeat Rows 34–42.
Cast off.

Colour:
■ A

Medium

Mix and match: **128 + 18**

129 GARTER HEART

STORING KNIT AND CROCHET

Apart from dust and dirt, the main enemy of knit and crochet fabrics is direct sunlight, which can cause yarn colours to fade and fibres to weaken. Excessive heat, too, makes yarn dry and brittle, damp rots fibres and moths damage woollen yarns.

Avoid storing yarns or finished crochet items in polyethylene as it attracts dirt and dust particles that will transfer readily to your work. Polyethylene bags prevent yarns with natural fibres, such as cotton and linen, from breathing, which can result in mildew attacks that will eventually weaken or rot the fibres. Store small items wrapped in white, acid-free tissue paper or an old cotton pillowcase. Large, heavy items will probably drop and stretch out of shape if stored on hangers, so fold them loosely between layers of white tissue paper, making sure that each fold is padded.

Store all items in a drawer, cupboard, or other dark, dry and moth-free place. Check them regularly, refolding the larger garments. It is also a good idea to make small cloth sachets filled with dried lavender flowers to tuck into your drawer or cupboard along with your knit and crochet, as the smell deters moths.

Cast on 2 stitches.
Row 1: K1f&b, place marker, k1. (3 sts)
Row 2: K1f&b, slip marker, k2. (4 sts)
Row 3: K1, k1f&b, slip marker, k2. (5 sts)
Row 4: K1, k1f&b, slip marker, k3. (6 sts)
Row 5: Knit to one st before marker, k1f&b, slip marker, k to end of row.
Repeat Row 5 until there are 30 sts.

Row 29 (RS): K15, turn.
Work on these 15 sts only, place remaining sts onto a stitch holder.
Row 30: K1, k2tog, k to end. (14 sts)
Repeat Row 30 until 5 sts remain. Cast off.
With RS facing, rejoin yarn to work the remaining 15 sts.
Row 29 (RS): Knit.
Repeat Row 30 until 5 sts remain. Cast off.

Colour:
☐ A

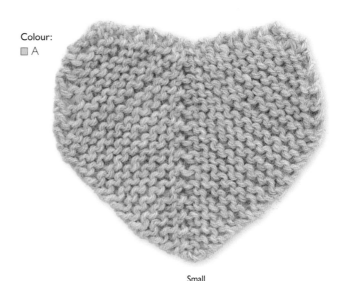

Small

SHELLS

130 LACY SHELL

Foundation ring: Ch 3, join with ss to form a ring.

Row 1 (RS): Ch 3 (counts as first tr), 6 tr into ring, turn. (7 tr)

Row 2: Ch 5 (counts as first tr and ch 2) skip next tr, [1 tr in next tr, ch 2, skip next tr] twice, 1 tr in third ch of beg ch-3, turn. (4 tr and 3 ch-2 sps)

Row 3: Ch 3 (counts as first tr), [3 tr into next ch-2 sp, 2 tr in next tr] twice, 3 tr in next ch-2 sp, 1 tr in third ch of beg ch-5, turn. (15 tr)

Row 4: Ch 5 (counts as first tr and ch 2), skip next 2 tr, [1 tr in next tr, ch 2, skip next tr] 5 times, 1 tr in third ch of beg ch-3, turn. (7 tr and 6 ch-2 sps)

Row 5: Ch 3 (counts as first tr), [2 tr in next ch-2 sp, 1 tr in next tr] 5 times, 2 tr in next ch-2 sp, 1 tr in third ch of beg ch-5, turn. (19 tr)

Row 6: Ch 5 (counts as first tr and ch 2), skip next tr, [1 tr in next tr, ch 2, skip next tr] 8 times, 1 tr in third ch of beg ch-3, turn. (10 tr and 9 ch-2 sp)

Row 7: Ch 3 (counts as first tr), [2 tr in next ch-2 sp, 1 tr in next tr] 4 times, 3 tr in next ch-2 sp, [1 tr in next tr, 2 tr in next ch-2 sp] 4 times, 1 tr in third ch of beg ch-5, turn. (29 tr)

Row 8: Ch 5 (counts as first tr and ch 2), skip next 2 tr, [1 tr in next tr, ch 2, skip next tr] 12 times, skip next tr, 1 tr in third ch of beg ch-3, turn. (14 tr and 13 ch-2 sps)

Row 9: Ch 3 (counts as first tr), [2 tr in next ch-2 sp, 1 tr in next tr] 12 times, 2 tr in next ch-2 sp, 1 tr in third ch of beg ch-5.
Fasten off.

Colour:
■ A

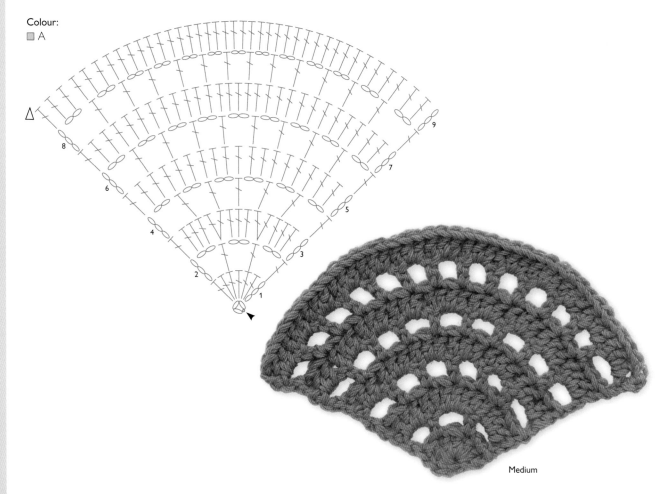

Medium

Symbols and abbreviations
Turn to pages 140–141 for a full explanation of the symbols and abbreviations used.

131 TWO-TONE SEASHELL

Using A, cast on 36 stitches.
Row 1 (RS): Purl.
Row 2: Knit.
Change to B.
Row 3: [K2tog] 18 times. (18 sts).
Row 4: Purl.
Change to A.
Rows 5 and 6: Knit.
Row 7: Purl.
Row 8: Knit.
Change to B.
Row 9: [K2tog, k1] 6 times. (12 sts)
Repeat Rows 4–8.

Change to B.
Row 15: [K2tog, k2] 3 times. (9 sts).
Repeat Rows 4–8.
Change to B.
Row 21: [K2tog, k1] 3 times. (6 sts).
Repeat Rows 4–8.
Fasten off A. Change to B.
Row 27: [K2tog] 3 times. (3 sts)
Row 28: Purl.
Row 29: K3tog.
Fasten off.

Colours:
- A
- B

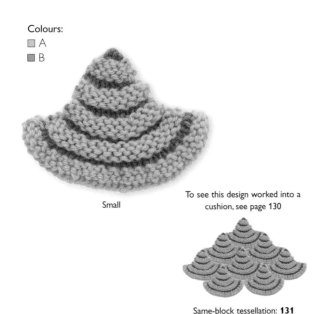

Small

To see this design worked into a
cushion, see page 130

Same-block tessellation: **131**

132 HORIZONTAL RIBBED SHELL

Cast on 44 stitches.
Row 1 (WS): Knit.
Row 2 [K2tog, yo] to last 2 sts,
k2tog. (43 sts)
Row 3: Knit.
Row 4: [K2tog, yo] to last st, k1.
Row 5: Knit.
Row 6: K3, k2tog, knit to end of
row. (42 sts)
Row 7: K3, k2tog, purl to last 4 sts,
k4. (41 sts)
Rows 8 and 9: Repeat Row 6.
(39 sts)

Repeat Rows 6–8 10 times more.
(9 sts)
Rows 40 and 41: Repeat Row 6.
(7 sts)
Row 42: K3, k2tog, k2. (6 sts)
Row 43: K3, k2tog, k1. (5 sts)
Row 44: K2, k2tog k1. (4 sts)
Row 45: K1, k2tog, k1. (3 sts)
Row 46: Sl 1, k2tog, psso (1 st).
Fasten off.

Colour:
- A

Large

133 VERTICAL RIBBED SHELL

LAUNDERING KNIT AND CROCHET

Always follow the washing and pressing instructions given on the ball band.

If the yarn you are using is machine washable, put the item into a zippered mesh laundry bag to keep it from stretching and snagging during the wash cycle. If you do not have a mesh bag, use an old, clean white pillowcase instead. Secure the open end with an elastic ponytail band or work a row of running stitches across the opening to close the pillowcase.

For crochet pieces made from yarns that are not machine washable, handwash in hot water with a mild, detergent-free cleaning agent. Most purpose-made wool or fabric shampoos are ideal but check that the one you choose does not contain optical brighteners, which will cause yarn colours to fade. Rinse the piece thoroughly in several changes of water at the same temperature as the washing water to avoid felting. Without wringing, squeeze out as much surplus water as you can, roll the damp item in a towel, and press to remove any moisture. Gently ease the item into shape and dry it flat out of direct sunlight. For very lacy items, you will probably need to block (see page 138) every time they are washed.

Cast on 2 stitches.
Row 1: K1f&b, knit to end. (3 sts)
Repeat the last row 4 times more. (7 sts)
Row 6: K1f&b, k1, yo, k2, yo, k3. (10 sts)
Row 7: K4, p2, k4.
Row 8: K3, yo, p1, k2, p1, yo, k3. (12 sts)
Row 9: K5, p2, k5.
Row 10: K3, yo, p2, k2, p2, yo, k3. (14 sts)
Row 11: K3, p1, k2, p2, k2, p1, k3.
Row 12: K3, yo, k1, p2, k2, p2, k1, yo, k3. (16 sts)
Row 13: K3, [p2, k2] twice, p2, k3.
Row 14: K3, yo, [k2, p2] twice, k2, yo, k3. (18 sts)
Row 15: K4, [p2, k2] twice, p2, k4.
Row 16: K3, yo, p1, [k2, p2] twice, k2, p1, yo, k3. (20 sts)
Row 17: K5, [p2, k2] twice, p2, k5.
Row 18: K3, yo, [p2, k2] 3 times, p2, yo, k3. (22 sts)
Row 19: K3, p1, [k2, p2] 3 times, k2, p1, k3.
Row 20: K3, yo, k1, [p2, k2] 3 times, p2, k1, yo, k3. (24 sts)
Row 21: K3, [p2, k2] 4 times, p2, k3.
Row 22: K3, yo, [k2, p2] 4 times, k2, yo, k3. (26 sts)
Row 23: K4, [p2, k2] 4 times, p2, k4.
Row 24: K3, yo, p1, (k2, p2) 4 times, k2, p1, yo, k3. (28 sts)

Row 25: K5, [p2, k2] 5 times, k3.
Row 26: K3, yo [p2, k2] 5 times, p2, yo, k3. (30 sts)
Row 27: K3, p1, [k2, p2] 5 times, k2, p1, k3.
Row 28: K3, yo, k1, [p2, k2] 5 times, p2, k1, yo, k3. (32 sts)
Row 29: K3, [p2, k2] 6 times, p2, k3.
Row 30: K3, yo, [k2, p2] 6 times, k2, yo, k3. (34 sts)
Row 31: K4, [p2, k2] 6 times, p2, k4.
Row 32: K3, yo, p1, [k2, p2] 6 times, k2, p1, yo, k3. (36 sts)
Row 33: K5, [p2, k2] 7 times, k3.
Row 34: K3, yo, [k2, p2] 7 times, p2, yo, k3. (38 sts)
Row 35: K3, p1, [k2, p2] 7 times, k2, p1, k3.
Row 36: K3, yo, k1, [p2, k2], 7 times, p2, k1, yo, k3. (40 sts)
Row 37: K3, [p2, k2] 8 times, p2, k3.
Row 38: K3, yo, [k2, p2] 8 times, k2, yo, k3. (42 sts)
Row 39: K4, [p2, k2] 8 times, p2, k4.
Row 40: K3, [yo, k2tog, yo, ssk] 9 times, yo, k3. (43 sts)
Rows 41–43: Knit.
Cast off loosely knitwise.

Colour:
☐ A

Large

Foundation chain: Ch 18.
Row 1: Skip 2 ch (counts as first htr), 1 htr into the third ch from the hook, 1 htr into each ch to last ch, 3 htr into last ch, 1 htr in each of the next 15 ch loop on opposite side of the foundation chain, turn.
Row 2: Ch 2, (counts as first htr), skip first st, 1 htr into each st up to centre st of 3-htr on the previous row, 3 htr into centre st, 1 htr into each st to last 4 sts, turn.
Repeat the last row 4 times more. Fasten off.

Colour:
■ A

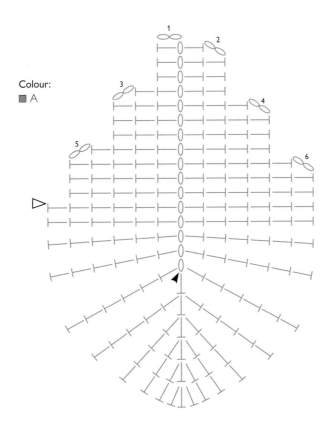

Large

For an edging

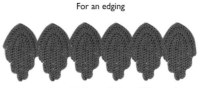

Same-block tessellation: **134**

Symbols and abbreviations Turn to pages 140–141 for a full explanation of the symbols and abbreviations used.

LEAVES

135 SINGLE CLOVER LEAF

Foundation chain: Ch 2.
Row 1: 2 dc into second ch from hook, turn. (2 dc)
Row 2: Ch 1, 2 dc in each of next 2 dc, turn. (4 dc)
Row 3: Ch 1, 2 dc in next dc, 1 dc in each of next 2 dc, 2 dc in next dc, turn. (6 dc)
Row 4: Ch 1, 1 dc in each st, turn. (6 dc)
Row 5: Ch 1, 2 dc in next dc, 1 dc in each of next 4 dc, 2 dc in next dc, turn. (8 dc)

Row 6: Ch 1, 1 dc in each st, turn. (8 dc)
Row 7: Ch 1, skip dc at base of beg ch-1, [1 dc, 1 htr, 1 tr] into next dc, [1 tr, 1 htr, 1 dc] into next dc, ss in next dc, ch 1, skip 1 dc, [1 dc, 1 htr, 1 tr] into next dc, [1 tr, 1 htr, 1 dc] into next dc, ss in next dc.
Fasten off.
Make 3 or 4 leaves depending on clover or shamrock desired. Use the ends to sew the leaves together.

Colour:
◻ A

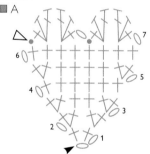

Small

Same-block tessellation: **135**

136 SIMPLE PAISLEY

Foundation ring: Using A, ch 4, join to form a ring.
Round 1: Ch 3 (counts as first tr), 9 tr into ring, join with ss to beg ch-3. (10 tr)
Fasten off A. Join B into any tr.
Round 2: Ch 2 (counts as first htr), 1 blo htr into the st at the base of beg ch-2, 2 blo htr into each of next 9 tr; join with ss to top of beg ch-2.
Fasten off B. Join C into any htr.
Round 3: Ch 9, 1 dc into the second ch from the hook, 1 htr in each of the next 2 ch 1tr in

each of the next 2 ch, 1 dtr in each of the next 2 ch, skip 1 ch, working into the sts of Round 2, [1 blo htr in next st, 2 blo htr in next st] 10 times, working in each ch loop on opposite side of beg ch-9, skip 1 ch, 1 dc in each of the next 7 ch, ss in last ch.
Fasten off C. Join D with ss at point of the block.
Row 4: 1 Htr in each of the next 37 sts, skip 1 dc, ss in each of the next 6 dc, ss in last ss.
Fasten off.

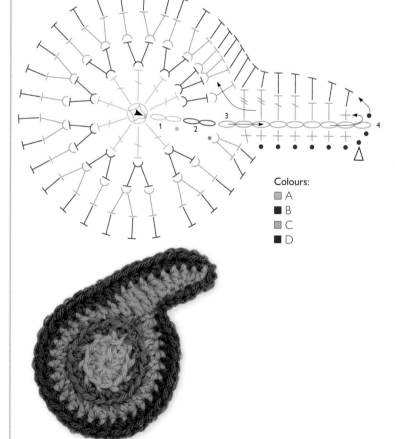

Colours:
◻ A
■ B
◻ C
■ D

Medium

137 CABLED TWO-TONE LEAF

NOTE

This block is worked with 2 colours on every row. Work the C4B maintaining the colours set.

Using A, cast on 3 stitches, using B cast on 3 stitches onto same needle.

Row 1 (RS): K3A, k3B.

Row 2: K1B, p2B, p2A, k1A.

Row 3: K1A, yo, k2A, k2B, yo, k1B. (8 sts)

Row 4: K1B, p3B, p3A, k1A.

Row 5: K1A, yo, k3A, k3B, yo, k1B. (10 sts)

Row 6: K1B, p4B, p4A, k1A.

Row 7: K1f&bA, yo, k4A, k4B, yo, k1f&bB. (14 sts)

Row 8: K2B, p5B, p5A, k2A.

Row 9: K2A, yo, k3A, C4F, k3B, yo, k2B. (16 sts)

Row 10: K2B, p4B, p2A, p2B, p4A, k2A.

Row 11: K2A, yo, k4A, k2B, k2A, k4B, yo, k2B. (18 sts)

Row 12: K2B, yo, p5B, p2A, p2B, p5A, yo, k2A. (20 sts)

Row 13: K2A, yo, k6A, k2B, k2A, k6B, yo, k2B. (22 sts)

Row 14: K2B, p7B, p2A, p2B, p7A, k2A.

Row 15: K2A, yo, sskA, k5A, C4F, k5B, k2togB, yo, k2B.

Row 16: k2B, p9B, p9A, k2A.

Row 17: K2A, yo, sskA, k7A, k7B, k2togB, yo, k2B.

Row 18: as Row 16.

Row 19: as Row 17.

Row 20: as Row 16.

Row 21: K2A, yo, sskA, k5A, C4F, k5B, k2togB, yo, k2B.

Row 22: K2B, p7B, p2A, p2B, p7A, k2A.

Row 23: K2A, yo, sskA, k5A, k2B, k2A, k5B, k2togB, yo, k2B.

Row 24: as Row 22.

Row 25: as Row 23.

Row 26: as Row 22.

Row 27: K2A, yo, sskA, k5A, C4F, k5B, k2togB, yo, k2B.

Row 28: K2B, p9B, p9A, k2A.

Row 29: K2A, sskA, k7A, k7B, k2togB, k2B. (20 sts)

Row 30: K2B, p8B, p8A, k2A.

Row 31: K2A, sskA, k6A, k6B, k2togB, k2B. (18 sts)

Row 32: K2B, p7B, p7A, k2A.

Row 33: K2A, sskA, k3A, C4F, k3B, k2togB, k2B. (16 sts)

Row 34: K2B, p4B, p2A, p2B, p4A, k2A.

Row 35: K2A, sskA, k2A, k2B, k2A, k2B, k2togB, k2B. (14 sts)

Row 36: K2B, p3B, p2A, p2B, p3A, k2A.

Row 37: K2A, sskA, k1A, k2B, k2A, k1B, k2togB, k2B. (12 sts)

Row 38: K2B, p2B, p2A, p2B, p2A, k2A.

Row 39: K2A, sskA, C4F, k2togB, k2B. (10 sts)

Row 40: K2B, p3B, p3A, k2A.

Row 41: K2A, sskA, k1A, k1B, k2togB, k2B. (8 sts)

Row 42: K2B, p2B, p2A, k2A.

Row 43: K2A, sskA, k2togB, k2B. (6 sts)

Row 44: K2B, p1B, p1A, k2A.

Row 45: With A sl 2tog, k1, p2sso, k3togB. (2 sts)

Row 46: P2togA.

Fasten off.

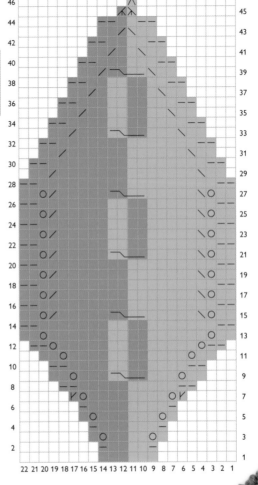

Colours:
A
B

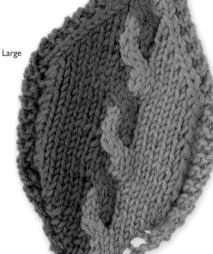

Large

138 GARTER LEAF

Cast on 5 stitches.

Row 1: K1, yo, k3, yo, k1. (7 sts)

Row 2 (and all even-numbered rows): Knit.

Row 3: [K1, yo] twice, sl 1, k2tog, psso, [yo, k1] twice. (9 sts)

Row 5: K1, yo, k2, yo, sl 1, k2tog, psso, yo, k2, yo, k1. (11 sts)

Row 7: K1, yo, k3, yo, sl 1, k2tog, psso, yo, k3, yo, k1. (13 sts)

Row 9: K1, yo, k4, yo, sl 1, k2tog, psso, yo, k4, yo, k1. (15 sts)

Row 11: K1, yo, k5, yo, sl 1, k2tog, psso, yo, k5, yo, k1. (17 sts)

Row 13: K1, yo, k6, yo, sl 1, k2tog, psso, yo, k6, yo, k1. (19 sts)

Row 15: K1, yo, k7, yo, sl 1, k2tog, psso, yo, k7, yo, k1. (21 sts)

Row 17: K1, yo, ssk, k6, yo, sl 1, k2tog, psso, yo, k6, k2tog, yo, k1. Repeat the last row each odd-numbered row until Row 27 has been completed.

Row 29: Ssk, k7, yo, sl 1, k2tog, psso, yo, k7, k2tog. (19 sts)

Row 31: Ssk, k6, yo, sl 1, k2tog, psso, yo, k6, k2tog. (17 sts)

Row 33: Ssk, k5, yo, sl 1, k2tog, psso, yo, k5, k2tog. (15 sts)

Row 35: Ssk, k4, yo, sl 1, k2tog, psso, yo, k4, k2tog. (13 sts)

Row 37: Ssk, k3, yo, sl 1, k2tog, psso, yo, k3, k2tog. (11 sts)

Row 39: Ssk, k2, yo, sl 1, k2tog, psso, yo, k2, k2tog. (9 sts)

Row 41: Ssk, k1, yo, sl 1, k2tog, psso, yo, k1, k2tog. (7 sts)

Row 43: Ssk, yo, sl 1, k2tog, psso, yo, k2tog. (5 sts)

Row 45: K1, sl 1, k2tog, psso, k1. (3 sts)

Row 46: Sl 1, k2tog, psso. Fasten off.

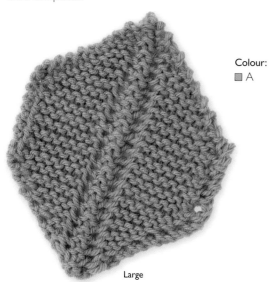

Colour:
■ A

Large

139 MITRED SOLID LEAF

Cast on 27 stitches.

Row 1 (RS): K12, sl 2tog, k1, p2sso, k12. (25 sts)

Row 2 (WS): P1, M1P, purl to last st, M1P, p1. (27 sts)

Row 3: Rep Row 1. (25 sts)

Row 4: K1, M1, k11, p1, k11, M1, k1. (27 sts)

Repeat the last 4 rows, 4 times more.

Row 21: Rep Row 1.

Row 22: Purl.

Row 23: K to 1 st before centre st, sl 2tog, k1, p2sso, k to end.

Row 24: K to centre st, p1, k to end.

Row 25: Rep Row 23.

Repeat the last 4 rows until 3 sts remain, ending with a WS row.

Next row: Sl 2tog, k1, p2sso. Fasten off.

Colour:
■ A

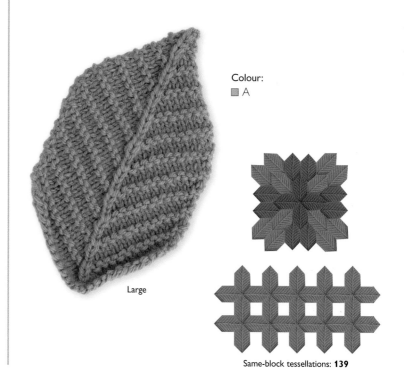

Large

Same-block tessellations: **139**

140 TWO-TONE LEAF

Using A, cast on 20 stitches.
Row 1 (WS): Knit.
Join B.
Row 2 (RS): K8, ssk, k2tog, k to end.
(18 sts)
Row 3: Knit.
Change to A.
Row 4: K7, ssk, k2tog, k to end.
(16 sts)
Row 5: Knit.
Change to B.
Row 6: K6, ssk, k2tog, k to end.
(14 sts)
Row 7: Knit.

Change to A.
Row 8: K5, ssk, k2tog, k to end.
(12 sts)
Row 9: Knit.
Fasten off A.
Row 10: K4, ssk, k2tog, k to end.
(10 sts)
Row 11: Ssk, cast off to last 2 sts,
k2tog, cast off last st.
Make 3 or 4 leaves depending on
clover or shamrock desired.
Use the ends to sew the leaves
together.

Colours:
■ A
■ B

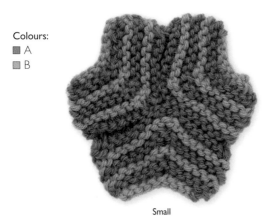

Small

Same-block tessellation: **140**

141 GARTER LEAF

Cast on 19 stitches.
Row 1 (RS): K8, sl 2tog, k1, p2sso,
k8. (17 sts)
Row 2 (WS): K8, sl 1 purlwise wyf,
k8.
Row 3: K7, sl 2tog, k1, p2sso, k7.
(15 sts)
Row 4: K7, sl 1 purlwise wyf, k7.
Row 5: K6, sl 2tog, k1, p2sso, k6.
(13 sts)
Row 6: K6, sl 1 purlwise wyf, k6.
Row 7: K5, sl 2tog, k1, p2sso, k5.
(11 sts)

Row 8: K5, sl 1 purlwise wyf, k5.
Row 9: K4, sl 2tog, k1, p2sso, k4.
(9 sts)
Row 10: Ssk, cast off to last 2 sts,
k2tog,
Cast off last st.
Make 3 or 4 leaves depending on
clover or shamrock desired.
Use the ends to sew the leaves
together.

Colour:
■ A

Small

142 GARTER TWO-TONE LEAF

Using A, cast on 21 stitches, mark centre stitch.
Row 1: Knit.
Row 2: K9, sl 2tog, k1, p2sso, k9. (19 sts)
Row 3: K1f&b, k8, p1, k7, k1f&b, k1. (21 sts)
Change to B.
Row 4: K9, sl 2tog, k1, p2sso, k9. (19 sts)
Row 5: K1f&b, k8, p1, k7, k1f&b, k1. (21 sts)
Repeat the last 4 rows, 4 times more.
Fasten off B. Change to A.
Row 22: K9, sl 2tog, k1, p2sso, k9. (19 sts)
Row 23: K9, p1, k9.
Row 24: K8, sl 2tog, k1, p2sso, k8. (17 sts)
Row 25: K8, p1, k8.
Row 26: K7, sl 2tog, k1, p2sso, k7. (15 sts)
Row 27: K7, p1, k7.
Row 28: K6, sl 2tog, k1, p2sso, k6. (13 sts)
Row 29: K6, p1, k6.
Row 30: K5, sl 2tog, k1, p2sso, k5. (11 sts)
Row 31: K5, p1, k5.
Row 32: K4, sl 2tog, k1, p2sso, k4. (9 sts)
Row 33: K4, p1, k4.
Row 34: K3, sl 2tog, k1, p2sso, k3. (7 sts)
Row 35: K3, p1, k3.
Row 36: K2, sl 2tog, k1, p2sso, k2. (5 sts)
Row 37: K2, p1, k2.
Row 38: K1, sl 2tog, k1, p2sso, k1. (3 sts)
Row 39: K1, p1, k1.
Row 40: Sl 2tog, k1, p2sso.
Fasten off.

Colours:
■ A
■ B

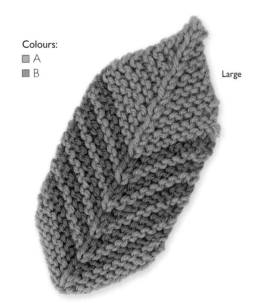

Large

143 LACE LEAF

Cast on 5 stitches.
Row 1: K2, yo, k1, yo, k2. (7 sts)
Row 2 (and all even-numbered rows): K1, p to last st, k1.
Row 3: K3, yo, k1, yo, k3. (9 sts)
Row 5: K4, yo, k1, yo, k4. (11 sts)
Row 7: K5, yo, k1, yo, k5. (13 sts)
Row 9: K3, k2tog, [yo, k1] 3 times, yo, ssk, k3. (15 sts)
Row 11: K2, k2tog, yo, k3, yo, k1, yo, k3, yo, ssk, k2. (17 sts)
Row 13: K1, k2tog, yo, k5, yo, k1, yo, k5, yo, ssk, k1. (19 sts)
Row 15: K6, k2tog, [yo, k1] 3 times, yo, ssk, k6. (21 sts)
Row 17: K5, k2tog, yo, k3, yo, k1, yo, k3, yo, ssk, k5. (23 sts)
Row 19: K4, k2tog, yo, k11, yo, ssk, k4.
Row 21: K3, k2tog, yo, k13, yo, ssk, k3.
Row 23: K2, k2tog, yo, k4, k2tog, yo, k3, yo, ssk, k4, yo, ssk, k2.
Row 25: K1, k2tog, yo, k4, k2tog, yo, k5, yo, ssk, k4, yo, ssk, k1.
Row 27: K6, k2tog, yo, k2, sl 2tog, k1, p2sso, k2, yo, ssk, k6. (21 sts)
Row 29: K5, k2tog, yo, k2, sl 2tog, k1, p2sso, k2, yo, ssk, k5. (19 sts)
Row 31: K4, k2tog, yo, k2, sl 2tog, k1, p2sso, k2, yo, ssk, k4. (17 sts)
Row 33: K3, k2tog, yo, k2, sl 2tog, k1, p2sso, k2, yo, ssk, k3. (15 sts)
Row 35: K2, k2tog, yo, k2, sl 2tog, k1, p2sso, k2, yo, ssk, k2. (13 sts)
Row 37: K1, k2tog, yo, k2, sl 2tog, k1, p2sso, k2, yo, ssk, k1. (11 sts)
Row 39: K4, sl 2tog, k1, p2sso, k4. (9 sts)
Row 41: K3, sl 2tog, k1, p2sso, k3. (7 sts)
Row 43: K2, sl 2tog, k1, p2sso, k2. (5 sts)
Row 45: K1, sl 2tog, k1, p2sso, k1. (3 sts)
Row 47: Sl 2tog, k1, p2sso.
Fasten off.

Colour:
■ A

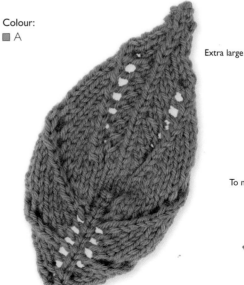

Extra large

To make an appliqué design

Mix and match: **143 + 121**

CONNECTORS

Designing a project and combining block shapes can often be a creative challenge. You find one block you like, which you would like to make the feature of your design, and you need to find a way of connecting it to itself or to another block in a way that satisfies your design vision. A connector is any block that is used to connect two or more blocks together. A connector can echo part of the feature block design, it can introduce another design element, or it can act simply as a scaffold. A connector block can contrast with the weight and drape of the feature block design or match it. There are no rules, just design choices.

ADAPTING BLOCK DESIGNS

Any block design worked from a corner or from the centre can easily be adapted to become a connector block because the block can usually be bound or fastened off when the desired dimensions have been reached. Blocks worked from the outside edge inwards can also be adapted to create smaller blocks but it often requires a bit of charting and a few gauge calculations. Adapting larger blocks works particularly well if the block has a short row repeat but common sense can always override this rule.

BASIC CONNECTOR BLOCKS

Over the years, crafters have developed a series of blocks that are easily adapted to fit any shape. Some rely on the stretch of the fabric, others on long chains or loops. So, when looking for inspiration in finished projects, don't just look at the blocks but the connector blocks, if there are any, and don't just look at the connector blocks from a design point of view but from a technique point of view. Why does that connector work? Is it easily adapted to another shape? You will soon build up a library of ideas and solutions, which will stand you in good stead in the future.

Symbols and abbreviations
Turn to pages 140–141 for a full explanation of the symbols and abbreviations used.

NOTE

Appropriate for connecting pieces with curved edges, this shape works best over an arc equivalent to a quarter of a circle and over only a few rows but it can be worked over greater arcs and to a greater depth.

Measure the exposed curved edge or the length you wish to join and calculate, using a gauge swatch, the number of stitches required. The single crochet stitches will flatten the exposed edge of the feature block slightly, so examine the feature block, measure the distance you think will tolerate this distortion, and calculate the number of single crochet stitches required. The remaining stitches will be half treble crochet stitches.

This pattern will work using any number of stitches plus 3 stitches for the turning chain.

Foundation chain: Ch 22 (or chain to the desired width).

Set-up row: Insert the hook into the third chain from the hook, work 1 blo htr, 1 blo htr in each of next 3 ch, 1 blo dc in each of next 10 ch, 1 blo htr in last 5 ch, turn.

Row 2: Ch 2 (counts as first htr), 1 blo htr in each of next 4 htr, 1 blo dc in each of next 10 dc, 1 blo htr in each of next 5 htr, turn. Repeat Row 2 until desired depth. Fasten off.

Repeat Row 2 until desired depth

Colour:
A ■

Medium

145 SMALL SQUARE

NOTE

This is a good base for a connector. To make it larger, work more rounds, working extra stitches into the corner stitches. To make it smaller, work only the central roundel. To adapt it to fit any gap, on the last round, work a chain of stitches to reach the neighbouring block and join the chain to it with a slip stitch; work an equal number of chain stitches as the outward chain and continue working around the last round until you reach the next position from which you would like to make another chain loop to link the feature blocks.

Foundation ring: Ch 6, join with ss to form a ring.
Round 1: Ch 3 (counts as first tr), 19 tr into ring, join with ss in top of beg ch-3. (20 tr)
Round 2: Ch 1, 1 dc into base of ch-1, 1 dc in each of next 4 tr, *ch 2, 1 dc in each of next 5 tr; rep from * 2 times more, ch 2, join with ss in beg dc.
Round 3: Ch 1, *1 dc in each of next 5 dc, 4 dc in next ch-2 sp; rep from * 3 times more, join with ss in beg dc. (36 dc)
Fasten off.

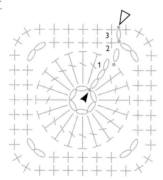

Colour:
A ■

Small

146 TRI-COLOUR RECTANGLE

NOTE

This connector is shown in an extreme form. It is, in fact, a classic centre-out connector block, which could equally be used to fill a square-shaped gap by simply working a shorter foundation chain.

This shape will work using any number of stitches plus 1 stitch for the turning chain.

Foundation chain: Using A, ch 21. Do not turn.
Round 1: Insert the hook into the second ch from hook, work 3 dc, 1 dc in each of the next 18 ch 6 dc in last ch. working along opposite side of foundation ch, 1 dc in each of next 18 ch, 3 dc in same ch as first dc, join with ss in beg dc and change to B in join. Fasten off A.
Round 2: Ch 3 (counts first tr), [1 tr, ch 2, 1 tr] in next dc, 1 tr in each of next 20 dc, [1 tr; ch 2, 1 tr] in next dc, 1 tr in each of next 20 dc, [1 tr; ch 2, 1 tr] in next dc, 1 tr in each of next 20 dc, [1 tr; ch 2, 1 tr] in next dc, 1 tr in next dc, join with ss in top of beg ch-3 and change to C in join: (52 tr and 4 corner ch-2 sps.)
Fasten off B.
Round 3: With C, ch 3, (counts first tr), *1 tr in each st to next corner ch-2 sp, [1 tr; ch 2, 1 tr] in corner ch-2 sp; rep from * 3 more times, 1 tr in each st to end of round, join with ss in top of beg ch-3.
Fasten off.

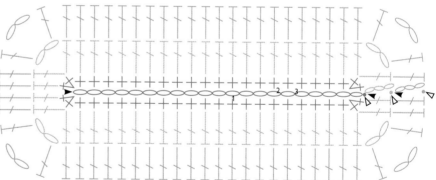

Colours:
■ A
■ B
■ C

Extra large

147 ELONGATED GRANNY TRIANGLE

NOTE

A connector that works well with straight edges is this classic variation on a larger block; it can be made smaller or larger by altering the number of repeats. The principles of this connector can easily be applied to other blocks; see working half or quarter blocks, page 134.

Foundation chain: Using A, ch 4, join with sl st to form a ring.

Row 1 (RS): Ch 3 (counts as first tr), 3 tr into ring, ch 1, 4 tr into ring. (8 tr)

Fasten off A. Do not turn. Join B with ss to top of ch-3 of previous row.

Row 2 (RS): Ch 3 (counts as first tr), 3 tr into the base of ch-3, ch 1, skip next 3 tr, [3 tr, ch 1, 3 tr] into next ch-1 sp, ch 1, skip 3 tr, 4 tr in last tr.

Fasten off B. Do not turn.

Join C with ss to top of ch-3 of previous row.

Row 3 (RS): Ch 3, (counts as first tr), 3 tr into the base of ch-3, ch 1, skip next 3 tr, 3 tr in next ch-1 sp, ch 1, [3 tr, ch 1, 3 tr] into next corner ch-1 sp, ch 1, skip next 3 tr, 3 tr into next ch-1, ch 1, skip 3 tr, 4 tr in last tr.

Fasten off C. Do not turn.

Join A with ss to top of ch-3 of previous row.

Row 4 (RS): Ch 3, (counts as first tr), 3 tr into the base of ch-3, [ch 1, skip next 3 tr, 3 tr into next ch-1 sp] twice, ch 1, [3 tr, ch 1, 3 tr] into next ch-1 sp, [ch 1, skip next 3 tr, 3 tr into next ch-1 sp] twice, ch 1, skip 3 tr, 4 tr in last tr.

Fasten off A.

Colours:
- ■ A
- ■ B
- ■ C

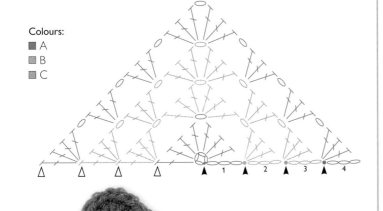

Medium

148 DOUBLE GARTER CONNECTOR

NOTE

This connector works equally well with curved or straight edges. For even more flexibility, work the block in garter stitch throughout. Garter stitch is useful for connectors because one stitch over two rows usually forms a square shape when worked to the recommended gauge. Measure the space you wish to fill and calculate, using a gauge swatch (see page 138), the number of stitches and rows required. Using squared paper and allowing one square to represent one stitch and two rows, plot the corners of the shape and join the points following the grid lines. Work the shape from the chart created – increasing and decreasing the number of stitches as required. On larger shapes it may be useful to work the occasional purl row to improve the drape.

This shape will work using any number of stitches.

Cast on 30 stitches loosely.

Row 1 (WS): Knit.

Rows 2 and 3: Purl.

Row 4: Knit.

Repeat Rows 1–4 5 times more or until it is the required depth.

Repeat Rows 1–2 once more.

Cast off loosely.

Colour:
- ☐ A

Large

149 RIBBED CONNECTOR

NOTE

This connector works well with curved edges. It relies on the elastic nature of rib and its desire to contract when relaxed. The connector shown below will work well along a long, shallow curve. For a deeper curve, increase the number of stocking stitch rows at the beginning and end and reduce the number of rib rows. If placed between two firmer fabrics, the rib will contract to fit the space but if placed between two lighter fabrics the rib may distort the shape of the lighter blocks.

This shape will work to various lengths. It will also work with stitch multiples of 4 stitches plus 2 stitches.

Cast on 30 stitches loosely.
Row 1 (RS): Purl.
Row 2: Knit.
Row 3: [K2, p2] 7 times, k2.
Row 4: [P2, k2] 7 times, p2.
Repeat the last 2 rows until the work measures 15cm (6in) from the cast-on edge, ending with a wrong-side row.
Next row: Purl.
Next row: Knit.
Cast off loosely.

Colour:
■ A

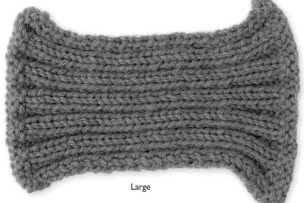

Large

150 KNIT LACE TRAPEZOID

NOTE

This connector works well with straight edges. The stitch pattern used for this connector creates a light, flexible fabric and is easily contorted into the same stitch proportion as garter stitch – one stitch over two rows to form a square. For more ideas on how to use this stitch pattern see block 148.

This shape will work using any odd number of stitches.

Cast on 17 stitches loosely.
Row 1 (WS): Purl.
Row 2 (RS): K1, *yo, k2tog; rep from * to last 2 sts, [yo, k1] twice: (19 sts)
Repeat the last 2 rows until there are 35 sts or it is the width required.
Cast off loosely.
Weave in ends and gently block to trapezoid shape before assembling.

Colour:
■ A

Extra large

CHAPTER TWO
PROJECTS & TECHNIQUES

This chapter opens with some beautiful and imaginative project ideas, made using the blocks in the book. The Techniques section covers everything from fitting the different-shaped blocks together, to blocking and joining blocks, and choosing and calculating yarn. A complete list of the abbreviations and chart symbols used is also included.

THE PROJECTS

The blocks in this book can be combined and used in a multitude of ways. The projects on these pages are just a few examples to start you off and provide inspiration for your own ideas.

PENTAGON STAR AFGHAN

w = 152cm (59¾in); h = 145cm (57in)

Garter pentagon	Garter pentagon	Garter pentagon	Garter pentagon	Garter pentagon	Ribbed starfish
Pink = 1 block	Peach = 5 blocks	Yellow = 30 blocks	Blue = 40 blocks	Green = 10 blocks	Green = 15 blocks

This shape is ideal for a baby blanket. It is narrower at the top around the shoulders, widens around the body, and then tapers towards the bottom edge, and those sensitive, kicking feet.

SIZE
■ 152 x 145cm (60 x 57in) not including the edging.

MATERIALS
■ Knitting needles 4.5mm (US 7).
■ Worsted-weight Superwash or acrylic, or an easily laundered and light fibre in the yarn shades indicated below.
See page 138 for information on how to calculate yarn amounts.

TENSION
■ Garter pentagon 13cm (5⅛in) high – the drape is light.
■ Ribbed starfish 10cm (4in) wide – the drape is medium.
See page 138 for information on tension.

KNIT
Work each of the garter pentagon (block 85, page 81) and ribbed starfish blocks (block 109, page 97) as described in the pattern, in the yarn shades, and the number of times indicated below.
The gaps between the blocks give this afghan a light drape. If you would like a more solid afghan add a connector of your choice.

FINISHING
Block all the pieces (page 138) and allow them to dry. Lay out the blocks following the diagram (left) or in drifts of colour. Stitch or crochet together (page 139) using matching yarn. Weave the ends into the seams. Lightly apply steam or press.

EDGING
Following the outer edge, work one round of single crochet or a narrow edging of your choice. This afghan is quite heavy and a weighted edging or deep edging is not required.

HALF-MOON BAG

This bag has a stylish shape, which looks equally good as a handbag, purse or shoulder bag. For extra security buy a waterproof drawstring bag – often found in camping shops – and sew the bottom edge of the bag to the inside of the bag project.

SIZE
51 × 30cm (20 × 12in) not including the edging.

MATERIALS
■ Crochet hook J–10 (6mm).
■ DK-weight cotton, or a fibre with very little elasticity, in the yarn shades indicated below.
■ The appropriate bag hardware for the style of bag required.

TENSION
■ Classic hexagon 18cm (7in) wide – the drape is firm.
■ Double triangle 9cm (3½in) wide – the drape is firm.

CROCHET
Work each of the classic hexagon (block 60, page 64) and double triangle blocks (block 53, page 58) as described in the pattern, in the yarn shades, and the number of times indicated below, to create a back and front and a side and base panel.

FINISHING
Block all the pieces (page 138) and allow them to dry. Lay out the blocks following the diagram (below). Stitch or crochet together (page 139) firmly using matching yarn. The seaming adds to the strength of the bag. Weave the ends into the seams. Lightly apply steam or press. Attach bag hardware.

ALTERNATIVE DESIGN
Work in near shades or a single shade and embellish with the heart, flower and leaf blocks found in this book.

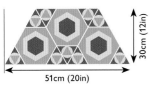

30cm (12in)

51cm (20in)

Classic hexagon
3 blocks

Double triangle
Front = 9 blocks
Back = 27 blocks
Base and sides = 50 blocks
Total = 85 blocks

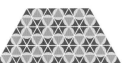

104cm (41in)

5½in (14cm)

HEARTS AND FLOWERS SCARF

A vision of fluff and frill, this cosy scarf is easy to make and fun to wear. This is a very adaptable design and looks great as a narrow scarf – work the sweet heart blocks in a fine-weight sock yarn and the flower-power posy blocks in a fine-weight mohair-mix yarn.

SIZE
35 × 200cm (13¾ × 78¾in) not including the edging.

MATERIALS
■ Crochet hook J–10 (6mm).
■ Worsted-weight mohair or mohair mix in the yarn shades indicated below.

TENSION
■ Sweet heart 13cm (5⅛in) wide – the drape is medium.
■ Flower power posy 11cm (4¼in) wide – the drape is light.

CROCHET
Work each of the sweet heart blocks (block 126, page 110) as described in the pattern in the yarn shades, and the number of times indicated below. Join each heart to its neighbour with a slip stitch on the last round at the point, the end of each straight edge, and the centre stitch of each curve.

Work the single flower-power posy blocks (block 114, page 100) indicated in the centre of the group of sweet heart blocks as described in the pattern the number of times shown below. You may want to make double in order to attach them to the right side and wrong side.

FINISHING
Block each piece (page 138) and allow them to dry. Attach the flower-power posy blocks in the centre of the group of sweet heart blocks. Weave the ends into the seams. Lightly apply steam or press.

EDGING
Work each of the flower-power posy blocks as described in the pattern the number of times indicated below, looping each new block to the last as shown. Attach to the outer edge of the sweet heart blocks.

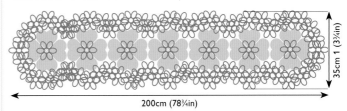

35cm 1 (3¾in)

200cm (78¾in)

Sweet heart
28 blocks

Flower-power posy
Frill = 80 blocks
Centres = 14 blocks (7 each side)
Total = 94 blocks

SHELL CUSHION

Reminiscent of a Japanese print, the texture of this block creates the illusion of waves and an ever-changing ripple of colour.

SIZE
40 x 40cm (15¾ x 15¾in).

MATERIALS
- Knitting needles 4.5mm (US 7).
- Worsted-weight pure wool yarn or cotton.
- 4 buttons.

TENSION
- Two-tone seashell 10cm (4in) wide – the drape is medium to firm.

KNIT
Work each of the whole two-tone seashell blocks (block 131, page 114) as described in the pattern, using the yarn shades indicated below.

HALF BLOCK
Using the yarn colours indicated below as a guide and A, cast on 18 stitches.
Work Rows 1–2 as for whole block.
Row 3: [K2tog, k1] 6 times. (12 sts)
Work Rows 4–8 as for whole block.
Row 9: [K2tog, k2] 3 times. (9 sts)
Work Rows 10–14 as for whole block.
Row 15: [K2tog, k1] 3 times. (6 sts)
Work Rows 16–20 as for whole block.
Row 21: [K2tog] 3 times. (3 sts)
Work Rows 22–26 as for whole block.
Row 27: Knit.

Complete as for whole block. Start by working individual blocks for each of the bottom row shell shapes.
For the second row of blocks, working from right to left with the right-side facing, pick up and knit 18 stitches along the edge of the left-edge of the block to the right and 18 stitches along the edge of the right-edge of the block to the left. Knit one row. Then, starting with Row 1, complete the block as directed in the directory.
For the third row of blocks, working from right to left, pick up and knit 18 stitches along the edge of the right-edge of the block to the left. Knit one row. Then, starting with Row 1, complete the block as directed in the directory. Work the next block as described in second row of the blocks. Work the last block as for the first block in the third row of blocks.
Continue until all the blocks have been completed.
Work buttonholes on blocks indicated.

FINISHING
Weave in the ends. Block the knitted fabric (page 138) and allow it to dry. Fold along the lines in the diagram, so that the letters match as indicated. Stitch the bottom edge to the corresponding gaps along the top edge (page 139) and stitch the side edges together using matching yarn. Attach the buttons securely.

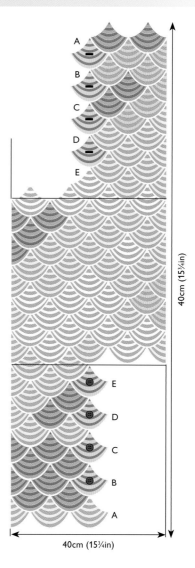

Two-tone seashell
8 blocks

Two-tone seashell
6 blocks

Two-tone seashell
14 blocks

Two-tone seashell
18 blocks

Two-tone seashell
29 blocks

Two-tone seashell
4 blocks

Two-tone seashell
4 blocks

Two-tone seashell
12 blocks; 6 facing left, 6 facing right

FLOWER BED AFGHAN

This afghan design is the perfect project for using up any leftover or odd balls of yarn you may have. Choose a colour palate for each block design and arrange the tilted square blocks randomly or in drifts as shown.

SIZE
84 x 108cm (33 x 42½in) not including the edging.

MATERIALS
- Knitting needles 4.5mm (US 7).
- Worsted-weight pure wool yarn or, a light fibre with some elasticity, in the yarn shades indicated below.
- 126 plastic buttons.

TENSION
- Folk flower with button 12cm (4¾in) wide – the drape is light.
- Tilted square 5cm (2in) wide.

KNIT
Work each of the folk flower with button blocks (block 122, page 107) as described in the pattern, in the yarn shades, and the number of times indicated below. Work each of the tilted square blocks (block 42, page 50), Rounds 1–16, as described in the pattern, in the yarn shades, and the number of times indicated below, or using odd balls of your choice.

FINISHING
Attach securely one button to the centre of each folk flower with button block – on the wrong side and the right side. Block all the pieces (page 138) and allow them to dry. Lay out the blocks following the diagram (right) or in drifts of colour, stitch or crochet together (page 139) using matching yarn. Weave the ends into the seams. Lightly apply steam or block.

EDGING
Following the outer edge, work one round of single crochet or a narrow edging of your choice. This afghan is quite heavy and a weighted or deep edging is not required.

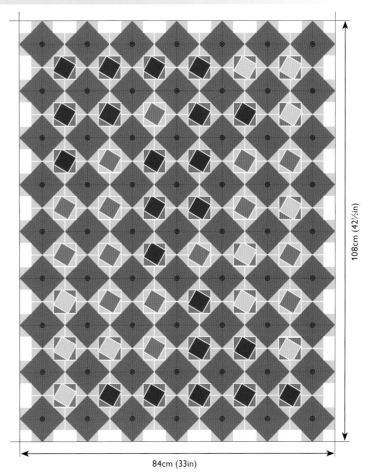

108cm (42½in)

84cm (33in)

Folk flower with button
63 blocks
126 buttons (1 on RS, 1 on WS)

Tilted square
22 blocks. Work Rounds 1–16 only.

Tilted square
15 blocks. Work Rounds 1–16 only.

Tilted square
11 blocks. Work Rounds 1–16 only.

TECHNIQUES

This section explains and demonstrates some useful techniques for creating and combining shaped blocks.

FITTING BLOCKS TOGETHER

Some block shapes fit together easily to make a continuous surface with no gaps. Other types of blocks will not interlock exactly; the spaces between them can be left empty for a lighter, more lacy effect. Alternatively, the spaces between blocks can be filled with small connector pieces.

UNUSUAL SHAPES
Shapes such as snowflakes have six points, and may therefore be treated as hexagons. Flowers may be treated as circles, and clover shapes as triangles.

SHELLS
Shells fit together as shown. Join each shell in place in turn, using the yarn tail left at the top point to join the seam to the left, around to the next point. It is usual to fill the spaces on the side edges with half-shells. The lower edge will be scalloped, and the top edge will have a series of points.

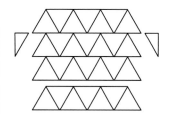

TRIANGLES
Here are just two of the ways in which triangles can be arranged. Join the triangles into strips, alternating the direction as required. Then join the strips. Add half-triangles to the side edges if desired.

SIMPLE ARRANGEMENTS

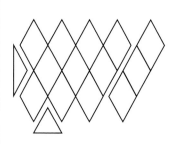

DIAMONDS
Assemble diamonds into diagonal strips as shown, then join the strips to make the whole. If you wish, work half-diamonds (triangles) to fit the gaps on the side edges.

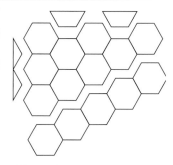

HEXAGONS
Hexagons have six sides. First join the hexagons into diagonal strips, then join the strips to make the whole. Shallow triangles can fill the spaces on the side edges. The gaps on the top and bottom edges can be filled with half-hexagons.

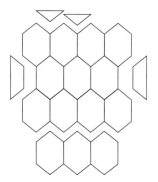

LEAVES
Join the leaves into strips, then fit the strips together as shown. The gaps at the side edges may be filled with half-leaves, or trapezoids. The top and bottom edges may be straightened by adding triangles.

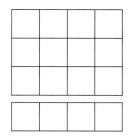

SQUARES
Join the squares into strips, then join the strips to make the size and shape you want.

ARRANGEMENTS WITH SPACES

HEARTS

Hearts can be joined into vertical lines, and if the lines are arranged as shown (one line pointing up, the next pointing down), they will fit together quite snugly with only small gaps between.

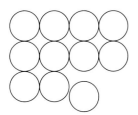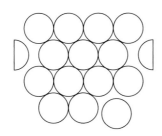

CIRCLES

Circles may be joined where they touch on four sides for an open, lacy effect. Join each circle in place in turn. If you want a firmer result, you can add connector pieces between the circles, as on the right.

ARRANGEMENTS WITH CONNECTORS

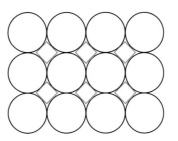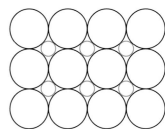

CIRCLES

For a solid arrangement of circles, the gaps may be filled with small square connectors, stretched slightly to fit. Alternatively, using smaller circles as connectors leaves only small gaps between the shapes.

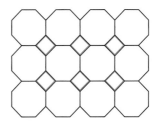

OCTAGONS

Eight-sided octagons can be joined as shown with small square connectors, set 'on point'. Join one strip of octagons, matching opposite faces. Join in the square connectors between them. Then add the octagons of the row below, one at a time. Repeat the last two steps as required. Triangles may be used to fill the gaps all around the edges.

STARS

Triangles added to a five-pointed star make a solid five-sided shape. Such shapes may then be arranged in rows and the spaces filled with more triangles.

WORKING LARGER OR SMALLER BLOCKS

BLOCKS WORKED IN ROUNDS

Both knit and crochet blocks worked in rounds are easy to adapt in size.
For a smaller shape: simply omit the last one or two rounds.
For a larger shape: work one or more extra rounds in a similar way to the last round given, increasing at the corners as set.

The proportions of this rectangle (block 146, page 123), worked in rounds, may be varied by starting with a longer or shorter foundation chain. The difference in length between a long side and a short side is always equal to the length of the foundation chain. For example, to make a rectangle 20 x 13cm (8 x 5in):

1. 20 − 13 = 7cm (8 − 5 = 3in).
2. Determine the number of stitches to 7cm (3in), and add 1 to this number for the foundation chain.
3. Work the rectangle in the same way as given, then work additional rounds (increasing at the corners as set), until the rectangle reaches the required size.

BLOCKS WORKED IN ROWS

Some blocks worked in rows are easily adapted.
To make a smaller diamond: work fewer increasing rows (choose an even number to subtract from the rows), and correspondingly fewer decreasing rows.
To make a larger diamond: work more increasing rows, and correspondingly more decreasing rows.
To make a larger diamond: add two or more stitches to the foundation chain. Then work the block with one half of the extra stitches at either side of the central decrease. Extra rows will be required to reach the point.
To make a smaller diamond: begin with a smaller number of foundation chains.

WORKING HALF OR QUARTER BLOCKS

To create connectors or to fill gaps at the tops or sides of projects, you may find it necessary to work half or quarter blocks.

To work a half or quarter block, start by familiarizing yourself with the pattern for the whole block by working a sample and charting the pattern. Then, on the chart carefully outline the area you require plus one column of edging stitches along each new edge. Charting can be laborious but it is far easier than working out repeats in an ever-changing number of stitches in a written pattern.

■ **If a block is worked in rows** it is often easy to identify the number of stitches required and how the shaping and stitch pattern should be worked.

■ Likewise, **if the block is a crochet block worked in the round and the work is turned after each round**, a fraction of each round is easy to identify and a new turning point can be marked.

■ If, however, **a block is crocheted in one direction without turning the work**, then turning the work to work a fraction of a round will show as a slightly different surface stitch texture. This can be avoided by breaking the yarn at the end of each fraction of the round and rejoining the yarn on the right-hand edge of the block—but the bulk of all those yarn ends may not be worth the improved appearance.

■ **If a block is knitted in the round** then, turning the work as required, work the chart from left to right as a wrong-side to the charted design.

This all sounds good in theory and it does usually work well the first time if you have already worked a swatch and you have just charted the block design. But as with everything in knit and crochet, swatch, and be prepared for surprises – block segments do not have the support of the rest of the block and a few adjustments may be needed.

> **TIP**
> For flat shapes in double crochet each round needs to increase by approximately 6 stitches, in stocking (stockinette) stitch and treble crochet each round needs to increase by approximately 12 stitches.

ARRANGING BLOCKS

Some blocks are 'directional' – they will form larger patterns if they are turned in different directions before assembly.

 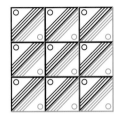 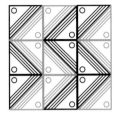

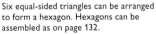

This knit bobble triangle (block 55, page 60) is just one example of a directional block. By turning the triangles in different directions, and working them in different colours, you can assemble larger patterns.

OTHER BLOCKS CAN BE ARRANGED TO FORM LARGER UNITS

Six equal-sided triangles can be arranged to form a hexagon. Hexagons can be assembled as on page 132.

Four hearts can be arranged to form a flower, which can then be treated as a large circle (page 133).

OTHER DIRECTIONAL BLOCKS
Other directional blocks in this book include the mitred garter square (block 39, page 49) and the elongated granny triangle (block 147, page 124). Try sketching different arrangements of these, as shown on page 136.

COLOURING BLOCKS

The colours you choose can totally alter the appearance of a block, and the 'feel' of the whole design. If you are not sure how to go about choosing colours, ask yourself a couple of questions:

How will the design be used? If you are making an afghan for your room, choose colours to suit your existing colour scheme and furnishings. If you are making a baby blanket, consider whether you want bright, cheerful colours or more traditional baby pastels. If you are making a wrap for a friend, choose colours your friend likes to wear.

Should the colours be bold or subtle? Strongly contrasting colours (such as bright pink with turquoise and black) will make a lively, boldly patterned design. Subtle tones of one colour (such as greys), or colours that are close in shade (such as pinks with lilacs) will look calmer, and the design will be more unified.

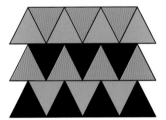 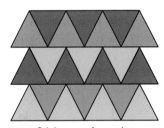

Strongly contrasting colours

Subtle tones of one colour

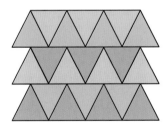

Colours close in shade

It is a good idea to buy sample balls of yarn and try out your colour choice before buying all the yarn you need for a large project – sometimes when colours are combined, they create a different effect to the one you expected. If possible, make several trial blocks before finally deciding on your colour choice. Lay out sample blocks in different arrangements and note down the combinations you like; you can take photographs to compare the different effects.

PLANNING YOUR DESIGN

Make a visual plan of your design, in order to check the final size and appearance, and to count how many blocks of each type and/or colour you will need.

1. Measure your sample block(s), and decide on the finished size required. How many blocks will be required in each direction?

2. Draw each block about 2.5 × 2.5cm (1 × 1in), or as appropriate (don't draw too small). Large sheets of graph paper are helpful when drawing shapes such as squares, diamonds, leaves and triangles. Other shapes are trickier to draw – if you have access to a computer with appropriate software, you can draw one shape such as a circle or heart, then copy and paste it to make the arrangement you need. Otherwise, draw the shape of your sample block onto thin

card, then cut out the outline to make a template. Draw around the template, fitting the outlines closely together.

3. Roughly colour in the plan to indicate the patterns and colours of your chosen blocks.

4. At the side of the plan, write a list of each block and colourway, and count how many blocks of each design will be needed.

5. To calculate yarn amounts, unravel a trial block and measure the yardage used for each colour, then compare this to the yardage of a whole ball (this information is usually printed on the ball band). If in doubt, always buy extra yarn!

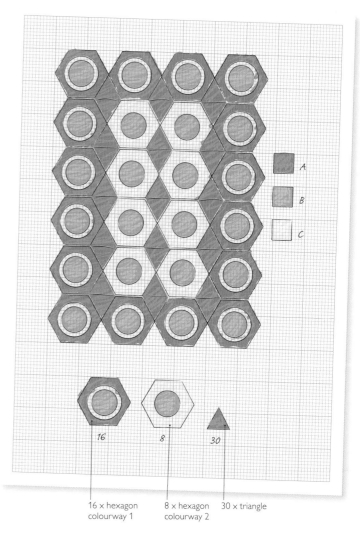

16 x hexagon colourway 1

8 x hexagon colourway 2

30 x triangle

Sketch for a hexagon blanket design

YARN CHOICES

Although each block in the book is worked in worsted-weight yarn, they can all be worked with the yarn that will work best for your project. But on entering a wool shop and faced with an abundance of rich colours, how do you choose the right yarn?

As well as colour, the fibre composition and the drape potential of a yarn are vital to the success of a project. Start by narrowing your options and consider carefully the characteristics you require of the finished knitted or crocheted fabric.

■ Would it be better if the fabric had some elasticity or not?

■ Would a fabric with a good drape be better or one with a firm tension and no drape?

If your proposed project is an afghan, then perhaps a soft, cosy fabric with good drape would be a most suitable. Some people consider pure wool yarns preferable when crocheting an afghan or large project because wool is lighter than cotton and improves the drape of the crochet

fabric; but there are times when synthetic yarns are better – particularly for baby items that may require frequent washing. For a bag, a firm, resilient fabric would be ideal, and for a cushion, well, the choice is up to you.

The next step is to indulge yourself! Select a range of single balls or hanks of yarn, from the shop or from your stash at home, and work a few sample blocks. With experience you will be able to gauge how a yarn may perform, but there are always surprises. Remember that the hook or needle size, and the block worked will influence the final result – so experiment with yarns, hook or needle sizes, and block shapes with more or less texture or loft.

4-ply wool with lots of loft has good drape.

Ribbon and worsted mohair combination has a contrast of textures but it could be a problem to launder.

The swatches show the large double snowflake (block 95, page 87) worked in a variety of yarn weights and fibres. By using different yarns, the appearance of the block changes considerably.

Cotton holds the shape of the block well and has good stitch definition.

TENSION

If you are working from a pattern, then matching the tension specified in the pattern is essential.

In order to do this, work a sample block using the recommended yarn weight and hook or needle size, and block and measure the block. As a rule, if your block is smaller than required, work another block using a hook or needle one size larger.

If your block is larger than required, make another block using a hook or needle one size smaller. Tension can be affected by the colour and fibre composition of the yarn and the size and brand of the crochet hook or needles, so you may need to make several blocks using different hooks and needles until you achieve a tension that matches that in the pattern.

If you are designing your own project then you need to establish the tension that you want for the project. Again, work a sample block using your chosen yarn and the hook or needle size that is recommended for the yarn, and block the piece. As a rule, if your block is smaller than required, make another sample using a hook one size larger. If your block fabric feels tight and hard, make another sample using a hook one size larger. If your block fabric feels loose and floppy, make another sample using a hook one size smaller. Continue to work sample blocks until you are happy with the size and feel of your crochet fabric.

CALCULATING YARN AMOUNTS

The most reliable way to work out how much yarn you need to buy for a specific project is to buy a ball of each yarn you are going to use for your project and make some sample blocks.

The amount of yarn per ball or skein can vary considerably between colours of the same yarn because of the different dyes that have been used, so it's a good idea to make the samples using the actual colours you intend to use.

1. Using the yarn and a suitable size of hook or needles, work three samples in each block you intend to use, making sure that you allow at least 8cm (3in) of spare yarn at every colour change. This will compensate for the extra yarn you'll need when weaving in the ends.
2. Pull out the three blocks and carefully measure the amount of yarn used for each colour in each block.
3. Take the average yardage and multiply it by the number of blocks you intend to make. Don't forget to add extra yarn to your calculations for joining the blocks together and for working any edgings.

BLOCKING

Blocking involves pinning blocks out to the correct size then, depending on the yarn fibre content, either steaming them with an iron or moistening them with cold water.

Always be guided by the information given on the ball band of your yarn and, when in doubt, choose the cold water blocking method below.
1. To block the pieces, make a blocking board by securing one or two layers of quilter's wadding, covered with a sheet of cotton fabric, over a 60 × 90cm (23½ × 35½in) piece of flat board.
2. Pin out several blocks at the same time, using plenty of short metal pins. Gently ease the block into shape before inserting each pin.
3. To block woollen yarns with warm steam, hold a steam iron set at the correct temperature for the yarn about 2cm (¾in) above the surface of the block and allow the steam to penetrate for several seconds.
4. Lay the board flat and allow the block to dry completely before removing the pins.
5. To block acrylic and wool/acrylic blend yarns, pin out the pieces as above, then use a spray bottle to mist the crochet with cold water until it is moist, but not saturated.
6. Gently pat the fabric to help the moisture penetrate more easily. Lay the board flat and allow the block to dry completely before removing the pins.

Blocking pieces with the right side up allows you to adjust the picots and bobbles so they look their best.

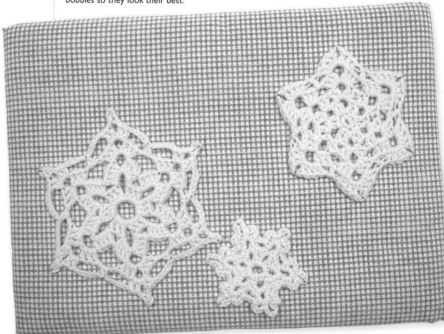

JOINING BLOCKS

Blocks can be joined by sewing or crocheting them together.

Always block the pieces before joining. Use the same yarn for joining as you used for working the blocks or a matching stronger yarn.

Begin by laying out the blocks in the correct order with the right or wrong side of each one facing upwards, depending on the joining method you have chosen. Working first in horizontal rows, join the blocks together, beginning with the top row. Repeat until all the horizontal edges are joined. Turn the work so the remaining edges of the blocks are now horizontal and, as before, join these edges together.

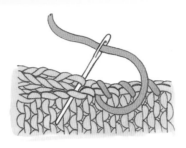

WORKING WHIP STITCH

Hold two blocks together with the right sides facing, pinning if necessary. Work a line of diagonal stitches from back to front under the strands at the edges of the blocks.

WORKING A WOVEN SEAM ON CROCHET FABRIC

Lay the blocks out with the edges touching and wrong sides facing upwards. Using matching yarn threaded in a tapestry needle, weave around the centres of the stitches as shown, without pulling the stitches too tightly.

WORKING A CROCHET SLIP STITCH SEAM

Joining blocks with wrong sides together gives a firm seam with an attractive ridge on the right side. If you prefer the ridge not to be visible, join the blocks with right sides together so the ridge is on the wrong side. Work a row of slip stitch through both loops of each block. When working this method along side edges of blocks worked in rows, work enough evenly-spaced stitches so the seam is not too tight.

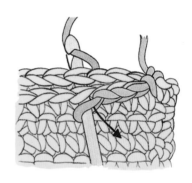

WORKING MATTRESS STITCH ON KNIT FABRIC

Lay the blocks out with the edges touching and right sides facing upwards. Using matching yarn threaded in a tapestry needle, weave under the bar between the outer stitch and the next stitch on each edge as shown.

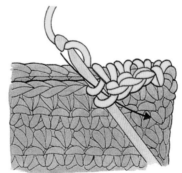

WORKING A SINGLE CROCHET SEAM

Work as for the slip stitch seam above, but work rows of single crochet stitches from the right or wrong side, depending on your preference.

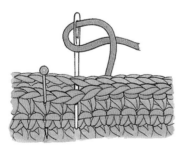

WORKING A BACK STITCH SEAM

Hold the blocks to be joined with right sides together, pinning if necessary. Using matching yarn threaded in a tapestry needle, work a back stitch seam along the edge.

READING PATTERNS AND CHARTS

Block patterns are worked using a combination of stitches. In order to make them easier to follow abbreviations are used. It may seem odd but once the abbreviations are understood, it is quicker and less frustrating to follow a well-abbreviated pattern. Check the abbreviations that accompany any pattern you work – we all have our good reasons for how we like to present patterns and we don't always agree.

KNIT PATTERN ABBREVIATIONS

This list includes some common knitting abbreviations. Any special abbreviations are described with the relevant pattern.

*	repeat indicator
[]	repeat indicator
alt	alternate
C3B	cable 3 back
C4B	cable 4 back
C4F	cable 4 front
cont	continue
dec	decrease
foll	following
inc	increase
k	knit
k2tog	knit 2 sts together
k2togtbl	knit 2 sts together through the back of the loops
k3tog	knit 3 sts together
k3togtbl	knit 3 sts together through the back of the loops
k1f&b	knit front and back
dp	double pointed
foll	following
M1	make 1 knit
M1P	make 1 purl
MB	make bobble as specified in pattern
oen	on each needle

p	purl
p2tog	purl 2 sts together
p2togtbl	purl 2 sts together through the back of the loops
p3tog	purl 3 sts together
patt	pattern
psso	pass sl st over
p2sso	pass 2 sl sts over
rem	remainder/remaining
rep	repeat
RS	right side
sl	slip st
s2kp	sl 2tog, k1, p2sso
skpo	sl 1, k1, psso
sk2po	sl 1, k2tog, psso
ssk	sl 1, sl 1, k2 sl sts togtbl
st(s)	stitch(es)
tbl	through the back of the loop
tog	together
WS	wrong side
wyf	with yarn forward
wyb	with yarn back
yo	yarn over needle to make a st.

KNITTING CHARTS AND JACQUARD CROCHET CHARTS

A chart is sometimes used to express complicated patterns. Sometimes, seeing what has to be done and its relation to the other stitches makes it easier to follow.

Charts also often use less space. To read a chart, start at the bottom and check on which side Row or Round 1 is indicated. If it is on the left the stitch pattern starts on a wrong side row and if it is on the right, the stitch patterns starts on a right-side row. Each square on the chart represents one stitch. Work upwards from the bottom of the chart, reading right side rows or rounds from right to left and wrong wide rows from left to right. There are no jacquard crochet charts in this book but it is always useful to know that some things apply to both crafts.

KNITTING SYMBOLS

☐	k on RS, p on WS
⊟	p on RS, k on WS
Ⓞ	yo
◩	ssk
◩	k2tog
Ⅴ	inc (kfb)
⟍	c4f
◩	sk2p
◩	k3tog
Λ	p2tog
◮	p3tog

CROCHET ABBREVIATIONS AND SYMBOLS

This list includes the common crochet abbreviations. Any special abbreviations are described with the relevant pattern.

▲		fasten off
△		join in new yarn
←		direction of working
*		start of repeat
[ ]		repeat the instruction within the brackets the stated number of times
-		hyphen grouping symbol
	alt	alternate
	beg	beginning
	blo	back loop only
	BPtr	treble crochet round the back post
	cl	cluster
	cont	continue
	dc	double crochet
	dc2tog	double crochet together
	dec	decrease
	dtr	double treble
	dtr2tog	double treble crochet 2 sts together
	dtr3tog	double treble crochet 3 sts together
	foll	following
	FPtr	treble crochet round the front post
	htr	half treble crochet
	MB	make bobble as specified in pattern
	patt	pattern
		popcorn
	rem	remainder/remaining
	rep	repeat
	RS	right side
	sl st	slip stitch
	tr	treble crochet
	tr2tog	treble crochet together
	trtr	triple treble
	WS	wrong side
	yrh	yarn round hook

READING A CROCHET CHART

These often look more daunting than a crochet pattern but what you see is what you get and actually once crochet charts have been mastered they are quicker and easier to follow.

Using yarn A, ch 9 and join with a sl st to form a ring. Reading from the centre out and anticlockwise.

Round 1 (RS): Ch 10 (counts as 1 tr and half a picot) *sl st into the 5th ch from the hook, (this completes a picot) ch 2, 3 tr into the centre of the ring, ch 7; rep from * five more times, sl st into the 5th ch from the hook, ch 2, 2 tr into the centre of the ring, join with a sl st into the 3rd ch of beg-ch. Fasten off yarn.

Round 2: Join B in any picot, ch 10 (counts as 1 tr and half a picot) sl st into the 5th ch from the hook, ch 2, 3 tr into the picot, *ch 1, 3 tr into the next picot, sl st into the 5th ch from the hook, ch 2, 3 tr in picot (this is a star point), rep from * 4 more times, 2 tr into the next picot, join with a sl st into the 3rd ch of beg-ch. Fasten off yarn.

Round 3: Join C in any point, ch 10 (counts as 1 tr and half a picot), sl st into the 5th ch from the hook, ch 2, 3 tr in next point, *ch 3, 1 trtr in ch1-sp, ch 3, 3 tr in next point, ch 7, sl st in 5th ch from hook, ch 2, 3 tr into point, rep from * 4 more times, ch 3, 1 trtr in ch1-sp, ch 3, 2 tr in first point, join with ss into the 3rd ch of beg-ch.
Fasten off yarn.

In this book the colors represent the yarn color used.

KEY
- ch in yellow
- ch in pale blue
- ch in blue
- dc in yellow
- dc in pale blue
- dc in blue
- trtr in yellow
- trtr in pale blue
- trtr in blue

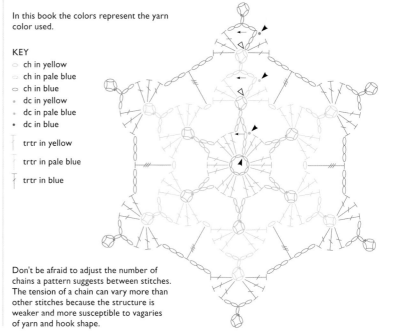

Don't be afraid to adjust the number of chains a pattern suggests between stitches. The tension of a chain can vary more than other stitches because the structure is weaker and more susceptible to vagaries of yarn and hook shape.

INDEX

Fold out this flap

CREDITS

There are so many people who contributed to this book and I am grateful to all from Buffalo, NY to London.

I would like to thank everyone at Quarto in London, especially Victoria Lyle, Kate Kirby, Sorrel Wood and the many talented people there who helped guide me through my first book. I also would like to thank everyone at Lion Brand Yarn in New York for their support in this project and for supplying the yarn used in all 150 of the blocks.

A very special thank you to Rebecca Lennox who knitted many of the blocks in this book. Her agility and ability never cease to amaze me!

My gratitude and love goes to all of my family and friends who supported me, especially my husband, Greg, and our daughters Lizzie and Caroline.

And thank you to all of my students at the Elmwood Yarn Shop in Buffalo. Their enthusiasm for this book has been constant and they are the ones who make me a better teacher and designer.

Finally, this book is dedicated to my very own knitting teacher – my mother, Ramona Dunn.

Quarto would like to thank Luise Roberts for all her help and for supplying the blocks and images on pages 137 and 141. All other photographs and illustrations are the copyright of Quarto Inc.